Knowledge Management

Historical and Cross-Disciplinary Themes

Danny P. Wallace

Libraries Unlimited Knowledge Management Series

LIBRARIES
U N L I M I T E D
A Member of the Greenwood Publishing Group

Westport, Connecticut • London

Library of Congress Cataloging-in-Publication Data

Wallace, Danny P.
  Knowledge management : historical and cross-disciplinary themes /
Danny P. Wallace.
        p. cm. — (Libraries Unlimited knowledge management series)
  Includes bibliographical references and index.
  ISBN 978–1–59158–502–2 (hardcover : alk. paper)
  1. Knowledge management.   2. Organizational learning.   3. Information resources
management.   I. Title.
  HD30.2.W344   2007
  658.4'038—dc22   2007037825

British Library Cataloguing in Publication Data is available.

Library of Congress Catalog Card Number: 2007037825
ISBN: 978–1–59158–502–2

First published in 2007

Libraries Unlimited, 88 Post Road West, Westport, CT 06881
A Member of the Greenwood Publishing Group, Inc.
www.lu.com

Printed in the United States of America

The paper used in this book complies with the
Permanent Paper Standard issued by the National
Information Standards Organization (Z39.48–1984).

10 9 8 7 6 5 4 3 2 1

Contents

Introduction

Knowledge Management: Historical and Cross-Disciplinary Themes

Danny P. Wallace

> **knowledge management,** *n.* Econ. and Business the effective management of the sharing and retention of information in an organization; the use of management techniques to optimize the acquisition, dissemination, and use of knowledge.
>
> **1971** *D. SMITH* in E. Hopper Readings in Theory Educ. Syst. vii. 139 (heading) Selection and *knowledge management in education systems.

WHY THIS BOOK?

Knowledge management (KM) gained prominence during the 1990s as an innovative approach to redirecting the energies and activities of organizations by enhancing the generation, flow, and use of internal knowledge. Knowledge management has generally been presented as transformative in nature and fundamentally different from prior models for organizational management. In particular, knowledge management has been described as being radically different from information management and especially different from information technology management.

Knowledge management is frequently presented as a recent development born entirely of the business world. Gamble and Blackwell, writing in 2001, described knowledge management as having "come to the fore over the last 8–10 years."[1] Other experts have offered slightly differing opinions on the origins. Sveiby suggested that knowledge management began in 1992.[2] Prusak traced the origin of knowledge management to a 1993 conference.[3] Ponzi associated the beginning of interest in the concept to Drucker's 1993 book *The Post-capitalist Society*.[4] Even those authors who recognize that the precedents and foundations of knowledge management have deeper origins tend to focus on the influences of business management, appropriately citing Taylor, Drucker, and

Nonaka as major thinkers, but ignoring the work of both earlier scholars and contemporary work in domains other than management.

The intellectual origins of knowledge management, however, are both deeper and broader than the explorations that have appeared in the literature to date. The influences of philosophy, economics, education, psychology, information and communication theory, and library and information studies have been almost completely overlooked. Furthermore, the historical chain of antecedents to current knowledge management thought and practice is either exaggerated (the history of knowledge management is coterminous with the history of knowledge) or truncated (knowledge management began with the 1995 publication of Nonaka and Takeuchi's *The Knowledge-Creating Company*.[5]

Although knowledge management has been largely explored, explained, and expounded from the point of view of the corporate sector, it has found its way into such diverse environments as the military, government, health care, education, and library and information science. Knowledge management has had a mixed impact on the philosophies and practices of the library and information professions. Although knowledge management mavens frequently have couched knowledge management as being wholly different from what came before, the argument for fundamental differences frequently seems strained and even shallow. Librarians and other information professionals have a lengthy, robust, and distinguished history of supporting the generation, flow, dissemination, and use of knowledge and may justifiably be quite skeptical of contentions that knowledge management constitutes something truly new. Just as the documentation movement of the 1950s was dismissed as "librarianship practiced by amateurs" and the information science movement of the 1970s was described as "librarianship practiced by men," the knowledge management movement of the 1990s is subject to categorization as "library and information science practiced by businessmen."[6] Like documentation and information science, knowledge management does not seem likely to just go away because library and information professionals can readily see within it clear and definite links to what they pioneered in earlier decades and centuries. The goal of this book is to link current and historical works of importance to the development and understanding of knowledge management across domains and disciplines.

KNOWLEDGE MANAGEMENT IN CONTEXT

Definitions of Knowledge Management

What exactly have experts said about knowledge management? There is no one standardized, accepted definition of knowledge management. Where they do exist, dictionary and encyclopedia definitions are sparse. The *Encyclopedia of Business and Finance* offers no definition. *Encyclopaedia Britannica* mentions knowledge management systems in the article on "Information Systems" but provides no explicit definition of knowledge management. The *Encyclopedia of Communication and Information* describes the "basic challenge in knowledge management" as "learning how to design an organization's strategy, structure, and systems so that the organization can use what it knows to innovate and adapt."[7] The *Encyclopedia of Library and Information Science* defines knowledge management as "a management practice that uses an organization's intellectual capital to achieve its organizational mission."[8] The *Encyclopedia of Communities of Practice in Information and Knowledge Management* defines knowledge management variously as "the processes necessary to capture, codify, and transfer knowledge across the organization to achieve competitive advantage" and "a combination of management awareness, attitudes, processes, and practices for creating, acquiring, capturing, sharing, and using knowledge to enhance learning and performance in organisations."[9]

Some authors have deliberately sidestepped the need to define knowledge management. Barclay and Murray contended that it was not surprising that "knowledge management is hard to define precisely and simply," and queried whether health professionals can precisely define health care, CEOs can provide a concise definition for management, or CFOs can define compensation.[10] Another expert, Wiig, defined knowledge management only by implication.[11]

Firestone and McElroy employed a very simple and straightforward definition. "KM is a management discipline that seeks to enhance organizational knowledge processing."[12] Tiwana defined knowledge management as "management of organizational knowledge for creating business value and generating a competitive advantage."[13] According to Pan, Newell, Huang, and Galliers, "Knowledge management involves a range of processes including creating, sharing, integrating, storing, and reusing knowledge."[14]

In categorizing definitions of knowledge management, Dillon found that they tended to emphasize (1) return on investment, (2) knowledge integration, (3) information assets, or (4) knowledge management goals. He noted that the plethora of definitions and viewpoints makes a consolidated understanding of the core concept difficult and that none of the definitions is fully satisfactory.[15]

Terminological Origins and Early Works in Knowledge Management

The origin of the expression "knowledge management" is no clearer than the definition of the concept. The *Oxford English Dictionary* traces the term's first use to a 1971 chapter in the book *Readings in the Theory of Educational Systems.* The closely parallel expression "management of knowledge," the gerund "knowledge-managing," and the more personalized "knowledge manager" appeared in a 1967 article by Lynton Caldwell in *Public Administration Review.*[16] Caldwell's use of these terms had a remarkably modern flavor that would not seem out of place in an article published 40 years later. One of the first authors to emphasize the emerging importance of knowledge, Caldwell asserted that, "to a degree never before experienced, the critical element and basic source of power in this new age is knowledge."[17] In describing the sweeping nature of this "knowledge breakthrough," Caldwell emphasized the broad-based nature of "the managers of knowledge. . . . Government bureau chiefs, college professors, librarians, computer technicians, television engineers and physicians, for example, can now be found as consciously interdependent co-workers in the same knowledge-managing enterprise, even though they may be employed in different organizations and at geographically diverse locations."[18]

A 1970 panel on science and technology commissioned by the U.S. House of Representatives called its eleventh meeting "The Management of Information and Knowledge." Keynote speaker McGeorge Bundy summarized the motivations for the conference as implying "a problem, a capability, and a potential, if unrealized, benefit." He said, "The problem is that in most, if not all spheres of inquiry and choice, the quantities of raw information which are needed and are increasingly available overwhelm in magnitude the few comprehensive and trusted bodies or systems of knowledge that have been perceived and elaborated by man." He went on to say, "Yet, if streams of unassimilated, and certainly unmanaged, information inundate us in the midst of this kind of thirst for understanding, computer information systems, taken comprehensively, do seem to offer an unprecedented capability of addressing this age-old problem. . . . The faith of modern man reasons that we can reap important social benefits if we harness the capabilities of modern systems of information analysis and storage to convert data into knowledge, and then apply the product as widely as possible to issues of social and personal choice."[19]

In 1974 Henry extended the notion of knowledge management to public administration, noting "that new patterns of information and new information technologies (1) can change the content and quality of public policies and (2) may cultivate a new strain on politics and policy making."[20] Henry defined knowledge management as "public policy for the production, dissemination, accessibility, and use of information as it applies to public policy formulation."[21] He also identified knowledge management as "metapolicy," or "policy for policy-making procedures."[22] Later, Henry revisited knowledge management in a 1974 discussion of "the utility of copyright as a public policy for knowledge management in a society that possesses a high level of information technology."[23]

In another 1974 article, Freeman addressed the management of knowledge in the *Journal of Higher Education*. Although Freeman's intent was not particularly well aligned with current notions of knowledge management, there are definite points of congruence. He was greatly concerned that management structures and processes in higher education were substantially at odds with the purposes of higher education.

"Instead of an open, morphogenic system as the rhetoric of liberal education requires, we find a management system that is homeostatic and characterized by its capacity to provide negative but not positive feedback."[24] Freeman was particularly critical of the notion of the academic department, which he described as "an arbitrary, unpredictable outgrowth of particular social problems and processes."[25]

In 1975, the editorial board of the *Public Administrative Review* organized a symposium on knowledge management, and symposium articles appeared in the November 1975 issue of the *Review*.[26] James D. Carroll and Nicholas Henry, the editors of the symposium issue, identified its central theme as the "old notion" that "knowledge is power." They identified three major sub-themes in the articles: "the relationships between knowledge, society, and bureaucracy," "the implications of knowledge management for theories of public administration," and "knowledge management in relation to specific policy and administrative development."[27] Articles in the symposium issue included Lynton Caldwell's "Managing the Transition to Post-modern Society," James D. Carroll's "Service, Knowledge, and Choice: The Future as Post-industrial Administration," Bruce L. Gates's "Knowledge Management in the Technological Society: Government by Indicator," Nicholas Henry's "Bureaucracy, Technology, and Knowledge Management," William Thomas Keating's "On Managing Ignorance," and Jerry McCaffery's "Knowledge Management in Fiscal Policy Formulation."[28]

Although education and public administration dominated the use of the term "knowledge management" during the 1970s, in 1975 Goerl related knowledge management to cybernetics.[29] In 1977, Freeman consciously adopted the concept as it had been developed in public administration and applied it to the management of information about oceans and the environment.[30]

Growth of the Knowledge Management Literature

As of March 28, 2007, the *Social Sciences Citation Index* included 3,566 records containing the term "knowledge management." A decade-by-decade breakdown indicates that 7 of those records were published during the 1970s, 9 were published during the 1980s, 425 were published during the 1990s, and 3,125 have been published since the beginning of the 2000s.

This pattern reveals a remarkably rapid literature growth, but it is a limited indicator of the real growth of the field in that it relies exclusively on one terminological expression of the field. A more realistic assessment of growth would be difficult to achieve, given the wide variety of language used to describe concepts that are central to knowledge management and the intensely interdisciplinary nature of the field. Furthermore, any true picture of the growth of the knowledge management literature would have to take into account the growth in areas that constitute the intellectual and conceptual antecedents and foundations of knowledge management but can't really be considered subfields within knowledge management—for example, artificial intelligence, cognitive science, education, epistemology, industrial and organizational psychology, library and information science, and systems analysis.

Conceptual Foundations of Knowledge Management

According to the *Encyclopedia of Knowledge Management*, "Knowledge management . . . is a multidisciplinary subject, with contributions from such disciplines as information systems . . . and information technology . . . , strategic management, organizational theory, human-resource management, education science, psychology, cognitive science, and artificial intelligence."[31] Prusak found the "intellectual antecedents" of knowledge management in economics, sociology, and philosophy and psychology, in that order of importance.[32] He further traced the influences of three areas of practice: "information management, the quality movement, and the human factors/human capital movement."[33] Ponzi's analysis of knowledge management works published between 1994 and 1998 identified the top 10 interdisciplinary influences, listed here in rank order, as (1) management, (2) business, (3) computer information systems, (4) library and information science, (5) planning and development, (6) computer science theory and methods, (7) industrial engineering, (8) operations research and management science, (9) applied psychology, and (10) public administration.[34] Ponzi's categorization was limited by his reliance on the categories used by *Journal Citation Reports*. Gu's bibliometric analysis employed a method somewhat similar to that used by Ponzi but examined articles published from 1975 to 2002, representing 462 journals and spanning 110 *Journal Citation Reports* categories.[35]

Day took a considerably longer view that grounded knowledge management in the documentation movement of the late nineteenth and early twentieth centuries, noting similarities in the knowledge management literature to ideas first presented by Paul Otlet and Suzanne Briet. Day also noted the influences of Martin Heidegger's phenomenology, William Benjamin's experiential view of knowledge, and the concept of post-Fordism, a term used to describe the transition from a primarily industrial economy to a primarily knowledge-based one.[36] Black found antecedents to many of the principles of knowledge management in the special libraries movement of the early twentieth century, noting that "formal recognition was given to the importance of knowledge as a prime factor of production by firms that pioneered the in-house technical and commercial library."[37] Wilson viewed knowledge management primarily as an outgrowth of the "scientific management" movement led by Taylor in the late nineteenth century and the "human relations school" that arose in the 1930s. Wilson also noted the vast number of management trends that characterized the twentieth century and questioned whether knowledge management represented something new or simply a fusion of preexisting techniques.[38]

Critiques of Knowledge Management

Spender's review of knowledge management led to the conclusion that "much of [knowledge management] is old-style systems analysis, human resource management, or organization development, updated and re-labeled. There is a great deal of hype, not only in the trade press."[39] According to Alvesson and Kärreman, "knowledge management is an ambiguous, unspecific and dynamic phenomenon, intrinsically related to meaning, understanding and process, and therefore difficult to manage. There is . . . a contradiction between knowledge and management."[40]

Perhaps the most extensive critique of knowledge management was provided by Wilson, who titled his article "The Nonsense of 'Knowledge Management.'"[41] Although Wilson did not dismiss all management trends as fads, he noted that many of them arose and disappeared rapidly enough to qualify as fads. Wilson analyzed the literature of knowledge management and profiled corporate stances on knowledge management, ultimately concluding that "'knowledge management' is, in large part, a management fad, promulgated primarily by certain consultancy firms, and the probability is that it will fade away like previous fads."[42] To Wilson, the joint knowledge management principles of managing tacit knowledge, an environment that encourages the exchange of knowledge, individual autonomy to develop expertise, and a community orientation for work constitute a "Utopian idea" that has not been and probably cannot be achieved.[43]

OVERVIEW OF THE BOOK

This book provides a critical analysis of historically significant and more recent "classic" works related to nine major themes of knowledge management: (1) the nature of knowledge, (2) knowledge capital, (3) organizational learning and learning organizations, (4) knowledge sharing, (5) communities of practice, (6) knowledge representation, (7) content management, (8) taxonomies and ontologies, and (9) informatics and information technology. Each chapter provides a discussion of key concepts related to the topic of the chapter and detailed analyses of a set of key papers that provide a multidimensional perspective on the topic, thereby tracing the evolution of knowledge management concepts. The key papers that are the focus of the book were selected on the basis of (1) citation frequency data drawn from the *Social Sciences Citation Index,*

(2) assessment of historical precedent, and (3) uniqueness of viewpoint. Each chapter is introduced with a pertinent definition from the *Oxford English Dictionary* providing either the origin and basic definition of the chapter topic or one or more etymologies and definitions for key concepts found in the chapter.

This book is intended for all students of knowledge management and closely related fields and knowledge management practitioners who wish to place the field in context.

Most authors writing about knowledge management, beginning with Henry in 1975, seem to feel compelled to define knowledge and distinguish it from other related concepts. Chapter 1, "The Nature of Knowledge," addresses definitions and forms of knowledge and approaches to categorizing knowledge-related concepts. The chapter offers analyses of works by Michael Polanyi, Karl Popper, Robert S. Taylor, and Ikujiro Nonaka and Hirotaka Takeuchi.

The role of the community and the concept of organizations as communities are common themes in the literature of knowledge management. Achieving a sense of community is a goal of knowledge management practice. "Communities of Practice" are the focus of chapter 2, which explores the meaning of community, the varieties of community models that can be found in societal and organizational settings, and community as a model for learning. Works by John Dewey and Jean Lave and Etienne Wenger are analyzed.

Chapter 3, "Organizational Learning and Learning Organizations," explores the knowledge management concern with learning, comparing and contrasting organizational learning and learning organizations as concepts and exploring the role of learning in quality and continuous improvement initiatives. Works analyzed are authored by Vincent E. Cangelosi and William R. Dill, C. West Churchman, Chris Argyris and Donald A. Schön, and Peter Senge.

One of the foundational concepts of knowledge management is the principle that what was once a primarily industrial economy is shifting to or has shifted to an economy based primarily on knowledge. Chapter 4 explores "Intellectual Capital and the Knowledge Economy," defining the nature and origins of intellectual capital, the knowledge industries, the nature of the knowledge economy, knowledge markets, and the pricing of knowledge. The chapter provides analyses of works by John Locke, Fritz Machlup, Peter F. Drucker, and Thomas H. Davenport and Laurence Prusak.

It has long been held as axiomatic that knowledge in isolation has no meaningful value: knowledge is assigned value only when it is exchanged. The principles of knowledge exchange, the dangers of knowledge hoarding, and the nature of knowledge diffusion are explored in chapter 5, "Knowledge Sharing." Analyzed works are from Diana Crane, Dorothy Leonard-Barton, and Gabriel Szulanski.

Knowledge has no native form other than in the human mind. Chapter 6, "Knowledge Representation," reaches into the areas of cognition, artificial intelligence, and design to explore the processes by which knowledge can be transformed into forms that can be shared. Chapter 6 provides analyses of works by Vannevar Bush, William A. Woods, and Terrence A. Brooks.

Chapter 7, "Content Management," explores the ways in which the focuses of knowledge management are and are not different from those of earlier concepts, initiatives, and practices. The chapter explores the distinctions among data management, records management, and content management and relates knowledge management to libraries, in particular digital libraries. Particular attention is given to the prospect for global knowledge management. Writings by Paul Otlet, H. G. Wells, Tim Berners-Lee, and John M. Budd and Bart Harloe are analyzed.

The functional aspects of knowledge management in practice require the development and implementation of systematic approaches to the organization of knowledge. Those approaches are examined in chapter 8, "Taxonomies and Ontologies." The chapter explores the nature of categorization and classification, the roles and problems of natural and artificially constructed languages, metadata, and the function of ontologies in defining purpose. The chapter offers analyses of works by Charles A. Cutter, Jesse Shera, and B. C. Vickery.

Chapter 9 is devoted to "Informatics and Information Technology." The concepts of cybernetics and informatics are introduced, and the sometimes uncertain and difficult role of information technology in knowledge management is explored. Key papers examined in this chapter were authored by Norbert Wiener and Rob Kling.

As dangerous and uncertain as is any attempt at prognostication, the final chapter points to the future of knowledge management as a means of bringing the historical and cross-disciplinary origins of the field into perspective.

NOTES

1. Paul R. Gamble and John Blackwell, *Knowledge Management: A State of the Art Guide* (London: Kogan Page, 2002), 6.

2. Sveiby, Karl-Erik. "What Is Knowledge Management?" http://www.sveiby.com/articles/KnowledgeManagement.html (accessed December 14, 2005).

3. L. Prusak, "Where Did Knowledge Management Come From?" *IBM Systems Journal* 40, no. 4 (2001): 1003.

4. Leonard J. Ponzi, "The Intellectual Structure and Interdisciplinary Breadth of Knowledge Management: A Bibliometric Study of Its Early State of Development," *Scientometrics* 55, no. 2 (2002): 259.

5. Ikujiro Nonaka and Hirotaka Takeuchi, *The Knowledge-Creating Company: How Japanese Companies Create the Dynamics of Innovation* (New York: Oxford University Press, 1995).

6. Eugene B. Jackson, "Inside Documentation," *Special Libraries* 45 (April 1954): 151; Michael Gorman, "A Bogus and Dismal Science; Or, the Eggplant That Ate Library Schools," *American Libraries* 21 (May 1990): 463.

7. Chun Wei Choo, "Knowledge Management," *Encyclopedia of Communication and Information,* ed. Jorge Reina Schement (New York: Macmillan, 2002).

8. Guy St. Clair, "Knowledge Management," *Encyclopedia of Library and Information Science,* 2nd ed., ed. Miriam Drake (New York: Marcel Dekker, 2003).

9. Noam Archer, "A Classification of Communities of Practice," in *Encyclopedia of Communities of Practice in Information and Knowledge Management,* edited by Elayne Coakes and Steve Clark (Hershey, PA: Idea Group, 2006), 29; Lizzie Bellarby and Graham Orange, "Knowledge Sharing through Communities of Practice in the Voluntary Sector," in *Encyclopedia of Communities of Practice in Information and Knowledge Management,* edited by Elayne Coakes and Steve Clark (Hershey, PA: Idea Group, 2006), 306.

10. Rebecca O. Barclay and Philip C. Murray, "What Is Knowledge Management?" *Knowledge Praxis* (1997), www.media-access.com/whatis.html (accessed December 14, 2005).

11. Karl Wiig, *People-Focused Knowledge Management: How Effective Decision Making Leads to Corporate Success* (Amsterdam: Elsevier, 2004).

12. Joseph W. Firestone and Mark W. McElroy, *Key Issues in the New Knowledge Management* (Burlington, MA: Elsevier Science, 2003), 70.

13. Amrit Tiwana, *The Knowledge Management Toolkit: Practical Techniques for Building a Knowledge Management System* (Upper Saddle River, NJ: Prentice Hall PTR, 2000), 5.

14. Shan L. Pan, Sue Newell, Jimmy Huang, and Robert D. Galliers, "Overcoming Knowledge Management Challenges during ERP Implementation: The Need to Integrate and Share Different Types of Knowledge," *Journal of the American Society for Information Science and Technology* 58, no. 3 (2007): 405.

15. Martin Dillon, "Knowledge Management: Chimera or Solution?" *Portal: Libraries and the Academy* 2, no. 2 (2002): 331.

16. Lynton K. Caldwell, "Managing the Scientific Super-Culture: The Task of Educational Preparation," *Public Administration Review* 27 (June 1967): 128–33.

17. Ibid., 129.

18. Ibid., 130.

19. Panel on Science and Technology, *The Management of Information and Knowledge: A Compilation of Papers Prepared for the Eleventh Meeting of the Panel on Science and Technology* (Washington, DC: U.S. Government Printing Office, 1970), 4.

20. Nicholas L. Henry, "Knowledge Management: A New Concern for Public Administration," *Public Administration Review* 34 (May/June 1974): 189.

21. Ibid.

22. Ibid., 190.

23. Nicholas L. Henry, "Copyright: Its Adequacy in Technological Societies," *Science* 186 (December 13, 1974): 993–94.

24. Lawrence D. Freeman, "The Management of Knowledge," *Journal of Higher Education* 45 (February 1974): 86.

25. Ibid., 88.

26. Dwight Waldo, "Editorial: About the Review," *Public Administrative Review* 35 (March/April 1975): 129.

27. James D. Carroll and Nicholas Henry, "Introduction: Symposium on Knowledge Management," *Public Administration Review* 35 (November/December 1975): 567.

28. Lynton K. Caldwell, "Managing the Transition to Post-modern Society," *Public Administration Review* 35 (November/December 1975): 567–72; James D. Carroll, "Service, Knowledge, and Choice: The Future as Post-industrial Administration," *Public Administration Review* 35 (November/December 1975): 578–81; Bruce L. Gates, "Knowledge Management in the Technological Society: Government by Indicator," *Public Administration Review* 35 (November/December 1975): 589–93; Nicholas Henry, "Bureaucracy, Technology, and Knowledge Management," *Public Administration Review* 35 (November/December 1975): 572–78; William Thomas Keating, "On Managing Ignorance," *Public Administration Review* 35 (November/December 1975): 593–97; Jerry McCaffery, "Knowledge Management in Fiscal Policy Formulation," *Public Administration Review* 35 (November/December 1975): 598–602.

29. George Frederick Goerl, "Cybernetics, Professionalism, and Knowledge Management: An Exercise in Assumptive Theory," *Public Administration Review* 35 (November 1975): 581–88.

30. Robert R. Freeman, "Ocean and Environmental Information: The Theory, Policy, and Practice of Knowledge Management," *Marine Policy* 1 (July 1977): 215–29.

31. Nicolas Prat, "A Hierarchical Model of Knowledge Management," in *Encyclopedia of Knowledge Management,* edited by D. Schwartz (Hershey, PA: Idea Group, 2006), 211.

32. L. Prusak, "Where Did Knowledge Management Come From?" *IBM Systems Journal* 40, no. 4 (2001): 1003–5.

33. Ibid., 1005.

34. Ponzi, "The Intellectual Structure," 265.

35. Yinian Gu, "Global Knowledge Management Research: A Bibliometric Analysis," *Scientometrics* 61, no. 2 (2004): 171–90.

36. Ronald E. Day, "Totality and Representation: A History of Knowledge Management through European Documentation, Critical Modernity, and Post-Fordism," *Journal of the American Society for Information Science and Technology* 52, no. 9 (2001): 725–35.

37. Alistair Black, "Hidden Worlds of the Early Knowledge Economy: Libraries in British Companies before the Middle of the 20th Century," *Journal of Information Science* 30, no. 5 (2004): 419.

38. T. D. Wilson, "The Nonsense of 'Knowledge Management,'" *Information Research* 8, no. 1 (2002), 1, http://informationr.net/ir/8–1/paper144.html (accessed March 29, 2007).

39. J. C. Spender, "Review Article: An Essay on the State of Knowledge Management," *Prometheus* 23 (March 2005): 101.

40. Mats Alvesson and Dan Kärreman, "Odd Couple: Making Sense of the Curious Concept of Knowledge Management," *Journal of Management Studies* 38 (November 2001): 995.

41. Wilson, "The Nonsense of 'Knowledge Management.'"

42. Ibid., 12.

43. Ibid., 12–13.

1

The Nature of Knowledge

knowledge, *n.* The fact of knowing a thing, state, etc., or (in general sense) a person; acquaintance; familiarity gained by experience.

a1300 *Cursor M.* 15931 Coth petre, "knaulage [Gött. cnaulage, Fairf. knawlage] of him had i neuer nan."

IN THIS CHAPTER

KEY CONCEPTS

Definitions of Knowledge
Machlup's Classification of Knowledge
The Knowledge Hierarchy
The Search for Definition

KEY PAPERS

Michael Polanyi, "The Logic of Tacit Inference"
Karl Popper, "Epistemology without a Knowing Subject"
Robert S. Taylor, "Question-Negotiation and Information Seeking in Libraries"
Ikujiro Nonaka and Hirotaka Takeuchi, *The Knowledge-Creating Company: How Japanese Companies Create the Dynamics of Innovation*

DEFINITIONS OF KNOWLEDGE

The meaning of "knowledge" is of sufficient importance that it defines a major branch of philosophy—epistemology, "the branch of philosophy that studies the nature of knowledge, its presuppositions and foundations, and its extent and validity."[1] Epistemology has traditionally defined knowledge as "justified true belief" or "warranted belief," although those terms apply only to what is known as propositional knowledge: knowledge regarding the veracity or accuracy of a stated proposition as distinguished from knowing a person or place or knowing how to accomplish a task.[2] This definition is generally held to imply that to be known, something must be true. Machlup, however, questioned that contention and described the "requirement that knowledge be 'true,' tested, verified" as "embarrassing."[3] To Machlup, the requirement of truth or verifiability "raises delicate questions about several types of knowledge, especially spiritual knowledge."[4] This concern also applies to scientific knowledge, since science grows and matures only by rejecting as false that which was previously held to be true. Machlup made some allowance for the possibility that "questions of truth, accuracy, and verifiability matter only for practical knowledge" but was clearly skeptical of an absolute need for truth even in the domain of practical knowledge.[5]

On the other hand, Adler contended that no precise definition of knowledge is needed. "For our purposes your present understanding of 'knowledge' is sufficient. You have knowledge. You know that you know and what you know. You know the difference between knowing and not knowing something."[6] Adler apparently felt compelled to devote two subsequent paragraphs to the defense of this position.

Echoing Adler in his proposal, Machlup asserted "that we get rid of the duplication 'knowledge and information.'"[7] Machlup went on to devote most of a page to further exploration of the distinction between knowledge and information as a means of defending his position. By 1980, Machlup had slightly modified his position in suggesting that "we get rid of the duplication 'knowledge and information' when we refer to *what* people know or are informed about."[8] This proposal was followed by three paragraphs of explanation and defense over almost two pages. Machlup's position apparently evolved substantially in a relatively short period of time. In an essay not yet finished at the time of his death in 1983, Machlup devoted eight pages to the distinctions among information, knowledge, and data.[9]

MACHLUP'S CLASSIFICATION OF KNOWLEDGE

Machlup's extensive exposition on knowledge production addressed the nature of knowledge in a wide variety of ways, contrasting basic knowledge with applied knowledge, scientific knowledge with historical knowledge, general-abstract knowledge with particular-concrete knowledge, analytical knowledge with empirical knowledge, and enduring knowledge with transitory knowledge, among other approaches to the categorization of knowledge. One of the most important components of Machlup's analysis is the identification of five classes of knowledge:

Using then the subjective meaning of the known to the *knower* as the criterion, I propose to distinguish five types of knowledge:

1. Practical knowledge: useful in his work, his decisions, and actions can be subdivided, according to his activities, into
   a. Professional knowledge
   b. Business knowledge

      c. Workman's knowledge

      d. Political knowledge

      e. Household knowledge

      f. Other practical knowledge

2. Intellectual knowledge: satisfying his intellectual curiosity, regarded as part of liberal education, humanistic and scientific learning, general culture; acquired, as a rule, in active concentration with an appreciation of the existence of open problems and cultural values.

3. Small-talk and pastime knowledge: satisfying the nonintellectual curiosity or his desire for light entertainment and emotional stimulation, including local gossip, news of crimes and accidents, light novels, stories, jokes, games, etc.; acquired, as a rule, in passive relaxation from "serious" pursuits; apt to dull his sensitiveness.

4. Spiritual knowledge: related to his religious knowledge of God and of the ways to the salvation of the soul.

5. Unwanted knowledge: outside his interests, usually accidentally acquired, aimlessly retained.[10]

THE KNOWLEDGE HIERARCHY

The presentation of the relationships among data, information, knowledge, and sometimes wisdom in a hierarchical arrangement has been part of the language of information science for many years. Although it is uncertain when and by whom those relationships were first presented as a hierarchy, the ubiquity of the notion of a hierarchy is embedded in the use of the acronym DIKW as a shorthand representation for the data-to-information-to-knowledge-to-wisdom transformation. Adler at least implied a hierarchy in his description of the "goods of the mind," which include "knowledge, understanding, prudence, and even a modicum of wisdom."[11] Although Adler's conceptualization of the "goods of the mind" wasn't presented in this form until 1970, its seeds can be found in much earlier works, most notably in the 1927 *Dialectic* and the 1941 *A Dialectic of Morals*. Boulding presented an early form of the hierarchy in his 1955 essay "Notes on the Information Concept." Boulding's hierarchy consisted of signals, messages, information, and knowledge. Boulding defined knowledge as a "mental structure" or "the subjective 'perception of the world and one's place in it.'"[12]

The first author to distinguish among data, information, and knowledge and to also employ the term "knowledge management" may have been Henry, whose 1974 article in *Public Administration Review* is among the earliest to describe a process called knowledge management. Henry defined data as "merely raw facts" and information as "data that change us." Although Henry didn't provide an explicit definition of knowledge or describe a structured hierarchy, the hierarchical transition from data to information to knowledge is strongly implied, and the notion that data, information, and knowledge are qualitatively different is explicit.[13]

Many commentators have related the data-information-wisdom hierarchy to a passage from the initial stanza of T. S. Eliot's 1934 "Choruses from 'The Rock,'" which contains the couplet

Where is the wisdom we have lost in knowledge?
Where is the knowledge we have lost in information?

This relationship was explicitly stated by Cleveland in a 1982 article in the *Futurist,* in which the author explored the relationships among information ("the sum total of all the facts and ideas that are available to be known by somebody at a given moment in time"), knowledge ("the result of somebody applying the refiner's fire to the mass of facts and ideas, selecting and organizing what is useful to somebody," and wisdom ("integrated knowledge—information made super-useful").[14] Although Cleveland's link between the hierarchy and Eliot's couplet was undoubtedly creative, it is not at all clear that poetry was on the mind of the unknown originator of the hierarchical model.

Zeleny explicitly presented data, information, knowledge, and wisdom as a hierarchy and has frequently been credited with proposing the DIKW pyramid, which presents data as the broad base of the pyramid and wisdom as its much smaller summit, although he actually made no reference to any such graphical model.[15] Zeleny's summary definition of knowledge is: "Knowledge should refer to an observer's distinction of 'objects' (wholes, unities) through which he brings forth from the background of experience a coherent and self-consistent set of coordinated actions."[16]

Ackoff has also been credited with responsibility for the DIKW pyramid, although Ackoff, like Zeleny, made no reference to such a structure. Ackoff's 1988 presidential address to the International Society for General Systems Research added "understanding" to the hierarchy, placing it between wisdom and knowledge.[17] Debons, Horne, and Cronenweth presented a more complex hierarchy that begins with events and progresses upward through symbols, rules and formulations, data, information, and knowledge, with wisdom taking its usual place at the top of the hierarchy.[18] This may be the first published version to present the hierarchy graphically. This view to some extent echoes that of Dewey and Bentley, who presented tentative definitions for a complex set of entities that included fact, event, designation, characterization, specification, definition, action (activity), self-action, interaction, transaction, behavior-agent, behavior-object, situation, occurrence, object, sign, signal, name, and symbol.[19] These "terminological guide-posts" were formulated in part to avoid the term "knowledge," which they identified as "a vague word."[20]

Many authors have attempted to define the distinctions among data, information, knowledge, and wisdom. Gamble and Blackwell describe "knowledge as a step on the road to wisdom" and provide the following definitions:

> "Data—refers to chunks of facts about the state of the world."
> "Classically, information is defined as data that are endowed with meaning and purpose."
> "Information connected in relationships may be described as knowledge."
> "Wisdom is the ability to make sound judgments and decisions apparently without thought."[21]

Gamble and Blackwell expanded each of these definitions substantially, but they are typical of attempts to define the four terms that make up the DIKW hierarchy.

More recently, Boiko reiterated the hierarchy by stating that "Data are material facts; information is matter-of-fact; knowledge is a matter of dispute; and wisdom is nonmaterial." Unfortunately, Boiko added confusion to the discussion by contending that "knowledge and wisdom can be information."[22]

THE SEARCH FOR DEFINITION

Ultimately, many—perhaps most—authors of works exploring the nature and implications of knowledge management appear to feel that some attempt at defining the term "knowledge" is necessary but at the same time recognize that providing a concise, precise definition is difficult, if not impossible. Many of the definitions that have found widespread use are neither concise nor precise.

One of the most frequently quoted definitions comes from Davenport and Prusak:

> Knowledge is a fluid mix of framed experience, values, contextual information, expert insight and grounded intuition that provides an environment and framework for evaluating and incorporating new experiences and information. It originates and is applied in the minds of knowers. In organizations it often becomes embedded not only in documents and repositories but also in organizational routines, processes, practices and norms.[23]

Firestone and McElroy dedicated an entire chapter to the "knowledge conundrum," citing a wide range of definitions and contexts and suggesting that meaningful definition is a product of the context within which knowledge is examined. They refer to three "worlds" based on the work of Popper and present these definitions:

> World 1 knowledge—encoded structures in physical systems (such as genetic coding in DNA) that allows those objects to adapt to an environment;
>
> World 2 knowledge—beliefs and belief predispositions (in minds) about the world, the beautiful, and the right that we believe have survived our tests, evaluation, and experience;
>
> World 3 knowledge—sharable linguistic formulations, knowledge claims about the world, the beautiful, and the right, that have survived testing and evaluation by the agent (individual, group, community, team, organization, society, etc.) acquiring, formulating, and testing and evaluating the knowledge claims.[24]

Firestone and McElroy reject the hierarchical structure of the DIKW pyramid in favor of a "knowledge life cycle" in which "data and knowledge are made from preexisting information."[25]

Michael Polanyi, "The Logic of Tacit Inference," in *Knowing and Being: Essays by Michael Polanyi,* edited by Marjorie Greene (Chicago: University of Chicago Press, 1969), 138–58. First published 1964.

Michael Polanyi (1891–1976), a Hungarian-born scholar whose career spanned physical chemistry and philosophy while touching on economics, is best known for his essays on the recurring theme of tacit knowing. This theme was first explored in his 1945 *Science, Faith and Society* and revisited in multiple works, including *Personal Knowledge* (1958) and *The Tacit Dimension* (1967). His 1964 essay, "The Logic of Tacit Inference," is frequently cited as the first comprehensive exploration of the concept of tacit knowledge and appears to have been the progenitor for the lengthier exposition found in *The Tacit Dimension.*

POLANYI AND EPISTEMOLOGY

Polanyi is the third most frequently cited author in the domain of knowledge management, which soundly establishes the importance and influence of his contribution. His work is also of great importance to epistemologists, who constitute an additional source of citation and recognition of his work. Epistemologists have understandably striven to position Polanyi's ideas in the dialectic framework of philosophy, in some cases tracing his ideas, as did Polanyi, to Aristotle and Plato. Polanyi certainly gave later writers on epistemology and related branches of philosophy much to explore, discuss, support, and refute. Writers on knowledge management have tended, however, to simultaneously exaggerate and trivialize Polanyi's concept of tacit knowing or tacit knowledge. Many writers reference tacit knowledge without even acknowledging that the basic notion originated with Polanyi, which is a further indicator of the significance the concept has assumed in the literature of knowledge management.

Polanyi was clearly uninterested in knowledge as input to any kind of management activity and would probably have been quite skeptical about the whole notion of knowledge management. He was, however, quite interested in the practical aspects and implications of his ideas. Building on his experience as a scientist, Polanyi was deeply interested in scientific knowledge and the ways in which his thoughts on knowledge and its nature influenced and were influenced by scientific discovery. The core issue of "The Logic of Tacit Inference" is established early in the essay in this statement:

> To hold a natural law to be true is to believe that its presence may reveal itself in yet unknown and perhaps yet unthinkable consequences; it is to believe that natural laws are features of a reality which as such will continue to bear consequences inexhaustibly.[26]

Knowledge, then, is explicitly about truth, and truth is explicitly about understanding the universe within which we live. "Discovery must be arrived at by the tacit powers of the mind, and its content, so far as it is indeterminate, can only be tacitly known."[27]

Polanyi was much influenced by gestalt psychology and viewed scientific knowledge as inherently synergistic. The premise that knowing is a process that inherently produces outcomes that are greater than the sum of its parts permeates Polanyi's writings and is critical to the concept of implicit knowledge.

KNOWLEDGE AND PERCEPTION

Much of "The Logic of Tacit Inference" is focused not on knowledge as an internalized process, but on perception and how perception determines and shapes knowledge. He cites the gestalt principle as evidence that perception is closely tied to conception, using examples such as the adult human's ability to codify experiences more quickly and more precisely than an infant is able to. Extending from this, Polanyi infers that scientific perception is an acquired ability and that the relationship between scientific perception and ordinary perception may be directly analogous to the relationship between adult perception and infantile perception.

One of the most important premises in Polanyi's work is the distinction between subsidiary and focal perception. Subsidiary perception involves subliminal clues that are not directly subject to conscious experience, and marginal clues that may be consciously experienced but normally are not, contribute to but do not define perception of an object of attention to an observer, although they do play a distinct role in shaping perception of that which is observed. Focal perception is the observer's central awareness of the object of attention. According to Polanyi, some combination of subsidiary and focal perception is essential to all understanding. Drawing again from gestalt psychology, Polanyi emphasizes that perception of the whole of an object and perception of its component parts are entirely separate and to some extent unrelated processes. A scientific discovery, then, "reduces our focal awareness of observations into a subsidiary awareness of them, by shifting our attention from them to their theoretical coherence."[28]

THE NATURE OF TACIT KNOWING

From this basis Polanyi builds to a succinct statement of the central premise of the essay and to his most noted contribution to the study of knowledge:

> This act of integration, which we can identify both in the visual perception of objects and in the discovery of scientific theories is the tacit power we have been looking for. I shall call it *tacit knowing*.[29]

Polanyi's use of the verb "knowing" rather than the more commonly used noun "knowledge" appears to be a deliberate effort to focus on the active meaning of the concept. Again, Polanyi is interested primarily in the processes of scientific discovery, and by extension other forms of perception and awareness. This very active approach to the central theme is a fundamentally important tenet of "The Logic of Tacit Inference" and of all of Polanyi's writing on the topic.

Polanyi returns to the notion of subsidiary and focal perception and distinguishes between two components of tacit knowing that he identifies as the proximal term and the distal term. In ordinary casual observation, no conscious distinction is made by the observer between subsidiary and focal perception; in this kind of perception, the proximal and distal terms serve extremely different functions and can be said to be separate functions "joined together by tacit knowing."[30] When an object is observed with the objective of thoroughly understanding the object, the observer deliberately integrates subsidiary and focal perception such that the proximal term plays the role of describing the object's component parts in isolation, and the distal term plays the role of describing the object as an integrated whole. Casually noticing that there is a bowl of apples on a table, for instance, requires no explicit, conscious recognition of the direction from which the apples, the bowl, and the table are viewed, the nature of the light that makes it possible to see and recognize the objects, or any other analytical detail. A painter or photographer interested in producing a still life or a researcher designing an approach to searching for and retrieving images from a database, however, must deliberately break the combination of objects, angle, and lighting into understandable component parts. According to Polanyi, the most important aspect of observation has not to do with looking at an object, but with looking from the proximal terms that define the object "to a distal term which is [the object's] meaning."[31] Rather than focusing attention on the object, the observer naturally focuses attention from the object to the meaning of the object. In fact, Polanyi contends, focusing on the nature of the object rather than the meaning of the object has the effect of destroying the meaning of the object.

TACIT AND EXPLICIT KNOWLEDGE

Building from this rather technical presentation of the nature of tacit knowing, Polanyi progresses to the aspect of tacit knowing that is perhaps most central to the integration of the concept in the domain of knowledge management by stating that tacit knowing frequently *"cannot be explicitly stated."*[32] The possessor of a skill (Polanyi uses the example of riding a bicycle) or a talent, such as innate artistic ability, may find it quite literally impossible to explain the nature or processes of that skill or talent. It is clear that such an individual knows how to do something but is not capable of joining the proximal and distal terms to make it possible to decompose that knowledge and describe both its subsidiary and focal elements. Furthermore, it is quite possible to acquire new knowledge without being able to explicitly state, describe, or even identify what it is that is now known that previously was not. Extending from this to the essay's basic focus on scientific discovery, Polanyi asserts that just as it is possible to learn without being consciously aware of doing so, there must also be a process of "discovery without awareness."[33] To a considerable extent, then, scientific knowledge may be acquired more through a predilection for unplanned discovery, which Polanyi terms "scientific intuition," than through deliberate efforts to discover.[34]

It is only from this basis in exploring the nature of tacit knowing that Polanyi progresses to the discussion for which he is most credited and most misunderstood: the distinction between tacit knowledge and explicit knowledge, which he very succinctly described:

> While tacit knowledge can be possessed by itself, explicit knowledge must rely on being tacitly understood and applied. Hence all knowledge is *either tacit* or *rooted in tacit knowledge*. A *wholly* explicit knowledge is unthinkable.[35]

Making use of an instance of explicit knowledge, then, such as a document, a recording, or a work of art, requires transforming that explicit knowledge into tacit knowledge; that is, a passive artifact can be said to contain explicit knowledge, but such an artifact can assume meaning only through the active process of *tacit knowing*.

Polanyi clearly views tacit and explicit knowledge as fundamental, essential, and inseparable components within the overall process of knowing. Artifactual, explicit knowledge is required for shared retention and sharing of knowledge, but the artifacts of explicit knowledge are of no value if they cannot be transformed into tacit knowing. This integration of the explicit and tacit dimensions of knowledge has largely been lost in the application of Polanyi's ideas to knowledge management.

CHARACTERISTICS OF TACIT KNOWLEDGE

Crowley synthesized the literature on tacit knowledge to create a list of commonly perceived characteristics of tacit knowledge. According to this analysis, tacit knowledge is commonly assumed to be

- Personal in origin
- Valuable to the possessor
- Job specific
- Related to context
- Difficult to fully articulate
- Both known in part and unknown in part to the possessor
- Transmitted, where transmission is possible, through interpersonal contact
- Operative on an organizational level
- Applied, in part, through "if-then" rules ("*if* certain conditions exist, *then* apply the following")
- Capable of becoming explicit knowledge and vice versa
- Intertwined with explicit knowledge along unstable knowledge borders
- Poorly reflected in contemporary knowledge literature[36]

These definitional characteristics or assumptions are indeed characteristic of the knowledge management literature. Few, however, can be supported by Polanyi's work; those that can be supported are supportable mostly by inference, not through direct reference to Polanyi's writings. To Crowley's credit, he does not contend that these *are* the defining characteristics of tacit knowledge, but only that the literature has assumed these characteristics and assigned them to tacit knowledge. A brief examination of each of these characteristics in relationship to "The Logic of Tacit Inference" is sufficient to call each of them into question.

Tacit knowledge is personal in origin. Many authors in the knowledge management domain distinguish between explicit knowledge, which can be codified and is acquired primarily through formal processes, and tacit knowledge, which defies codification and is acquired primarily or even exclusively through informal processes. Although some essentially personal, internalized element may contribute to the definition of tacit knowledge, Polanyi clearly allows for the notion that tacit knowledge may be impersonal in nature in his assertion that explicit knowledge must be transformed into tacit knowing to be useful. Tacit knowledge can have its origin in the artifacts of explicit knowledge, which may or may not be—and frequently are not—personal in origin. On the other hand, tacit knowledge is frequently quite personal in application: a baseball fan may cull a large variety of sources of explicit knowledge in an effort to develop a comprehensive knowledge of historical and contemporary scores and performance records, motivated entirely by a sense of a personal need to know.

Tacit knowledge is valuable to the possessor. If the contention that tacit knowledge is inherently personal in origin is rejected, then the notion that tacit knowledge is necessarily of special or specific value to its possessor must also be rejected. In fact, it seems self-evident that every individual must possess substantial tacit knowledge that is transitory or even trivial. Although much tacit knowledge may indeed be personally valuable, to assume that all tacit knowledge is valuable to its possessor requires the assumption of some process by which individuals can deliberately unlearn that which they tacitly know, a process that does not seem to exist in most people.

Tacit knowledge is job specific. This is refuted by Polanyi's examples, which focus on such applications of tacit knowing as the ability to ride a bicycle or float while swimming. More importantly, however, Polanyi defines tacit knowing as the fundamental process by which all knowledge is acquired and internalized. It must therefore be the case that tacit knowledge can be either specific or general in nature and may very well be not only not job specific, but not even task specific except to the extent that possessing esoteric knowledge such as a comprehensive memory of baseball scores can be defined as providing an approach to a task.

Tacit knowledge is related to context. This assertion is accurate but essentially trivial. Polanyi's exploration of the interrelationship of the proximal term and the distal term in knowing makes it clear that all knowledge is related to context, as it fairly obviously must be. The value to knowledge management of exploring or understanding the role of context is questionable: an encyclopedic knowledge of baseball scores is probably of limited application to the daily work of database administration but may be of paramount importance to the on-the-job contentment and performance of a specific database administrator.

Tacit knowledge is difficult to fully articulate. Polanyi would probably agree that tacit knowledge may be or is frequently difficult to fully articulate, but not that it is necessarily difficult to fully articulate. As anyone who has ever prepared a synthetic research paper based on the works of others knows, it is frequently difficult to fully articulate explicit knowledge. It seems probable that like-minded individuals can at least sometimes quite fully articulate tacit knowledge for purposes of sharing it, thereby expanding the tacit knowledge of those with whom it is shared.

Tacit knowledge is both known in part and unknown in part to the possessor. This is a difficult assumption to interpret but does not seem to be supported by Polanyi's work. If all knowledge is, as Polanyi clearly indicated, a fusion of tacit and explicit, and if the fundamental nature of the tacit dimension is the active process of knowing, then the concept of any aspect of knowledge being unknown is at best paradoxical and at worst nonsensical. This assertion may be better expressed in terms of the extent to which the possessor of knowledge is consciously aware of the totality of the knowledge possessed. Polanyi would clearly contend that in ordinary observation the observer is fully cognizant of the distal term but not of the proximal term of the object under observation.

Tacit knowledge is transmitted, where transmission is possible, through interpersonal contact. Polanyi's description of the necessity of converting explicit knowledge to use through the process of tacit knowing is clearly in conflict with this assumption. If all knowledge must be internalized through tacit knowing, then the transmission mechanism is irrelevant. In fact, interpersonal contact frequently introduces matters of personality, politics, and culture that are not present in the transformation of the explicit knowledge codified in artifacts into tacit knowing.

Tacit knowledge is operative on an organizational level. The implication of this assumption is presumably that tacit knowledge can be put to work to benefit an organization in addition to providing a direct benefit to the individual who possesses the knowledge in question. This is probably true in some cases and not true in others. It might be accurate to assert that tacit knowledge is sometimes to some extent operative on an organizational level, but to contend that tacit knowledge is always and under all circumstances operational on an organizational level implies a unitary role for tacit knowledge that cannot reasonably be expected to pertain.

Tacit knowledge is applied, in part, through "if-then" rules. This is another assumption that is probably true but not of any particular import. The deductive principle of syllogistic reasoning permeates virtually all formal decision-making processes and is probably programmed into human reasoning. It is undoubtedly the case that the application of explicit knowledge also takes place largely through "if-then" rules used to assess the value and implications of documentary evidence. Crowley does not expand on the assumption to provide an example of an alternative to the application of "if-then" rules, which makes thoroughly understanding the validity or role of this assumption difficult.

Tacit knowledge is capable of becoming explicit knowledge and vice versa. "The Logic of Tacit Inference" firmly supports the notion that explicit knowledge can become tacit knowledge; in fact, Polanyi describes the process whereby explicit knowledge *must* be converted to tacit knowledge through the process of tacit knowing to render the explicit knowledge usable. The reverse, however, which is so fundamental to the knowledge management conception of tacit knowledge, is much less certain and much less predictable. Some tacit knowledge surely is capable of becoming explicit knowledge; there is no possible alternative mechanism by which explicit knowledge can come into being other than that an individual chooses to express tacit knowledge in an explicit form. That does not, however, promise a great deal for the introduction of formal programs for comprehensively transforming the tacit knowledge of an organization's workforce into explicit knowledge products.

Tacit knowledge is intertwined with explicit knowledge along unstable knowledge borders. This is another assumption that is difficult to interpret. The notion that tacit knowledge and explicit knowledge are intertwined is so fundamental to Polanyi's work as to be axiomatic. The concept of the "unstable knowledge border" doesn't arise in Polanyi. At the level of an individual, the border between tacit and explicit knowledge is probably stable within the limits that allow for the acquisition of new tacit knowledge; a lack of stability at the individual level would result in cognitive dysfunction and would at its extreme be reflected in externally visible mental instability. Within the context of an organization, the stability of the border between tacit knowledge and explicit knowledge is presumably quite variable, but excessive instability at the organizational level would surely lead to the same sort of dysfunctionality as at the individual level. Organizations that are in any sense stable surely must exist in an environment in which the border between tacit and explicit knowledge is reasonably stable, even though that stability may be more a function of accident than of design.

Tacit knowledge is poorly reflected in contemporary knowledge literature. A search of the *Social Sciences Citation Index* reveals that the works of Michael Polanyi have been cited in more than four thousand articles, only four of which are self-citations. Most of these citations are to Polanyi's various works in the arena of tacit knowing/tacit knowledge. As Crowley points out, the concept of tacit knowledge has found fertile intellectual ground in a wide variety of disciplines and professional domains, "including business, human resource management, information science, library science, law, military science, philosophy, psychology, public administration, and sociology."[37] The clear majority of citations to Polanyi come from the literature of epistemology, the branch of philosophy dedicated to the theory of knowledge. It is unquestionably accurate to state that the nature of tacit knowledge is inconsistently and incompletely reflected in the knowledge literature, but to expect such consistency or completeness for what is necessarily an abstract construct is hardly reasonable. It is also accurate to state that tacit knowledge is poorly understood in the knowledge management literature, a problem not of Michael Polanyi's making, but in great need of a solution.

Karl Popper, "Epistemology without a Knowing Subject," in *Objective Knowledge: An Evolutionary Approach* (Oxford: Clarendon, 1972), 106–52. (An address given on 25 Aug. 1967, at the Third International Congress for Logic, Methodology and Philosophy of Science, 25 Aug. to 2 Sept. 1967; first published in the proceedings of this Congress, ed. B. van Rootselaar and J. F. Staal, Amsterdam, 1968, pp. 333–73.)

Philosopher Sir Karl Raimund Popper (1902–94) was born in Vienna and educated at the University of Vienna, where he earned a PhD in philosophy in 1928. He spent most of his academic career at the London School of Economics. Popper was an extremely prolific author whose works focused largely on social philosophy and the philosophy of science. He is widely recognized as one of the most influential philosophers of the twentieth century; evidence of that status lies in the more than 9,500 references to Popper's works found in the *Social Sciences Citation Index*. Although his works have been cited substantially on a less frequent basis in the knowledge management literature, his "Epistemology without a Knowing Subject" provides a view of the nature of knowledge that has direct pertinence to knowledge management.

SCIENTIFIC KNOWLEDGE AND CONJECTURE

Virtually all of Popper's works are grounded in the sciences. One of the fundamental tenets of Popper's approach to philosophy is his contention that all science and all scientific knowledge are conjectural. The role of the scientist is to formulate conjectures, which at times take on the form of truly wild guesses, which are then challenged by further probing and ultimately are either supported or refuted. Popper explicitly disallows the notion that any such conjecture can ever be conclusively demonstrated to be true. To Popper, therefore, knowledge itself is a matter of conjecture. Although there is recognition in his writing that there must be a physical universe that is nonconjectural, his position is that the physical universe can be understood only in conjectural terms.

POPPER'S THREE WORLDS

"Epistemology without a Knowing Subject" begins with the definition of three conceptual areas Popper terms "worlds":

1. The world of physical objects or states
2. The world of states of consciousness
3. The world of objective contents of thought

Popper emphasizes that his identification of these conceptual areas as worlds is entirely a matter of choosing a convenient term to use in describing them.

"Epistemology without a Knowing Subject" is primarily an explication and defense of the concept of the third world, in which ideas have an objective rather than a purely subjective nature. In contrast to Polanyi's tacit knowing, which is fundamentally a subjective process, Popper's third world is an objective conceptual space in which ideas exist independently of any subjective process. To Popper, knowledge as a process in the ordinary sense, as expressed in the phrase "I know," belongs to the second world, the world of subjects. "Scientific knowledge belongs to the third world, to the world of objective theories, objective problems, and objective arguments."[38]

Knowledge in the second world is inherently subjective in nature and has primarily to do with the consciousness of a subject or a predilection to a particular pattern of behavior in response to a subject. The classical Cartesian model of knowledge explicitly distinguishes between the subject (the person who knows) and the object (that which is known), with a distinct focus on the subject. Knowledge in the third world, though, is objective in nature and consists "of problems, theories, and arguments as such."[39] From this explanation Popper extends to the central theme of "Epistemology without a Knowing Subject," which is that "knowledge in a objective sense is *knowledge without a knower; it is knowledge without a knowing subject.*"[40] By this, Popper means that scientific knowledge is independent of the mind of any particular individual and truly exists in and belongs to the objective universe, as do the physical entities and physical states that make up the first world. Knowledge, then, is not a process of developing content but is the content itself as it exists in the natural world.

Popper provides a pair of "experiments" in the form of scenarios to help explain the nature of the third world. In the first of these experiments, all global society and its artifacts are destroyed, as well as all knowledge of those artifacts and of how to use them, but libraries and the ability to use them survive. The scenario of the second experiment is the same, except that libraries and the ability to use them are also lost. The difference, of course, is that in the first scenario "after much suffering, our world may get going again," but in the second scenario "there will be no re-emergence of our civilization for many millennia."[41] The collections of libraries and all other artifacts of human knowledge are objective entities that express ideas in the form of content.

This notion of the independence of the objective third world of knowledge as content and the subjective second world of the processes of knowing may be a bit difficult to assimilate but is absolutely essential to Popper's understanding of scientific knowledge. Popper contends "that traditional epistemology with its concentration on the second world, or on knowledge in the subjective sense, is irrelevant to the study of scientific knowledge."[42] He further argues that "what is relevant for epistemology is the study of scientific problems and problem situations, of scientific conjectures (which I take as merely another word for scientific hypotheses or theories), of scientific discussions, of critical arguments, and of the role played by evidence in arguments; and therefore of scientific journals and books, and of experiments and their evaluation in scientific arguments; or, in brief, that the study of a *largely autonomous* third world of objective knowledge is of decisive importance for epistemology."[43]

THREE ESSENTIAL THESES

Popper summarizes the central theme of "Epistemology without a Knowing Subject" in three fundamental theses:

1. Subjective epistemology based on understanding of the second world is irrelevant.
2. Objective epistemology based on understanding of the third world is relevant.

3. Study of the third world helps inform understanding of the second world, but study of the second world does nothing to inform understanding of the third world.

The most important element of Popper's analysis of the relationship between the subjective second world and the objective third world is that knowledge is fundamentally evolutionary in nature and that although a specific scientific discovery may seem to be revolutionary, every discovery is in fact the inevitable result of an evolutionary process. The third world is truly organic and natural and consists both of knowledge that has already been discovered and knowledge not yet discovered. The nature or the sequence of the events that led to Newton's codification of the laws of gravity, which are processes of the second world, are independent of the nature of gravity itself. The laws of gravity were in a very real sense waiting for Newton's discovery and subsequent analysis.

Ultimately, Popper's contention is that the content of knowledge, regardless of how the knowledge is produced or codified, is both independent of and more important than the processes of discovery or codification. In Popper's third world, objective knowledge exists in and of itself and has autonomous importance. His discussion of the objectivity and autonomy of the third world is of particular importance to the domain of knowledge management. As an example, Popper refutes "the feeling that a book is nothing without a reader; only if it is understood does it really become a book; otherwise it is just paper with black spots on it."[44] A document—a book, a report, a record in a database, a video or audio recording, or any other codified artifact—contains objective knowledge regardless of the way in which the document was produced or stored, and regardless of how the document is used or even whether it is ever used. The objectivity of the document is independent of the truth or falsity of its content. The objective knowledge contained in a document exits in "its possibility of being understood or interpreted, or misunderstood or misinterpreted. . . . and this potentiality may exist without ever being actualized or realized."[45]

Popper's third world does not consist entirely of what is generally understood as explicit knowledge, however: "I assert that even though this third world is a human product, there are many theories in themselves and arguments in themselves and problem situations in themselves which have never been produced or understood and may never be produced or understood by men."[46] Just as the discovery of new species of plants and animals, new celestial bodies, and new physical processes expands the human knowledge base, so does the discovery of new theories, arguments, and problems.

The autonomy of the third world—its independence from the context of the mind—can be illustrated by many examples from mathematics. An example presented by Popper is the concept of prime numbers, which is fundamentally a human product. There was probably no pressing pragmatic gap in the collective knowledge base of society to be solved by the discovery of prime numbers. Once they were discovered and defined, however, prime numbers assumed an existence independent of the discovery and definition processes.

Popper graphically illustrates the process by which objective knowledge is developed and cumulated in the form of a simple formula:

$$P_1 \rightarrow TT \rightarrow EE \rightarrow P_2$$

A problem (P_1), identified by a person, generates a tentative theory (TT), which is subject to error elimination (EE), "which may consist of critical discussion or experimental activity."[47] The outcome is identification of additional problems (P_2) that can be addressed in the same way. These new problems, unlike the originally identified problem, "are not in general intentionally created by us, they emerge autonomously from the field of new relationships which we cannot help bringing into existence with every action, however little we intend to do so."[48]

EVERYTHING IS CONNECTED TO EVERYTHING ELSE

Ultimately, then, the knowledge of Popper's third world is—rather than a subjective, artificial outcome of the processes of knowing—an objective, organic, natural, integrated product of the physical universe that is purposive and pragmatic. All knowledge, since it derives from the same fundamental resources and processes, is directly interrelated to all other knowledge. In the words of *The Last Whole Earth Catalog,* "everything is connected to everything else."[49] Knowledge, whether tacit or explicit, is an essential component of the framework and web of the universe. Fuller distinguished between embodied knowledge and embedded knowledge. "Knowledge is embodied by being placed in a material container, whereas knowledge is embedded by being situated in a social context. Science, according to epistemologists, was both disembodied and disembedded."[50] Badaracco explicitly related embedded knowledge to tacit knowledge.[51] Madhavan and Grover described the essential management task as focusing on "the transition from embedded to embodied knowledge."[52] Popper's integrated view of knowledge, however, suggests that all knowledge is inherently embedded, that either tacit or explicit knowledge can be either embedded or embodied, and that the distinction between embodied and disembodied knowledge is largely immaterial.

Robert S. Taylor, "Question-Negotiation and Information Seeking in Libraries," *College and Research Libraries* 29 (May 1968): 178–94.

Robert S. Taylor was born in Ithaca, New York, and received a bachelor's degree in history in 1940 and a master's degree in library science in 1950, both from Cornell University. Taylor's 1968 article "Question-Negotiation and Information Seeking in Libraries" is required reading in many schools of library and information science as well as in other programs such as business administration and knowledge management; having received more than 230 entries in the *Social Sciences Citation Index,* it has been identified as a "citation classic."[53] The value of Taylor's work has not diminished in any way since its publication almost 40 years ago; more than 60 citation entries in *SSCI* are from articles published in the twenty-first century. Taylor did not set out to explore the nature of knowledge and in no way presents a conscious contribution to epistemology. The article is focused primarily on information in the specific form of answers to questions. Taylor does, however, provide substantial insight into the practical processes of seeking knowledge that has meaning for the understanding of knowledge in the context of knowledge management.

INFORMATION SEEKING

Taylor's primary goal was to create an evidence-based analysis of what happens when an individual needs and eventually seeks information. Although Taylor's exploration was grounded in the context of libraries, specifically special libraries and information centers, the result is applicable to any information-seeking environment. Taylor's work, although highly theoretical in nature, was solidly grounded in empirical data gathered from extensive structured interviews with special librarians and information specialists. Taylor derived three primary products from the interview data: (1) a graphic representation of the decisions an information seeker must make prior to entering into either a self-executed search or a process of question negotiation, (2) a model of four levels of question development or information need, and (3) the identification of five "filters" that must be applied to successfully answer a question or meet an information need.

Taylor's graphic model of the decision-making process, with minor modifications to extend beyond the library context, is reproduced as figure 1.1. In this process chart, an individual with an information need faces three primary decision points, labeled A, B, and C. "At decision point A, the inquirer decides whether to discuss his problem with a colleague or to go to whatever literature or information center may be available."[54] The information seeker will probably make some attempt to use whatever sources of information are readily at hand, assuming that the information need is adequately understood to do so.

At decision point B, the information seeker decides either to conduct a more exhaustive search of personal information files or to work with a formal information system. "This is an important choice and reflects a number of factors: previous experience, environment (is this an accepted procedure in his activity?), and ease of access."[55] Taylor echoes the research of Mooers and others, whose findings indicate that ease of use of an information system is typically a more important factor than the quantity or quality of information available from the system.[56] This is probably even more true in the era of Google.

Decision point C requires selection of a mode of information seeking: the information seeker may choose either to search independently or to enlist the assistance of an information professional. "Most important in this decision is the inquirer's image of the personnel, their effectiveness, and his previous experience with this or any other library and librarian."[57]

FOUR LEVELS OF INFORMATION NEED

Although Taylor's discussion of the "four levels of information need" is grounded primarily in the context of a process of negotiation between an information seeker and an information professional, it seems evident that some similar process must take place during a self-help search. In fact, these levels of need appear to be universals that are closely tied to the nature of knowledge.

1. The first level of need is "the conscious or even unconscious need for information not existing in the remembered experience of the inquirer. It may be only a vague sort of dissatisfaction. It is probably inexpressible in linguistic terms."[58] This is clearly analogous to Polanyi's notion of tacit knowledge; although Polanyi was focused more

Figure 1.1
Taylor's Model of Pre-negotiation Decisions

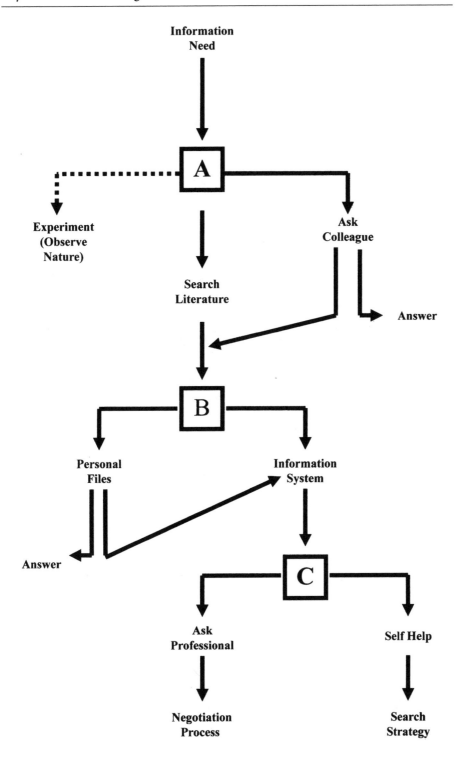

on what an individual knows than on what is not known, any awareness of a gap in knowledge must be a form of knowledge in and of itself. "This need . . . will change in form, quality, concreteness, and criteria as information is added, as it is influenced by analogy, or as its importance grows with the investigation."[59]

2. "At the second level of need there is a conscious mental description of an ill-defined area of indecision."[60] This amorphous, ambiguous, anomalous state of conscious awareness stands at the transition from tacit knowledge to explicit knowledge in that it is amenable to verbalization. It is most likely at this point that the information seeker will "talk to someone else to sharpen his focus."[61] Verbalizing this conscious need will probably help clarify the nature of the need and reduce ambiguity but is not likely to satisfy the information need.

3. The process of clarification and reduction of ambiguity leads to the third level of need, which involves more careful verbalization of the need in an attempt to more fully represent it. "At this level an inquirer can form a qualified and rational statement of his question. Here he is describing his area of doubt in concrete terms and he may or may not be thinking within the context or constraints of the system from which he wants information."[62] At this level the information need definitely constitutes explicit knowledge.

4. "At the fourth level the question is recast in anticipation of what the files can deliver. The searcher must think in terms of the organization of particular files and of the discrete packages available—such as books, reports, papers, drawings, or tables."[63] A common characteristic of the fourth level of information need is a loss of the clarity of the third level due to excessive attention to anticipated results rather than retention of focus on the true nature of the information need. This level then represents a reduction in the extent to which the question represents explicit knowledge. "This is where the process of negotiation starts."[64]

Taylor more succinctly presents "these four levels of question formation" as

Q1—the actual, but unexpressed need for information (the visceral need)
Q2—the conscious, within-brain description of the need (the *conscious* need)
Q3—the formal statement of the need (the *formalized* need)
Q4—the question as presented to the information system (the *compromised* need)[65]

THE NEGOTIATION PROCESS

The goal of the negotiation process, mediated by an information professional, is to move backward from the compromised statement of need (Q4) "to the formalized need (Q3), possibly even to the conscious need (Q2), and *then* to translate these needs into a useful search strategy."[66] The outcome of this process is a statement of a negotiated need that is amenable to searching. This negotiation process is effected through the application of Taylor's five filters. Although Taylor was primarily concerned with the role the filters play in guiding the negotiation process, they also provide a useful model for understanding the nature of knowledge.

1. *Determination of subject.* Most people probably think of knowledge primarily in terms of the specific subject of what is known. Subjects are most commonly understood in terms describable by nouns, although knowledge can also take the form of "know-how" as well as "know-what." Knowledge is additionally defined by "the *limits and structure of the subject.*"[67] The limits and structure are delimited partly by the nature of the subject and partly by the factors defined in the other four filters.

2. *Exploration of motivation and objective.* Taylor identified this filter as "probably the most critical: Why does the inquirer want this information? What is his objective? What is his motivation?"[68] Knowledge is defined by some combination of the subject itself and the individual's reasons for knowing. This relates well to Polanyi's view of the tacit-explicit continuum, and to Nonaka and Takeuchi's exposition of the oneness of the individual and what the individual knows, but calls into question some aspects of Popper's notion of knowledge "without a knowing subject."

3. *Identification of pertinent personal characteristics of the information seeker.* In Taylor's analysis, knowing the characteristics of the information seeker is an essential component in question negotiation. "What is his status in the organization? Has he been in the library before? What is his background? What relationship does his query have to what he knows? What is his level of critical awareness?"[69] In addition to the nature of the subject and the motivation for knowing, an individual's overall state of knowledge and capacity for knowing play a substantial role in determining the potential for converting from tacit to explicit or from explicit to tacit. Conversion from explicit to tacit knowledge requires a state of readiness on the part of the individual that is determined more by the personal characteristics of that individual than by motivation of the objective nature of the subject.

4. *Relationship of the negotiated need to the information system.* Conversion from tacit to explicit knowledge requires translation of tacit knowledge into terms that can be accommodated by the systems that support explicit knowledge. There is a core linguistic element to the translation process, but there are also intervening factors related to technology, culture, and politics. Polanyi's assertion that "we know more than we can tell" has as much to do with the imposition of these factors into the translation from tacit to explicit as with the linguistic factors.[70]

5. *Encapsulation of anticipated or acceptable answers.* An information seeker "has some picture in mind as to what he expects his answer to look like, *i.e.* format, data, size, etc. The problem of the inquirer's acceptability of an answer is an important filter in the process of answering queries."[71] The acceptability of knowledge to an individual is a key determiner of the successful conversion from explicit to tacit knowledge. It is influenced by the essentially physical factors identified by Taylor but is also driven by the objective nature of the subject, the motivation for learning, the individual's personal characteristics, and the relationship between the system of explicit knowledge and the ability of the individual to transform explicit knowledge into tacit knowledge. That ability may be shaped as much by preexisting tacit knowledge as by the nature of the explicit knowledge to be learned; new knowledge that is in conflict with preexisting knowledge may be rejected outright.[72]

Taylor's model, extended to the nature of knowledge, adds substantially to the concepts of tacit and explicit knowledge as well as to Popper's view of third-world knowledge by linking knowledge to the action modality of information seeking.

Ikujiro Nonaka and Hirotaka Takeuchi, *The Knowledge-Creating Company: How Japanese Companies Create the Dynamics of Innovation* (New York: Oxford University Press, 1995).

Ikujiro Nonaka and Hirotaka Takeuchi are professors of international business strategy at Hitotsubashi University in Tokyo. Nonaka is the most frequently cited author in the domain of knowledge management. With more than 1,300 references to the book listed in the *Social Sciences Citation Index*, *The Knowledge-Creating Company* is one of the most influential works in the field of knowledge management.

EAST IS EAST AND WEST IS WEST

The initial and guiding premise of *The Knowledge-Creating Company* is that there are fundamental differences between the philosophies and patterns of thought of Japanese people—and by extension Japanese business leaders—and their Western counterparts. These differences are so striking that they have inevitably resulted in radically different approaches to corporate management. The success of Japanese companies, particularly their success relative to the success of Western companies, is attributed to "their skills and expertise at 'organizational knowledge creation.'"[73] The authors address the fundamental differences in culture from a number of different perspectives, but the essential recurring theme is that there is a deeply ingrained difference in the ways in which Japanese and Western cultures view knowledge.

According to Nonaka and Takeuchi, there is a fundamental "paradox" related to the role of epistemology in the intellectual traditions of the two cultures: "While there is a rich epistemological tradition in Western philosophy, there is almost none to speak of in Japan."[74] Most of chapter 2 of *The Knowledge-Creating Company*, "Knowledge and Management," is devoted to a summarization of the comparative history of the role of epistemology in Western philosophy and the "Japanese intellectual tradition." Interestingly, Nonaka and Takeuchi draw their comments on Western philosophy entirely from well-documented formal sources representing the works of mainstream philosophers, while their discussion of the Japanese intellectual tradition draws primarily from less formal sources and emphasizes explicit documentation to a much lesser degree. This is perhaps a source of support for the authors' assertion about the relative roles of the "epistemological tradition" in the two cultures, but it results in something of an apples-and-oranges comparison.

TACIT KNOWLEDGE

Nonaka and Takeuchi draw heavily on the language of Polanyi related to tacit knowledge and explicit knowledge, but they actually do little more than adopt Polanyi's terminology for the purpose of applying their own definitions to those terms. Although no explicit definition of terms is provided, the authors' view of tacit knowledge is closely congruent with those characteristics summarized by Crowley.

> Tacit knowledge is highly personal and hard to formalize, making it difficult to communicate or to share with others. Subjective insights, intuitions, and hunches fall into this category of knowledge. Furthermore, tacit knowledge is deeply rooted in an individual's action and experience, as well as in the ideals, values, or emotions he or she embraces.[75]

The authors divide tacit knowledge into two "dimensions." The technical dimension is encapsulated in the term "know-how," which closely correlates with Polanyi's statement that "we know more than we can tell" but has little foundation in most of Polanyi's reasoning.[76] The cognitive dimension "consists of schemata, mental models, beliefs, and perceptions so ingrained that we take them for granted."[77] This is very closely aligned with Popper's notion of objective knowledge but is less well aligned with Polanyi's ideas of tacit knowing.

Although it mentions a wide range of philosophers from Plato to Heidegger and Russell, the discussion of Western philosophy presented in chapter 2 essentially begins and ends with Descartes and the Cartesian split between subject and object. Neither Polanyi nor Popper is referenced in this discussion, although Polanyi's work plays a critical role elsewhere in *The Knowledge-Creating Company*. This omission is acknowledged later in the book: "We did not include Polanyi in Chapter 2, because he is still considered minor in Western philosophy because of his view and background."[78] The exposition of the Japanese intellectual tradition focuses on the "(1) oneness of humanity and nature; (2) oneness of body and mind; and (3) oneness of self and other."[79] The comparison of Western and Japanese traditions concludes by suggesting "that the ultimate reality for the Japanese lies in the delicate, transitional, process of permanent flux, and in visible concrete matter, rather than in an eternal, unchanging, invisible, and abstract entity," which presumably characterizes the Western view of the ultimate reality.[80]

Chapter 2 concludes with a commentary on the role of knowledge in Western management theory. "We have found a paradox in that most of these theories scarcely mention knowledge itself, while they supposedly pursue scientific, objective knowledge under the strong influence of the Western epistemological tradition. . . . At the core of concern of these theories is the acquisition, accumulation, and utilization of *existing* knowledge; they lack the perspective of 'creating new knowledge.'"[81] Western management theory therefore has no potential for guiding the creation of explicit knowledge from tacit knowledge.

Ultimately, the arguments regarding epistemology and the differing philosophical approaches of Japanese and Western cultures seem hollow and somewhat specious. The authors have provided a dismal and depressing view of a unitary, inflexible, unchanging straw man in the form of Western philosophy and knocked it down with a glorified image of the Japanese viewpoint, which is presented as integrated, organic, and simultaneously universal and personal. The comparison is overly simple, resting on the assumption that the two systems of philosophy are both accurately depicted and pervasive in the societies compared. Although the principle of "oneness" may be pervasive in the collective and individual consciousnesses of the Japanese people, the Cartesian split between subject and object is probably virtually unknown among even highly educated citizens of Western nations and is certainly not part of daily or even occasional personal consciousness. The dominance of this model among business leaders, other than those who have read Nonaka and Takeuchi, is likewise probably virtually nonexistent.

FOUR MODES OF KNOWLEDGE CONVERSION

Chapter 3, "Theory of Organizational Knowledge Creation," concentrates on the variable relationships between tacit knowledge and explicit knowledge that Nonaka and

Takeuchi refer to as "knowledge conversion."[82] Four "modes" of knowledge conversion are described:

1. Conversion from tacit knowledge to tacit knowledge is "socialization."[83] Examples of socialization are presented primarily in the form of learning through observation. "Apprentices work with their masters and learn craftsmanship not through language but through observation, imitation, and practice."[84] This is an unfortunate example, in that it seems extremely unlikely that there has ever been a relationship between apprentice and master, or in the business world between protégé and mentor, that was not based both in discussion and in observation. The more specific examples provided, of a brainstorming session and a situation in which a researcher posed as an apprentice for the purpose of gaining insight not achievable through less formal observation, are not illuminative. It is clear from these examples that there is no direct tacit to tacit conversion; the conversion actually takes place through the creation of experiences that make it possible to convert tacit knowledge to explicit knowledge and then to immediately reconvert the explicit knowledge to tacit. Nonaka and Takeuchi seem to have confused explicit knowledge with documented knowledge, ignoring the fact that any codification of knowledge, whether in the form of an informal sharing of ideas or a structured opportunity for observation, is a process of generating explicit knowledge.

2. Conversion from tacit knowledge to explicit knowledge is "externalization."[85] Externalization "is a quintessential knowledge-creation process in that tacit knowledge becomes explicit, taking the shapes of metaphors, analogies, concepts, hypotheses, or models."[86] The authors rely heavily on the role of metaphors in the conversion of tacit knowledge to explicit knowledge, although there is no real explanation of why metaphors are inherently more important than other constructs. Interestingly, the discussion of externalization doesn't address the processes of documentation of knowledge.

3. Conversion from explicit knowledge to explicit knowledge is "combination."[87] "Combination is a process of systematizing concepts into a knowledge system."[88] This "mode of knowledge conversion is most often seen when middle managers break down and operationalize corporate visions, business concepts, or product concepts."[89] Once again, Nonaka and Takeuchi seem to have ignored Polanyi's contention that "explicit knowledge must rely on being tacitly understood and applied."[90] Polanyi's model clearly makes any direct process of conversion from explicit knowledge to explicit knowledge nonsensical. The progression must necessarily be from explicit knowledge to tacit knowledge to new explicit knowledge.

4. Conversion from explicit knowledge to tacit knowledge is "internalization," which the authors clarify as being "a process of embedding explicit knowledge into tacit knowledge . . . [that is] closely related to 'learning by doing.'"[91] If one accepts Polanyi's definitions of tacit knowing and explicit knowledge, "internalization" is simply *learning*: the process of conversion from explicit knowledge to tacit knowing that necessarily precedes any understanding or application of explicit knowledge.

The goal of *The Knowledge-Creating Company* is to provide practical insight into the role of structured knowledge creation in a corporate setting, not to contribute to the literature of epistemology; this is the primary value of the book as well. Chapters 4 through 8 provide examples of how the processes of knowledge conversion can be operationalized and guidance on redefining business processes to facilitate knowledge creation. The examples, mostly drawn from a single corporation, are interesting and useful; the guidance is inherently sound and presents an insightful view of business process transformation that many of the book's reviewers and commentators have justifiably viewed as truly eye opening. To the extent that it is oriented toward the practical outcomes of knowledge generation, the book is abundantly successful, as is evident from both the explicit accolades and the citations it has received. At the same time, the grounding of such guidance in a rather fundamentally flawed conceptual model tends to undermine the impact of the main body of the book.

KNOWLEDGE CREATION

Early on, Nonaka and Takeuchi describe the focus of *The Knowledge-Creating Company* as being "on knowledge *creation,* not on knowledge per se."[92] They should perhaps have taken that definitive focus more to heart and avoided the extensive and largely untrue comparison of Western and Japanese philosophies. Similarly, their work would have been well served had they chosen to develop new terminology rather than drawing from philosophy. In particular, their use of "tacit knowledge" and "explicit knowledge" is so divergent from the views of Polanyi that the use of those terms is more a distraction than a strength. The authors would have done well to distinguish between internalized knowledge, which is created through the process they term internalization, and externalized knowledge, which is created through the process they term externalization. Focusing on the internalization and externalization processes as the defining characteristics of the two forms of knowledge would also have reduced or eliminated the ambiguous use of the words "tacit" and "explicit" that permeates *The Knowledge-Creating Company.* Although the authors' use of "tacit knowledge" seems to consistently align with both Polanyi's use of that term and Taylor's notion of a "visceral" information need, "explicit knowledge" is used in a way that corresponds variously to Taylor's "conscious," "formalized," and "compromised" needs. The processes they term socialization and combination are much better presented and understood as special cases of interaction between internalization and externalization. In the end, *The Knowledge-Creating Company* does much to portray a potentially useful approach to achieving some form of knowledge creation in companies but plays a primarily confounding role in depicting the nature of knowledge.

NOTES

1. *American Heritage Dictionary of the English Language,* 4th ed., s.v. "Epistemology."

2. "The Analysis of Knowledge," in *Stanford Encyclopedia of Philosophy,* edited by Edward N. Zalta (Stanford, CA: Metaphysics Research Lab), http://plato.stanford.edu.

3. Fritz Machlup, *The Production and Distribution of Knowledge in the United States* (Princeton, NJ: Princeton University Press, 1962), 23.

4. Ibid., 22.

5. Ibid., 24.

6. Mortimer Adler, *How to Read a Book* (New York: Simon and Schuster, 1940), 34.

7. Machlup, *Production and Distribution of Knowledge,* 8.

8. Fritz Machlup, *Knowledge and Knowledge Production,* vol. 1 of *Knowledge: Its Creation, Distribution, and Economic Significance* (Princeton, NJ: Princeton University Press, 1980), 8.

9. Fritz Machlup and Una Mansfield, *The Study of Information: Interdisciplinary Messages* (New York: Wiley, 1983), 642–49.

10. Machlup, *Production and Distribution of Knowledge,* 21–22.

11. Mortimer J. Adler, *The Time of Our Lives: The Ethics of Common Sense* (New York: Holt, Rinehart and Winston, 1970), 206.

12. Kenneth E. Boulding, "Notes on the Information Concept," *Explorations* 6 (1955): 104.

13. Nicholas L. Henry, "Knowledge Management: A New Concern for Public Administration," *Public Administration Review* 34 (May/June 1974): 189.

14. Harlan Cleveland, "Information as a Resource," *Futurist* 16 (December 1982): 34.

15. Milan Zeleny, "Management Support Systems: Towards Integrated Knowledge Management," *Human Systems Management* 7, no. 1 (1987): 60.

16. Ibid., 61.

17. R. L. Ackoff, "From Data to Wisdom: Presidential Address to ISGSR, June 1988," *Journal of Applied Systems Analysis* 16 (1989): 8.

18. Anthony Debons, Estner Horne, and Scott Cronenweth, *Information Science: An Integrated View* (Boston: G.K. Hall, 1988), 5.

19. John Dewey and Arthur F. Bentley, *Knowing and the Known* (Boston: Beacon Press, 1949), 72–74.

20. Ibid., 58.

21. Paul R. Gamble and John Blackwell, *Knowledge Management: A State of the Art Guide* (London: Kogan Page, 2002), 43.

22. Bob Boiko, *Content Management Bible,* 2nd ed. (Indianapolis, IN: Wiley, 2005), 57.

23. Thomas H. Davenport and Laurence Prusak, *Working Knowledge: How Organizations Manage What They Know* (Boston: Harvard Business School Press, 1998), 5.

24. Joseph W. Firestone and Mark W. McElroy, *Key Issues in the New Knowledge Management* (Burlington, MA: Elsevier Science, 2003), 5–6.

25. Ibid., 18.

26. Michael Polanyi, "The Logic of Tacit Inference," in *Knowing and Being: Essays by Michael Polanyi,* edited by Marjorie Greene (Chicago: University of Chicago Press, 1969), 138.

27. Ibid.

28. Ibid., 140.

29. Ibid.

30. Ibid.

31. Ibid., 146.

32. Ibid., 141.

33. Ibid., 143.

34. Ibid.

35. Ibid., 144.

36. Bill Crowley, "Tacit Knowledge and Quality Assurance: Bridging the Theory-Practice Debate," in *Knowledge Management for the Information Professional,* edited by T. Kanti Srikantaiah and Michael E. D. Koenig (Medford, NJ: Information Today, 2000), 212.

37. Ibid., 205.

38. Karl Popper, "Epistemology without a Knowing Subject," in *Objective Knowledge: An Evolutionary Approach* (Oxford: Clarendon, 1972), 107–8.

39. Ibid., 109.

40. Ibid.

41. Ibid., 108.

42. Ibid., 111.

43. Ibid.

44. Ibid., 115.

45. Ibid., 116.

46. Ibid.

47. Ibid., 119.

48. Ibid.

49. *The Last Whole Earth Catalog: Access to Tools* (Menlo Park, CA: Portola Institute, 1971), 43.

50. Steve Fuller, *Knowledge Management Foundations* (Boston: Butterworth Heinemann, 2002).

51. Joseph L. Badaracco Jr., *The Knowledge Link: How Firms Compete through Strategic Alliances* (Boston: Harvard Business School Press, 1991).

52. Ravindranath Madhavan and Rajiv Grover, "From Embedded Knowledge to Embodied Knowledge: New Product Development as Knowledge Management," *Journal of Marketing* 62 (October 1998): 2.

53. "This Week's Citation Classic," *Current Contents,* November 25, 1985, 24.

54. Robert S. Taylor, "Question-Negotiation and Information Seeking in Libraries," *College and Research Libraries* 29 (May 1968): 181.

55. Ibid.

56. Calvin N. Mooers, "Mooers' Law: Or, Why Some Retrieval Systems Are Used and Others Are Not," *American Documentation* 11 (July 1960): ii.

57. Taylor, "Question-Negotiation," 182.

58. Ibid.

59. Ibid.

60. Ibid.

61. Ibid.

62. Ibid.

63. Ibid.

64. Ibid., 183.

65. Ibid., 182.

66. Ibid., 183.

67. Ibid., 184.

68. Ibid., 185.

69. Ibid.

70. Michael Polanyi, *The Tacit Dimension* (London: Routledge & Kegan Paul, 1966), 4.

71. Taylor, "Question-Negotiation," 187.

72. Yu A. Schreider, "On the Semantic Characteristics of Information," *Information Storage & Retrieval* 2 (August 1965): 221–33.

73. Ikujiro Nonaka and Hirotaka Takeuchi, *The Knowledge-Creating Company: How Japanese Companies Create the Dynamics of Innovation* (New York: Oxford University Press, 1995), 3.

74. Ibid., 20.

75. Ibid., 8.

76. Polanyi, *The Tacit Dimension,* 4.

77. Nonaka and Takeuchi, *The Knowledge-Creating Company,* 8.

78. Ibid., 91.

79. Ibid., 27.

80. Ibid., 31–32.

81. Ibid., 49.

82. Ibid., 61.

83. Ibid., 62.

84. Ibid., 63.
85. Ibid., 64.
86. Ibid.
87. Ibid., 67.
88. Ibid.
89. Ibid., 67–68.
90. Polanyi, "The Logic of Tacit Inference," 144.
91. Nonaka and Takeuchi, *The Knowledge-Creating Company,* 69.
92. Ibid., 6.

2

Communities of Practice

practice, *n.* The carrying out or exercise of a profession, esp. that of medicine or law. Also as a count noun: the business or premises of a doctor or lawyer.

1421 *Rolls of Parl.* IV. 158/1 Many unconnyng . . . in the forsayd Science practiseth, and specialy in Fysyk, so that in this Roialme is every man, be he never so lewed, takyng upon hym practyse.

IN THIS CHAPTER

KEY CONCEPTS

Origins of "Communities of Practice"
The Meaning of Community
Professional Communities
Discourse Communities
Learning Communities
Schools as Learning Communities
Online Learning Communities
Experiential Learning

KEY PAPERS

John Dewey, *Democracy and Education: An Introduction to the Philosophy of Education*
Jean Lave and Etienne Wenger, *Situated Learning: Legitimate Peripheral Participation*

ORIGINS OF "COMMUNITIES OF PRACTICE"

Although the knowledge management literature generally traces the origin of interest in communities of practice to Lave and Wenger's 1991 book *Situated Learning,* the concept has been prevalent in medicine, law, psychology, education, and theology for quite some time. An 1864 article on the developing sense of community between the Society of Friends and the English Church described the relationship that occurs when "such widely differing theories . . . result in a community of practice."[1] An article published in *Littell's Living Age* in 1878 described the commonalities of the publishing industries in France and England as a "community of practice."[2] Brown referred to religious institutions as communities of practice in 1882.[3] Paterson referred to a community of practice in the religious context in 1932.[4] In a 1957 article, the *Stanford Law Review* described a community of practice of attorneys.[5] Dawidoff used the term to refer to psychiatrists in 1966.[6] It is quite clear that the expression was widely used long before Lave and Wenger adopted it.

THE MEANING OF COMMUNITY

A central issue in understanding communities of practice is the definition of the term "community." The *Oxford American Dictionary* lists three pertinent definitions: "a group of people living together in one place, esp. one practicing common ownership," "a group of people having a religion, race, profession, or other particular characteristic in common," and "a feeling of fellowship with others, as a result of sharing common attitudes, interests, and goal."[7] Graves defined community as "an inherently cooperative, cohesive and self-reflective group entity whose members work on a regular, face-to-face basis toward common goals while respecting a variety of perspectives, values, and life styles."[8] Lave and Wenger's definition is completely at odds with Graves's and defines community primarily in terms of those characteristics not required, which include "co-presence, a well-defined, identifiable group, or socially visible boundaries. It does imply participation in an activity system about which participants share understandings concerning what they are doing and what that means in their lives and for their communities."[9]

The concept of communities of practice is closely linked to and reflective of a number of other concepts, practices, and proposals having to do with learning and living in communities. Professional communities, discourse communities, and learning communities are all concept areas with strong relationships to communities of practice. Lave and Wenger's exposition on communities of practice is grounded in the principles of situated learning, which is a form of experiential learning. The role played by these concepts is sufficiently significant that understanding communities of practice is, if not dependent on understanding the other concepts, augmented by understanding them.

PROFESSIONAL COMMUNITIES

The notion that groups of people who share a professional or occupational responsibility constitute communities is probably ancient. Practitioners have long referred to the organizational structures that bind them together as communities. The first use of the word "community" in this sense listed in the *Oxford English Dictionary* is dated to 1797, but it seems likely that the term was in use to describe communities of practitioners before that time.

This principle of shared responsibility is also reflected in the use of the word "society" to describe a shared community of professionals or practitioners. The first *Oxford English Dictionary* entry for the use of the word "society" in this sense is dated 1548.[10]

Merton described the practices of field research in social anthropology as "private skills passed on through example and word of mouth to a limited number of apprentices."[11] Dodson described a series of fieldwork projects carried out at the Center for Human Relations Studies at New York University and their influence in creating a sense of community among faculty and students.[12] In an extensive exploration of the profession as community, Goode cited the following characteristics that make a body of professionals a community:

1. Its members are bound by a sense of identity.
2. Once in it, few leave, so that it is a terminal or continuing status for the most part.
3. Its members share values in common.
4. Its role definitions *vis-à-vis* both members and non-members are agreed upon and are the same for all members.
5. Within the areas of communal action there is a common language, which is understood only partially by outsiders.
6. The Community has power over its members.
7. Though it does not produce the next generation biologically, it does so socially through its control over the selection of professional trainees, and through an adult socialization process.[13]

According to Goode's analysis, "it is likely that as the profession comes into being, or as an occupation begins to approach the pole of professionalism, it begins to take on the traits of a community."[14]

Goode's colleague Merton also explored the nature of professional associations as communities, noting that an association's "manifest and latent social functions, not the structure designed to put these functions into effect, are its social excuse for being. . . . What the association professes as its aims may coincide with what it actually does—but again, it may not."[15] Merton noted that the functions and roles of professions are complex and varied, and that the functions and roles of professional associations are therefore necessarily complex and varied as well. Such complexity and variety sometimes result in situations in which the objectives of the association, "principled as they are, may collide, or may seem to collide, with the interests of the public."[16] Merton divided the social functions of a professional association into four major entities for which the association assumes responsibility: "individuals, subgroups, the organization, and the larger society."[17]

Work by Wilensky suggested that the work orientation of an individual, as defined by the distinction between an occupation and a professional career, was a better predictor of participation in the broader societal community than socioeconomic status, suggesting that inclusion in an immediate professional community may be a major determiner of commitment to the broader community.[18] Hagedorn and Labovitz's study of employees in a nonprofit research organization, however, found that professional employees were more likely than nonprofessional employees to be involved in both professional associations and community groups. They found no meaningful correlation between engagement in professional associations and involvement in community groups, though.[19]

Knowles expanded on Schön's work on learning systems to describe professional associations as learning communities. Knowles contrasted six traditional assumptions about the roles of education with six modern assumptions:

Table 2.1
Traditional and Modern Assumptions about Education

Traditional Assumption	Modern Assumption
The purpose of education is to produce a knowledgeable person.	The purpose of education is to produce a competent person.
Education consists of transmission of knowledge and skills from a teacher to a student.	Education is a process of acquisition of knowledge, skills, attitudes, and values by a learner with help from a facilitator and resource person.
Learning takes place most efficiently in a formal classroom or clinical instruction setting.	Learning takes place most effectively when learning resources of a rich variety are available to learners at their convenience in time and place.
A person is fully equipped to practice a profession for the rest of his/her life upon completing formal professional training.	With rapidly changing technology and societal conditions, a professional person becomes obsolete unless he/she engages in a lifelong program of professional development.
The education of children is the responsibility of society; the continuing education of adults is their own responsibility.	Our society has as a great stake in the continuing education of adults in a world of accelerating change as it had for children in a stable world.
There is only one model of learning: the pedagogical model, in which the learner is defined as a dependent personality and is put in the role of passively receiving the content transmitted by the teacher.	Another model, the andragogical model, is available in which the learner is defined as a self-directing organism and is put in the role of diagnosing his/her own needs for learning, translating these needs into learning objectives, identifying and using appropriate resources for accomplishing these objectives, and evaluating the extent to which assistance from a facilitator is needed.

Source: Malcolm Knowles, "The Professional Organization as a Learning Community," *Training and Development Journal* 33 (May 1979): 36–40.

In Knowles's analysis, the transition from the set of traditional assumptions to the modern assumptions redefines the role of professional associations from that of "purveyors of miscellaneous educational services" to that of true learning communities.[20]

DISCOURSE COMMUNITIES

Ronald referred to "professional discourse communities" and the premise that "language invents, and is invented by, the constraints of the community in which it is used.

This perspective assumes that language is a community-generated and community-maintained symbolic construct, not an individually acquired skill. Knowledge, in other words, is local, not universal, expanded and validated by a 'community of knowledgeable peers.'"[21] Porter defined a discourse community as "a group of individuals bound by a common interest who communicate through approved channels and whose discourse is regulated."[22] Freed and Broadhead explored the concept of the discourse community in their study of two large international firms, called Alpha and Omega to preserve anonymity, that served similar business segments but were not directly in competition with each other.[23] Their analysis found that the major differences between the two firms arose from different cultures and philosophies that produced divergent discourse communities reflected directly in the ways in which language was used. Specifically, the language of Alpha, rooted in an environment dominated by a driving emphasis on accounting, was extremely conservative and cautious. Individuals and teams within Alpha were explicitly subservient to accounting processes designed to protect the firm. Omega, on the other hand, was driven by results and operated in a much more flexible manner that emphasized the value of individuals and teams.[24] Although the notion of discourse communities arose and triggered much discussion in the literature of rhetoric and composition, it also found its way into the literature of business communication.[25] Burroughs, Schwartz, and Hendricks-Lee explicitly linked the concepts of communities of practice and discourse communities.[26]

Killingsworth pointed out that the dual essential elements of a discourse community—social interchange (discourse) and the context within which that exchange is situated (community)—are both social constructions rather than a naturally occurring entity. The identity of the community is determined in part by the members of the community and in part by the observer, such that "the act of identifying communities is never innocent, never free of ideological influences."[27] Although the term "community" is almost always used to confer a positive or beneficent connotation, it is clearly possible to identify groups of people to whom the term can apply in a negative manner, such as organized crime groups or communities of addicts. Lyon criticized the literature on discourse communities as presenting a static, two-dimensional view of communities, ignoring the complex dynamics that define communities.[28] Similarly, Kent described the literature in terms of "thin" and "thick" interpretations of the concept of community. "The thick formulation understands a community to be a system of social conventions that may be isolated and then codified. . . . The thin formulation understands community to be a chorus of polyphonous voices where, according to Joseph Harris, 'one is always simultaneously a part of several discourses, several communities, is always already committed to a number of conflicting beliefs and practices.'"[29]

LEARNING COMMUNITIES

The concept of the learning community arose in the education literature in the 1960s and was the subject of a minor flirtation that continued through the 1970s and 1980s. The concept, somewhat revised, reemerged in the 1990s and constitutes a major thread in the education literature of the first part of the twenty-first century.

The term arose in the business literature in the 1990s and has continued to attract attention in the business community. The literature on learning communities is focused on three areas: the transformation of formal education, the roles and functions of professional associations, and the creation and nurturing of online communities.

SCHOOLS AS LEARNING COMMUNITIES

In 1968 Miller contended that the crisis in education was primarily a crisis of community that could be addressed only through attention to the essential social nature of learning.[30] Graham commented on the role of schools as learning communities, noting that "if schools have in the past provided a sense of community, too few are now providing it; they have lost the ability to develop in each student a sense of self-realization in the community. . . . Most teachers are petty bureaucrats of the state, at the bottom of an educational hierarchy. Students are members of a mass controlled by the state."[31] It was Graham's contention that it is possible to create an alternative model in which schools "become cooperative centers of inquiry which, through community, will teach the uses of community."[32] Jones and Stanford presented a set of suggestions for how schools could be transformed into learning communities.[33] Graves noted that early efforts to introduce community-building practices in schools were frequently viewed as "a diversion from the real purpose of the school" or countered by the assumption "that community feelings would develop automatically as students studied together in small groups."[34] Graves also contended that it is possible and directly beneficial to deliberately build learning communities in school settings. She suggested that there are four essential stages in creating a learning community: (1) building community, (2) exploring community, (3) functioning productively, and (4) providing outreach beyond the community. She also noted that some communities must inevitably end.[35] Busher and others have identified the establishment of communities as a central approach to creating inclusive school environments.[36] MacGregor and Smith provided a reflective commentary based on their research regarding the learning communities movement in higher education, noting that, although much has been learned about the process of creating learning communities, every lesson learned reveals more lessons to be learned.[37]

A conundrum in the literature on schools as learning communities arises from the distinction between schools as learning communities that are inclusive of students, teachers, administrators, and sometimes the external community and professional learning communities with memberships comprised entirely of teachers and administrators. Secules, Cottom, Bray, and Miller described an initiative in which the "community includes students, teachers, administrators, business leaders and members of the surrounding community."[38] The model presented by Lieberman, however, was intended to "offer teachers and administrators an opportunity to discuss their work and tackle problems in an atmosphere of trust and support."[39]

ONLINE LEARNING COMMUNITIES

The notion of distributed online learning communities was foreshadowed by McLuhan in the 1970s and emerged as an area that provoked a great deal of excitement across many disciplines in the wake of the introduction of the World Wide Web in the early 1990s. Online communities have been proposed as a means of linking otherwise isolated individuals such as older adults, providing flexibility in professional development, extending the reach of formal education, and creating new social structures. Charalambos, Michalinos, and Chamberlain provided a comprehensive overview of the challenges of creating successful online learning communities, presented a set of practical approaches to addressing those challenges, and commented on the immediate need for research into the nature, roles, and practices of online communities.[40]

EXPERIENTIAL LEARNING

Lave and Wenger couch their exploration of communities of practice in terms of the nature and functions of situated learning, a term that emerged in the late 1980s in the context of instructional design and technology. Situated learning is clearly a form of experiential learning, or learning by doing. The notion of learning by doing appears to have been part of the education literature for as long as there has been an education literature. For example, *The New Departure,* published in 1883, touted a "natural system" for learning English.[41] Whipple commented in 1935 on the "assertion made by the more enthusiastic proponents of the new in education—that textbooks should be discarded altogether in favor of experiential learning."[42] A 1937 review by Ramsey noted that "the world is too large for every child to secure all his education through experiential learning."[43]

Fenwick identified five major classes of experiential learning: reflection, interference, participation, resistance, and coemergence. The first three are closely enough related to the concept of learning communities that they merit discussion; the final two will be briefly introduced but have not typically been linked to the notion of the learning community.

1. *Reflection* is understood by Fenwick to be a constructivist perspective that couches adult learning in terms of a self-directed effort to derive meaning from experience. "The learner reflects on lived experience and then interprets and generalizes this experience to form mental structures."[44] This is the model of experiential learning found in the classic works of Piaget, in Schön's reflective practice, and in Vygotsky's activity theory.

   Activity theory is a theory of psychology that arose in Russia in the early twentieth century and is most closely associated with Lev Vygotsky. "Activity theorists seek to analyze the development of consciousness within practical social activity settings. Their emphasis is on the psychological impacts of organised activity and the social conditions and social systems which are produced in and through such activity."[45] Like situated learning, activity theory addresses the problem of "understanding the interpenetration of the individual, other people, and artifacts in everyday activity."[46] Activity theory has been proposed as a valuable context resource for designing technology, especially technological approaches to learning.[47] Activity theory has also been suggested as an overall framework for understanding work.[48] Although some authors have addressed situated learning in the context of activity theory, Fenwick places activity theory and situated learning in different experiential learning categories.

   The central characteristic of all approaches to the reflection model of experiential learning is the notion that "a learner is believed to construct, through reflection, a personal understanding of relevant structures of meaning derived from his or her action in the world."[49]

The constructivist view of learning as reflection has been criticized as simplistic, as overemphasizing the role of conscious awareness in learning, as depersonalizing learning, and as separating the context in which learning takes place from learned content.[50]

2. The *interference* model of experiential learning incorporates a psychoanalytic approach. The interference model provides an emphasis on the role of the unconscious in learning that is absent in the reflection model, taking into account "the individual's relations to the outside world of culture and objects of knowledge and the inside world of psychic energies and dilemmas of relating to these objects of knowledge. . . . These dilemmas unfold through struggles between the unconscious and the conscious mind, which is aware of unconscious rumblings but can neither access them fully nor understand their language."[51]

   Criticisms of the interference model address the impossibility of directly assessing the impact of the unconscious on learning and the individual's rational ability to "overcome our logical contradictions and unjustifiable or inarticulable beliefs."[52] If the reflective perspective is too external, the psychoanalytical interference model is too internal and takes into account only the context of the unconsciousness, not the many other possible contextual influences on learning.

3. The *participation* model described by Fenwick encompasses the situated learning perspective supported by Lave and Wenger. Situated learning is closely linked to situated cognition, which emerged in the literatures of psychology and artificial intelligence in the 1980s. Although neither term has been greatly used, the meaning of each is fairly clear.

   The central premise of situated learning is that the content that defines any act of learning cannot be separated from the context within which learning takes place. Learning is a complex network in which "knowledge is embedded in individuals, in connections between individuals, and in artifacts."[53] In their pioneering work on situated cognition and learning, Brown, Collins, and Duguid argued that "knowledge is situated, being in part a product of the activity, context, and culture in which it is developed and used."[54] Situated learning is closely related to, but possibly not synonymous with, experiential learning or learning by doing. Proponents of situated learning typically criticize traditional approaches to learning as defining knowledge as "free from any social or contextual influence."[55] Situated learning is frequently associated with apprenticeship as a core value and process in learning. An essential claim for situated learning is that knowledge acquired via a context-sensitive process is fundamentally transferable to real-world experience in a manner that knowledge acquired through other processes is not.

   The research literature related to situated learning is very sparse. Anderson, Reder, and Simon examined the literature of situated learning and identified four recurring claims about situated learning:

   1. Action is grounded in the concrete situation in which it occurs.
   2. Knowledge does not transfer between tasks.
   3. Training by abstraction is of little use.
   4. Instruction needs to be done in complex, social environments.[56]

   Their review of prior research found little to support any of the four claims, noting among other things that "while cognition is partly context-dependent, it is also partly context-independent."[57]

   Hendricks's study of 220 seventh-grade students found that a situated learning approach was associated with higher levels of immediate learning than a more abstract approach to learning but found no evidence of a higher incidence of ability to transfer what was learned to real-life situations.[58] A possible counter to Hendricks's research is that situated learning in the knowledge management context is primarily a function of adult learning. Pope, Cuthbertson, and Stoddart were cautiously optimistic about the role of situated learning in professional education for nurses.[59]

The participation model, with its emphasis on situated learning, is limited by the inherently idiosyncratic nature of learning. "Critics claim that the extent to which learning is tightly bound to context depends on the kind of knowledge being acquired and the ways the material is engaged."[60] Although the participation model generally rejects the notion that knowledge can be transferred across contexts, research demonstrates that abstract knowledge acquired in one context can indeed be applied in other contexts. Anderson, Reder, and Simon contended that the inherent nature of learning lies in "what cognitive processes a problem invokes, and not what real-world trappings it might have."[61]

4. The resistance model views experiential learning from a "critical cultural perspective" that requires "the structures of dominance that express or govern the social relationships and competing forms of communication and cultural practices within that system" to be analyzed.[62] This model adds to the participation model the principle of power, which is variable within a particular situation. Learning, then, takes place within the context of a social system characterized by interpersonal and intergroup tensions and is shaped largely by the group(s) to which the individual belongs and the power conferred by the position(s) of the individual within the group(s). Borders and boundaries between groups are important influences on the learning experience. Learning is in part a matter of resisting power, a process through which "people can become open to unexpected, unimagined possibilities for work, life, and development."[63] Learning is a sort of "emancipatory process" through which the learner gains liberating power in the form of knowledge.[64]

5. *Coemergence,* the most recent of the five classifications of experiential learning, is an "enactivist" perspective in which the learner and the context for learning are viewed as converging to enable learning. The role of the individual in the environment is influenced largely by sensory input rather than by reflection or the conceptual nature of the environment. Learning is understood to be a function of a complex ecology that is difficult to understand or even to envision. Because learning is primarily a biological phenomenon, knowledge can be understood primarily in behavioral terms.

John Dewey, *Democracy and Education: An Introduction to the Philosophy of Education* (New York: Macmillan, 1928).

Philosopher and educator John Dewey (1859–1952) is one of the most significant influences on modern educational thought. Educated at the University of Vermont and at Johns Hopkins University, he served on the faculties of the University of Minnesota, the University of Michigan, and the University of Chicago before joining the faculty of Columbia University, where he stayed from 1904 until his retirement in 1930. He was a prolific author; *The Collected Works of John Dewey, 1882–1953,* published by Southern Illinois University Press, comprises 37 volumes. His more important books include *Psychology* (1890), *The School and Society* (1899), *How We Think* (1910), *The Public and Its Problems* (1927), *Experience and Nature* (1929), *Experience and Education* (1938), and *Problems of Men* (1946). *Democracy and Education* (1928) has generated more than one thousand entries in the *Social Sciences Citation Index. Democracy and Education* was listed as "Required Reading" in the cover story of the June 8, 1998, issue of *Time* magazine and was recognized by the Museum of Education as one of the "Books of the Century" in 2000.[65]

Dewey is the acknowledged father of experiential learning. The fundamental principle of active experiential learning is captured in the first sentence of *Democracy and Education:* "The most notable distinction between living and inanimate beings is that the former maintain themselves by renewal."[66] This concept of renewal, and particularly the continuous nature of renewal, is fundamental to the philosophy of education that emerges in *Democracy and Education.* Dewey places great, deliberate emphasis on continuity as an essential characteristic of learning and therefore as an essential characteristic of education.

EDUCATION AND CONTINUITY

Dewey pays virtually no attention to the potential difference between learning and education, and he explicitly dismisses the notion of a major distinction between education and training.[67] Although it is clear in *Democracy and Education* that learning is the key way in which knowledge is acquired, it is equally clear that education is to Dewey the sum of all those experiences and processes that result in learning. In referring to the continuous process of renewal and growth that defines not only individuals but also groups, Dewey summarizes the nature of education: "Education, in its broadest sense, is the means of this social continuity of life."[68] The continuity of the social experience leads Dewey to reject the notion that education in any form is preparation for anything. Learning to Dewey takes place in and has primarily to do with the present moment and its role in the continuum of experience. This does not imply that preparation for the future has no role in education, but "if education is growth, it must progressively realize present possibilities, and thus make individuals better fitted to cope with later requirements."[69]

This principle of education as growth arises naturally and inevitably from the notion of education as the continuity of social experience. Growth is essential to both the individual and the social group(s) to which the individual belongs. "In directing the activities of the young, society determines its own future in determining that of the young. . . . This cumulative movement of action toward a later result is what is meant by growth."[70]

The central condition for growth is immaturity, a term to which Dewey gives an unfamiliar but useful spin: immaturity, rather than a lack of the positive characteristics of maturity, is itself a positive indicator of the ability to grow and develop. "Our tendency to take immaturity as mere lack, and growth as something which fills up the gap between the immature and the mature is due to regarding childhood *comparatively,* instead of intrinsically."[71] "Taken absolutely rather than comparatively, immaturity designates a positive force or ability,—the *power* to grow."[72] Immaturity in Dewey's schema is composed of two important elements: (1) dependence, which Dewey carefully distinguishes from helplessness and impotence, and (2) plasticity, which is "the ability to learn from experience; the power to retain from one experience something which is of avail in coping with the difficulties of a later situation."[73] Based on his understanding of growth, Dewey defines education as "the enterprise of supplying the conditions which insure growth, or adequacy of life, irrespective of age."[74]

FORMAL VS. INFORMAL EDUCATION

The tension between formal and informal education is a recurring theme in *Democracy and Education*. "There is . . . a marked difference between the education which every one gets from living with others, as long as he really lives instead of just continuing to subsist, and the deliberate educating of the young. In the former case the education is incidental; it is natural and important, but it is not the express reason of the association."[75] This kind of education is not tied to any particular social structure: "any social arrangement that remains vitally social, or vitally shared, is educative to those who participate in it. Only when it is cast in a mold and runs in a routine way does it lose its educative power."[76] A great deal of learning clearly arises from the interaction between younger, less experienced members of a group and older, more experienced members. Essential though this informal education is, as civilization advances, the gap between the capacities of the young and the concerns of adults widens. Learning by directly sharing in the pursuits of grown-ups becomes increasingly difficult except in the case of the less advanced occupations. Much of what adults do is so remote in space and in meaning that playful imitation is less and less adequate to reproduce its spirit. The ability to share effectively in adult activities thus depends upon a priori training given with this end in view. Intentional agencies (schools) and explicit material (studies) are devised. The task of teaching certain things is delegated to a special group of individuals. Without such formal education, it is not possible to transmit all the resources and achievements of a complex society.[77]

There is to Dewey both a benefit and a danger in the development of formal approaches to education.

> As societies become more complex in structure and resources, the need of formal or intentional teaching and learning increases. As formal teaching and training grow in extent, there is the danger of creating an undesirable split between the experience gained in more direct associations and what is acquired in school. This danger was never greater than at the present time, on account of the rapid growth in the last few centuries of knowledge and technical modes of skill.[78]

ENVIRONMENTAL INFLUENCES

Dewey explicitly recognizes that learning is situated in the environment in which it takes place. Because education is a social function, the environment in which learning takes place plays a critical role in all aspects of learning. "The environment consists of all those conditions that promote or hinder, stimulate or inhibit, the *characteristic* activities of a living being."[79] From this basic definition of environment, Dewey builds to the importance of recognizing and understanding the influence of the social environment. "A being whose activities are associated with others has a social environment. What he does and what he can do depend upon the expectations, demands, approvals, and condemnations of others."[80] Furthermore, the "social environment forms the mental and emotional disposition of behavior in individuals by engaging them in activities that arouse and strengthen certain impulses, that have certain purposes and entail certain consequences."[81] Ultimately, he says, "the development within the young of the attitudes and dispositions necessary to the continuous and progressive life of a society cannot take place by direct conveyance of beliefs, emotions, and knowledge. It takes place through the intermediary of the environment."[82]

One of the key roles of the environment is the provision of "direction, control, and guidance."[83] Dewey selects the term "direction" as the best descriptor of the influence of the environment, rejecting "guidance" as implying an unachievable level of cooperation between the guiding influence and the individual being guided, and "control" as involving no cooperation. "Direction is a more neutral term and suggests the fact that the active tendencies of those directed are led in a certain continuous course, instead of dispersing aimlessly. Direction expresses the basic function, which tends at one extreme to become a guiding assistance and at another, a regulation or ruling."[84] This directive role is most apparent in the ways in which the environment shapes the learning of the young or uninitiated. "The natural or native impulses of the young do not agree with the life-customs of the group into which they are born. Consequently they have to be directed or guided."[85] The extension from chronological youth to experiential youth is easily made: the role of the environment in directing growth is as valid in andragogy or on-the-job learning as it is in pedagogy.

DEMOCRACY AND COMMUNITY

Learning and education are understood by Dewey to be inherently and exclusively social processes. Learning requires a social context and rarely or never takes place outside that social context. Even when an individual is isolated, reflection occurs within a social framework and connects the individual to the group or society from which he or she is isolated. As a result, the nature of education is a function of the nature of the group(s) to which the individual belongs. "To say that education is a social function, securing direction and development in the immature through their participation in the life of the group to which they belong, is to say that education will vary with the quality of life which prevails in a group."[86]

There is, therefore, no possible unitary model for understanding the role and nature of education within the societal context. Although the term "community" is frequently used to imply an explicitly positive connotation, especially in the literature on communities of practice, Dewey recognizes that there truly is "honor among thieves, and a band of robbers has a common interest as respects its members. Gangs are marked by fraternal feeling, and narrow cliques by intense loyalty to their own codes."[87] Even models that are generally ascribed wholesome characteristics, such as traditional family structures, can be marred by negative and dysfunctional traits. A group may possess remarkably positive, adhesive internal characteristics and relate to the outside environment in an entirely hostile and segregative manner. One of the essential functions of the group is socialization of individuals to the group, but the nature of such socialization depends directly on the nature of the group.

Dewey is particularly, but not exclusively, interested in the relationship between democracy and education. At the same time he is realistic, noting that the means by which the role of society in education is evaluated cannot be based on a purely idealized model, but that the desirable traits of existing societies must be extracted from the negative traits. Dewey defines the measurable quality of positive group characteristics in terms of the quantity and variety of consciously shared interests. When the quantity and variety of shared interests are low, the group possesses a primarily exclusionary nature and is likely to be of overall negative value. A group of thieves, for instance, may be characterized primarily by the acts and benefits of theft. A political action committee is frequently focused entirely and obsessively on a single societal issue. Groups that are characterized by substantial diversity of shared interests tend to have overall positive natures. Professional membership associations, although centered around relatively tightly defined purposes, tend to work toward an expansive and inclusive model of support for a broadly defined area of professional practice. Where the political action committee tends to be exclusive and isolationist, the professional association strives to be inclusive and open.

Dewey identifies two characteristics that define the democratic ideal: (1) numerous and diverse shared common interests among members of a group and (2) continuous readjustment and repurposing as a direct result of communication and interaction among groups. An important point in Dewey's argument has to do with the distinction between education in a democratic context and education in a totalitarian environment. His contention is that a totalitarian or exclusivist environment has little need for well-established systems and institutions of education and may in fact value a focused lack of knowledge among members. A democratic environment, on the other hand, requires a systematic, broad-based approach to education if it is to support the range and diversity of shared interests and facilitate communication and interaction.

EXPERIENCE AND THINKING

Perhaps the most important portion of Democracy and Education is chapter 11, "Experience and Thinking," which forms the core of Dewey's emphasis on experiential learning. Experience, experiential learning, and experimentation constitute the foundation of Dewey's philosophy of education. Dewey describes experience as having two characteristic qualities: the active characteristic of trying and the passive characteristic of undergoing. "When we experience something we act upon it, we do something with it; then we suffer or undergo the consequences."[88] Activity does not constitute experience unless it possesses these twin characteristics of deliberate action involving change and conscious reaction to the outcomes of change. "To 'learn from experience' is to make a backward and a forward connection between what we do to things and what we enjoy or suffer from things in consequence."[89] Although experience itself is "not primarily cognitive," there is a cognitive aspect that influences the value assigned to an experience, which is assigned primarily to the role of the experience in influencing the future.[90]

Dewey views much of formal education as being inadequately connected to experience. "In schools, those under instruction are too customarily looked upon as acquiring knowledge as theoretical spectators, minds which appropriate knowledge by direct energy of intellect."[91] Dewey equates the conflict between theoretical and experiential learning to a "dualism of mind and body" in which the role of the body is treated as primarily intrusive and negative.[92] In this excessively cerebral view of education, all learning takes place in the mind, not in the body, which is essentially a passive container for the mind. Dewey credits this dualism with the bulk of the tension between teacher and learner that occurs in formal education. "The nervous strain and fatigue which result with both teacher and pupil are a necessary consequence of the abnormality of the situation in which bodily activity is divorced from the perception of meaning."[93] The dualism of mind and body removes the element of purpose from education and renders learning mechanical and routine rather than exploratory and enlightening.

Much of Dewey's discussion of the mind-body separation focuses on the role of connections. "The separation of 'mind' from direct occupation with things throws emphasis on *things* at the expense of *relations* or connections. It is all too common to separate perceptions and even ideas from judgments."[94] This concept evolved in Dewey's later work in the form of the term "transaction," which he used to describe the convergence of content and method. Transaction acts as an umbrella term for relationships, connections, context, and related concepts.[95]

Dewey's views on the importance of perception and experience anticipate Polanyi's distinction between subsidiary and focal perception: "every perception and every idea is a sense of the bearings, use, and cause, of a thing. We do not really know a chair by inventorying and enumerating its various isolated qualities, but only by bringing these qualities into connection with something else—the purpose which makes it a chair and not a table; or its difference from the kind of chair we are accustomed to, or the 'period' which it represents, and so on."[96] At the same time, Dewey notes that words are commonly confused with the ideas they represent and that such confusion is exacerbated by the separation of body and mind. The mind-body dualism, rather than explicating ideas by abstraction, divides words and the ideas they represent.

Ultimately, to Dewey, all learning takes place in the context of relationships, and relationships can be understood only through experience. All learning, then, is tied to experience, and meaningful experience requires an element of judgment. The dualism of theory and experience, like the mind-body dualism, is false. "An ounce of experience is better than a ton of theory simply because it is only in experience that theory has vital and verifiable significance."[97]

KNOW-WHAT, KNOW-HOW, REFLECTION, AND RISK

Meaningful experience requires judgment and thought. "No experience having a meaning is possible without some element of thought."[98] Dewey anticipates Schön's reflective practice in his focus on the role of reflection in relation to experience, dividing experiences into two categories on the basis of the degree to which they require reflection: (1) knowing a course of action and its consequences and (2) understanding the relationship between the action and its consequences. This distinction is reflected in the common use in the knowledge management literature of the distinction between know-what and know-how. The distinction is grounded in the extent of deliberate observation and insight-producing reflection. "Thinking . . . is the intentional endeavor to discover *specific* connections between something which we do and the consequences which result, so that the two become continuous."[99] Reflection is acceptance of responsibility for the consequences of actions. Reflection is forward looking and predictive. It has to do not with what has happened but with what will happen.

Because it is concerned with the human and social factors of actions and consequences, reflective thinking has not so much to do with what or how much is known, but more with the quality of understanding. Reflection is a highly personal process, not a neutral processing of data. It is grounded in "the flagrant partisanship of human nature"; there is an element in reflection of "sympathetic identification of our own destiny . . . with the outcome of the course of events."[100] The personal nature of reflection leads to "one of the chief paradoxes of thought. Born in partiality, in order to accomplish its tasks it must achieve a certain level of detached impartiality."[101]

Reflection is also in part a function of uncertainty. In identifying it as such, Dewey anticipates the relationship between information and uncertainty explained in Shannon's mathematical theory of communication.[102] That which is thoroughly understood, rote, or trivial requires no reflection. Reflection "is a process of inquiry, of looking into things, of investigating."[103] The mere acquisition of knowledge, although essential to reflection, is secondary and subsidiary to inquisition. Dewey rejects the notion that "original research" is different from any other form of reflective thinking, noting that "all thinking is research, and all research is native, original, to him who carries it on, even if everybody else in the world already is sure of what he is still looking for."[104]

Because thinking entails uncertainty, there is additionally an inherent element of risk: the nature of inquiry is that the outcome cannot be precisely anticipated. Inquiry begins with a hypothesis, however informal, that must be tested and verified. The results of the inquiry may themselves be tentative and may still exhibit some element of uncertainty, such that acting on them involves further risk.

The nature of reflective inquiry can be summarized as constituting five "general features" that closely mimic the scientific method:

1. Uncertainty, confusion, or doubt arising from a poorly or incompletely understood situation
2. A "conjectural anticipation" or hypothesis regarding the situation and its consequences
3. A structured exploration of available knowledge regarding the situation
4. An iterative expansion of the hypothesis as knowledge expands
5. A plan of action for addressing the situation, based on inquiry and analysis[105]

REFLECTION AND EDUCATION

If learning takes place only through a process of reflective experience, then it follows that all educational experiences must encompass both experience and reflection. A central theme of Dewey's work is that traditional approaches to education—especially, but not restricted to, formal education—are wedded to the mind-body dualism and ignore both experience and the reflection that adds meaning to experience. "Thinking is often regarded both in philosophic theory and in educational practice as something cut off from experience, and capable of being cultivated in isolation."[106] Dewey rejects any such separation of thought and action and argues that "the first approach to any subject in school, if thought is to be aroused and not words acquired, should be as unscholastic as possible."[107] Not only must fundamental learning be experiential, but it must be based in experiences that are comprehendible to the learner: there should be no disconnect between the experiences that engage interest and invoke activity in the outside world and those that occur within the learning environment.

Dewey identifies two essential characteristics that tie an educational problem to meaningful experience: (1) the problem must have some aspect of reality—problems perceived by the learner to be purely academic in nature are not experiential; (2) the learner must be capable of establishing some sense of ownership for the problem—the problem must be perceived as relevant to the learner's experience and to the learner's immediate or future needs. Ultimately, Dewey finds that the entirety of the typical classroom-centric approach to formal education is directly antithetical in every way to experience-centered learning.

EXPERIENCE AND EXPERIMENTATION

Knowledge is "the working capital, the indispensable resources, of further inquiry; of finding out, or learning, more things."[108] Just as Dewey rejects the dualism of mind and body, he also rejects the dualism of intellectual knowledge and practical knowledge. This dualism, which dates from the time of Plato, pits reason and the authority that is perceived to arise from reason against custom, tradition, and experience. To Dewey, this dualism cannot stand in an environment that recognizes the legitimacy and value of experimentation as an approach to generating knowledge.

Dewey draws a close relationship between experiential learning and direct experimentation. He envisions the ideal learning environment as being a combination of the tools and processes necessary for experimental learning, the data that are necessary to answer reflective questions, and the ability to address problems that have direct meaning to the learner. He clearly understands that not all learning experiences can be based on observational experimentation: "Meaning, observation, reading, communication, are all avenues for supplying data. The relative proportion to be obtained from each is a matter of the specific features of the particular problem at hand."[109] Although direct observation is highly desirable in that it involves the most direct interaction between the learner and that which is observed and is viewed by Dewey as an essential component in experiential learning, he does recognize that direct observation has limitations and cannot be the sole avenue to learning. Ultimately, all forms of learning are experiential if they involve the essential aspects of action, consequence, and reflection. There is no fundamental distinction in Dewey's analysis between that which is learned from reading and that which is learned from doing, as long as the activity of reading is sufficiently dynamic to constitute an experience.

EXPERIENCE, VOCATIONAL EDUCATION, AND COMMUNITIES OF PRACTICE

Dewey begins his chapter on "Vocational Aspects of Education" with a definition of vocation, "which means nothing but such a direction of life activities as renders them perceptibly significant to a person, because of the consequences they accomplish, and also useful to his associates."[110] Dewey finds yet another disagreeable dualism in the tendency to distinguish between vocations and careers or professions. "The opposite of a career is neither leisure nor culture, but aimlessness, capriciousness, the absence of cumulative achievement in experience, on the personal side, and idle display, parasitic dependence upon the others, on the social side. Occupation is a concrete term for continuity."[111] Rejecting outright the validity or even the possibility of educating an individual for "only one line of activity," Dewey was seemingly prescient in his understanding that most people will pursue more than one career path during their working lives.[112] One of the goals of education should be to "train power of readaptation to changing conditions so that future workers would not become blindly subject to a fate imposed upon them."[113]

Dewey works toward a conclusion that is of central importance for understanding communities of practice: education for practice necessarily involves direct experience of the area of practice.

> The only adequate training for occupations is training through occupations. The principle ... that the educative process is its own end, and that the only sufficient preparation for later responsibilities comes by making the most of immediately present life, applies in full force to the vocational phases of education.[114]
>
> Education *through* occupations ... combines within itself more of the factors conducive to learning than any other method. It calls instincts and habits into play; it is a foe to passive receptivity. It has an end in view; results are to be accomplished. Hence it appeals to thought; it demands that an idea of an end be steadily maintained, so that activity cannot be either routine or capricious.[115]

This is reiterated in Dewey's later *Essays in Experimental Logic*:

> The object of knowledge is not something with which thinking sets out; but something with which it ends: something which the processes of inquiry and testing, that constitute thinking themselves produce. Thus the object of knowledge is practical in the sense that it depends upon a specific kind of practice for its existence.[116]

Dewey notes that education has historically been much more vocationally oriented, relying on apprenticeships and other approaches to building communities of practice, than it has been in the twentieth century. In Dewey's analysis, this was true both for the working class, for whom apprenticeships were formally defined, and for the ruling class, whose opportunities for learning arrived mostly through trial, error, and practice. He attributes the increased role of formal vocational education to the combined forces of the labor movement, the industrialization of society, advancing technology, the transition in the sciences from primarily dialectical to primarily experimental methods, and advances in educational and developmental psychology.

Dewey provides a specific definition of practice in *Essays in Experimental Logic*:

> It means that knowing is literally something which we do; that analysis is ultimately physical and active; that meanings in their logical quality are standpoints, attitudes and methods of behaving toward facts, and that active experimentation is essential to verifications.[117]

The later communities of practice movement is most directly predicted in Dewey's conviction that effective vocational education will require not only reshaping the nature of schools, but also redefining the relationship between school and work, and possibly fundamentally changing the nature of work.

Both practically and philosophically, the key to the present educational situation lies in a gradual reconstruction of school materials and methods so as to utilize various forms of occupation-typifying social callings and to bring out their intellectual and moral content. This reconstruction must relegate purely literary methods—including textbooks—and dialectical methods to the position of necessary auxiliary tools in the intelligent development of consecutive and cumulative activities.

> Our discussion thus far has emphasized the fact that this educational reorganization cannot be accomplished by merely trying to give a technical preparation for industries and professions as they now operate, much less by merely reproducing existing industrial conditions in the school. The problem is not that of making the schools an adjunct to manufacture and commerce, but of utilizing the factors of industry to make school life more active, more full of immediate meaning, more connected with out-of-school experience.[118]

Dewey envisioned a different sort of society, "a society in which every person shall be occupied in something which makes the lives of others better worth living, and which accordingly makes the ties which bind persons together more perceptible—which breaks down the barriers of distance between them."[119] The ultimate impact of achievement of such a societal reformation is the creation of a meta-community of practice where the ways people learn produce a "state of affairs in which the interest of each in his work is uncoerced and intelligent: based upon its congeniality to his own aptitudes."[120]

Jean Lave and Etienne Wenger, *Situated Learning: Legitimate Peripheral Participation* (Cambridge: Cambridge University Press, 1991).

Jean Lave, a professor of education and geography at the University of California, Berkeley, holds a PhD in social anthropology from Harvard University. She is the author of *Cognition in Practice* (1988) and coauthor of *Understanding Practice* (1993). Etienne Wenger is an independent researcher and consultant; he was formerly a research scientist at the Institute for Research on Learning. He holds a bachelor's degree in computer science from the University of Geneva and master's and doctoral degrees in information and computer science, both from the University of California, Irvine. He is the author of *Artificial Intelligence and Tutoring Systems: Computational and Cognitive Approaches to the Communication of Knowledge* (1987) and *Communities of Practice: Learning, Meaning, and Identity* (1998) and coauthor of *Cultivating Communities of Practice: A Guide to Managing Knowledge* (2002). *Situated Learning: Legitimate Peripheral Participation* has earned more than 1,750 entries in the *Social Sciences Citation Index*.

Although Lave and Wenger do not claim to have either invented the concept of or coined the expression "communities of practice," the influence of their thinking on the concept of communities of practice in the knowledge management context is so great that they stand as recognized pioneers. *Situated Learning* is a slender book at 138 pages, including an index and a fairly lengthy foreword written by anthropologist William F. Hanks.

DEFINITIONAL OBSTACLES

Situated Learning is primarily descriptive and consciously exploratory in nature, rather than prescriptive or analytical. Lave and Wenger move from their original intent of "rescuing" the concept of the apprenticeship to a broader principle based in the nature and value of situated learning as a means of building "legitimate peripheral participation" in an organization or occupational setting. Unfortunately, neither situated learning nor legitimate peripheral participation is adequately defined. The lack of definition appears to be deliberate but is nonetheless confounding. The authors explain the absence of definition as a redefinition of the "notion of a concept. . . . The concept of legitimate peripheral participation obtains its meaning, not in a concise definition of its boundaries, but in its multiple, theoretically generative interconnections with persons, activities, knowing and world."[121] This statement is presented near the end of the book, but reading the book does little to help clarify the nature of legitimate peripheral participation. The lack of definition was not lost to reviewers of the book, one of whom defined legitimate peripheral participation as "learning by being there and gradually getting the hang of things while being accepted by those involved," and situated learning as "much the same without the emphasis on the social."[122] The confusion over the meaning of terms is exacerbated by such statements as "There is no activity that is not situated," "There may very well be no such thing as an 'illegitimate peripheral participant,'" and "There may well be no such thing as 'central participation' in a community of practice."[123] Ultimately, although it is clear that the authors perceive a tangible difference between the narrower concept of the apprenticeship and the broader model of situated learning, they fail to articulate the difference.

Although Lave and Wenger discourage decomposing the meaning of the expression "legitimate peripheral participation" into its component parts—"legitimate versus illegitimate, peripheral versus central, participation versus nonparticipation"—the phrase is far from being sufficiently self-explanatory that the uninitiated can understand it without engaging in such decomposition. Doing so actually renders the term readily understandable and at the same time reduces terminological mystery. The ease with which the expression is made understandable makes the authors' failure to do so all the more difficult to interpret.

1. "Legitimate" could perhaps be better expressed as "legitimized." It means that the involvement of the individual—the learner—has been consciously, positively, and to at least some extent formally accepted by the community.
2. "Participation" means that the learner is more than an observer, more than a student of the practice supported by the community. The learner is actively engaged in the primary activities of the community.
3. "Peripheral" refers to the role of learning in the learner's interaction with the community. The primary or central role of the learner is furtherance of the primarily activities of the community. Learning is a peripheral activity that supports the community allowing the learner to build the knowledge and skills he or she requires to become a full member of the community. As the learner gains facility in the area of practice, the learner moves from a partially peripheral role to a fundamentally central role.

The concept of situated learning is contrasted with "conventional explanations [that] view learning as a process by which a learner internalizes knowledge, whether 'discovered,' 'transmitted' from others, or 'experienced in interaction' with others."[124] This focus on internalization "establishes a sharp dichotomy between inside and outside, suggests that knowledge is largely cerebral, and takes the individual as the nonproblematic unit of analysis."[125] This is one more of many startlingly Deweyan perspectives found in *Situated Learning*. There is in fact so much of Dewey in Lave and Wenger's work that it is surprising that they neither reference nor even mention Dewey. Dewey certainly would have agreed that all learning is situated, was sharply critical of any view of learning as primarily cerebral, and was a firm supporter of the kind of engaged learning that is engendered by apprenticeship and legitimate peripheral participation. Like Dewey, Lave and Wenger consciously reject dualist approaches to understanding learning, specifically calling attention to "abstract-concrete; general-particular; theory about the world, and the world so described."[126] They also echo Dewey in their assertion that "even so-called general knowledge only has power in specific circumstances" and thereby dismiss the dualism between the general and the specific.[127]

LEARNING AND SCHOOL

The absence of any explicit mention of Dewey in *Situated Learning* may arise from the authors' decision to avoid discussion of learning in schools: "Steering clear of the problem of school learning . . . was a conscious decision, which was not always easy to adhere to as the issue kept creeping into our discussions."[128] Lave and Wenger explain the decision to leave learning in schools out of the discussion in terms of a desire "to take a fresh look at learning" by avoiding becoming embroiled in the relationship between learning and schooling, the contention that "the organization of schooling as an educational form is predicated on claims that knowledge can be decontextualized," and the assertion that "pervasive claims concerning the sources of the effectiveness of schooling . . . stand in contradiction with the situated perspective we have adopted."[129] The first reason, simply staying out of the discussion regarding the link between school and learning, is reasonably persuasive and probably sufficient for the authors' purpose. The second and third reasons, however, beg the question.

The assertion regarding decontextualization is not backed by any data or reference to any specific claim that knowledge can be considered free of its context. In fact, the educational thinking of Dewey, Schön, and others very much suggests the opposite. Educational practice may result in separation of content from context, but even if that is true, it doesn't constitute a claim that decontextualization is desirable or even appropriate. Overall, the education and psychology literatures have consistently and continuously decried decontextualization of content.

The third reason given for avoiding a discussion of learning in school environments is even more problematic. If situated learning contradicts conventional understanding of effective learning, then presenting that contradiction in the form of a deliberate comparison and contrast seems to be an obvious and even necessary component of fostering understanding of situated learning.

Perhaps their most persuasive reason for not exploring the relationships among learning, situated learning, and schools is not actually presented as a reason: "legitimate peripheral participation is not itself an educational form, much less a pedagogical strategy or a teaching technique. It is an analytical viewpoint on learning, a way of understanding learning."[130] Placed in the context of a descriptive, potentially analytical approach to understanding situated learning, the decision to avoid consideration of learning in schools is legitimate, and the stated reasons for doing so are essentially unnecessary. The authors are not content to leave the subject alone, however, and they go on to say that "Even though we decided to set aside issues of schooling in this initial stage of our work, we are persuaded that rethinking schooling from the perspective afforded by legitimate peripheral participation will turn out to be a fruitful exercise."[131] At this juncture an appreciation of Dewey's thinking would have been especially beneficial, given that *Democracy and Education* essentially provides that rethinking.

COMMUNITIES OF PRACTICE

One of the interesting aspects of *Situated Learning* is that although the book is legitimately credited with arousing interest in the concept of communities of practice, the authors actually do not devote much attention to communities of practice, stating that "the concept of 'community of practice' is left largely as an intuitive notion, which serves a purpose here but which requires a more rigorous treatment."[132] The term is defined more explicitly in the context of a discussion of the "crucial and subtle" nature of "the concept of community underlying the notion of legitimate peripheral participation. . . . A community of practice is a set of relations among persons, activity, and world, over time and in relation with other tangential and overlapping communities of practice."[133] The index to the book provides entries for only 10 references to the term "community of practice," most of which are truly peripheral to the major discussion.

APPRENTICESHIP

In contrast, apprenticeship emerges early in *Situated Learning* as a focus of consideration, and it provides the major context for exploring the roles of situated learning, legitimate peripheral participation, and communities of practice. Chapter 3 devotes 29 pages—more than a fifth of the book—to description and discussion of apprenticeships in five specific environments: Yucatec midwives in Mexico, Vai and Gola tailors in West Africa, quartermasters in the U.S. Navy, butchers in a midwestern metropolitan area, and members of Alcoholics Anonymous. These descriptions are all based on the ethnographic work of researchers other than Lave and Wenger.

The picture of apprenticeship that emerges from the five studies summarized by the authors characterizes apprenticeship in terms of relationship and participation: "There are rich relations among community members of all sorts, their activities and artifacts. All are implicated in processes of increasing participation and knowledgeability."[134] Based on the five ethnographic studies, and grounded in these common characteristics of apprenticeships, Lave and Wenger proceed to a more theoretical approach to understanding legitimate peripheral participation in communities of practice.

OBJECTS OF ANALYSIS

Lave and Wenger identify five "objects to be analyzed" arising from their discussion of apprenticeships: (1) "the structuring resources that shape the process and content of learning possibilities and apprentices' changing perspectives on what is known and done," (2) the concept of "'transparency' of the sociopolitical organization of practice," (3) "the relation of newcomers to the discourse of practice," (4) "a discussion of how identity and motivation are generated as newcomers move toward full participation," and (5) "contradictions inherent in learning, and the relations of the resulting conflicts to the development of identity and the transformation of practice."[135] The discussion of these "objects" contributes only somewhat to the understanding a reader gains from reading the bulk of the book.

LEARNING STRUCTURES

In the context of "structuring resources for learning in practice," the authors encourage the adoption of a perspective on apprenticeship broader than the traditional master-apprentice relationship, which is supported well by the discussion of the five apprenticeship environments. The role of the master is varied, even within a single apprenticeship setting, and learning in an apprenticeship is frequently defined more by the nature of the work than by the role or influence of the master. Lave and Wenger's assessment is that "apprentices learn mostly in relation to other apprentices."[136] The authors further reject the dual roles of observation and imitation that are traditionally ascribed to apprenticeships, arguing that "legitimate periphery . . . crucially involves *participation* as a way of learning—of both absorbing and being absorbed in—the 'culture of practice.'"[137]

Again echoing Dewey, Lave and Wenger distinguish between a learning curriculum and a teaching curriculum but fail to effectively define either. "A learning curriculum consists of situated opportunities . . . for the improvisational development of new practice. A learning curriculum is a field of learning resources in everyday practice *viewed from the perspective of learners.* A teaching curriculum . . . is constructed for the instruction of newcomers."[138] This suggestion that the distinction is a function of whether the curriculum is viewed from the perspective of the learner or from the perspective of the teacher is neither sufficient nor helpful; nor does the authors' expansion on it provide clarity.

TRANSPARENCY AND SEQUESTRATION

The induction of newcomers into a community of practice takes place in an environment that balances transparency of access to knowledge—particularly access to technology—and sequestration of newcomers from full participation in the community. This balance varies within and across apprenticeship settings and is to some extent tied to access to the language of the community as well as the tools and techniques employed in practice.

DISCOURSE

The role of language in legitimate peripheral participation is evidenced in the development of the discourses of instruction and of practice. In a distinctly Deweyan vein, Lave and Wenger discuss the dualism between perceptions of formal learning via verbal instruction being associated with abstraction and breadth of learning, while learning from demonstration has "a literal and narrow effect."[139] In situated learning, however, "issues about language . . . may well have more to do with legitimacy of participation and access to peripherality than they do with knowledge transmission."[140] The primary role of language in a community of practice may revolve around "learning how to talk (and be silent) in the manner of full participants."[141] A fundamental difference between learning in the classroom and learning situated in a community of practice is that "there are no special forms of discourse aimed at apprentices or crucial to their centripetal movement toward full participation."[142] The language of the community and the language of learning to be a member of the community are the same. Language in a community of practice is a direct manifestation of Dewey's principal of learning *through* occupation.

MOTIVATION AND IDENTITY

Legitimate peripheral practice as evidenced in apprenticeship is a progressive process of moving from newcomer status to full participation in a community of practice. Both the abilities and the opportunities of newcomers are more limited than those of full participants. Over time, the learner becomes a member of the community and is allocated status accordingly. An essential component in the learning process is the development of the motives that lead to increased identity with the community of practice. Such motivation is provided in part internally by the learner and in part externally by other members of the community. Although Lave and Wenger do not use the term "mentor," they refer directly to the mentor-protégé relationship without naming it.

CONTINUITY AND DISPLACEMENT

To Lave and Wenger, "it is essential to give learning and teaching independent status as analytic concepts."[143] They reject the idea that teachers and learners possess a shared goal in the learning process as a notion that ignores "the conflicting viewpoints associated with teaching and learning" and obscures "the distortions that ensue," that reflects "too narrowly rationalistic a perspective on the person and motivation," and that makes "it difficult to explore the mechanisms by which processes of change and transformation in communities of practice and process of learning are intricately implicated in each other."[144]

Like Dewey, Lave and Wenger view learning as a fundamentally and inherently social process. Also like Dewey, they note the continuous process of displacement and replacement of members of the community that is necessary for sustenance and community growth, which Lave and Wenger view as "surely part of all learning."[145] They describe this as a "continuity-displacement contradiction," although it is not quite certain what is contradictory in the equation; however, the intra-community conflicts that can arise from the "contradiction" are described adequately. "Shared participation is the stage on which the old and the new, the known and the unknown, the established and the hopeful, act out their differences and discover their commonalities, manifest their fear of one another, and come to terms with their need for one another. . . . Conflict is experienced and worked out through a shared everyday practice in which differing viewpoints and common stakes are in interplay."[146] An important point raised by the authors is the evolutionary nature of every community of practice and the role of change, which means that "everyone can to some degree be considered a 'newcomer' to the future of the changing community."[147]

ALTERNATIVES TO THE APPRENTICESHIP MODEL

A limitation of Lave and Wenger's concentration on the apprentice-master relationship as the basis for exploring situated learning is that it ignores other possible models that may be of equal or even greater pertinence in understanding the social structure of professional relationships in modern society. Van Fleet discussed the paired roles of advising and mentoring in supporting professional growth and personal development in the workplace. In many ways these roles seem to constitute a more accurate view of how professional interaction in communities of practice actually functions.

> Advising and mentoring are similar, yet distinct functions. Advisors and mentors provide information about basic skills and requirements, knowledge about bureaucratic structures, and support during emotional or psychological difficulties. They act as guides for those who are less experienced in a given area, and even established leaders in a field seem to prefer this type of personal and person-embodied information.[148]

The fundamental differences between advising and mentoring have to do with "duration, level and nature of involvement, degree of personal risk or investment, and intended outcomes."[149] The specific role of an advisor may be either formal or informal but is almost always of defined duration and fundamentally linked to some institutionalized relationship between the advisor and the advisee. An obvious example provided by Van Fleet is that of the relationship between a student and an academic advisor, which is variable in nature and ultimately quite personal but is restricted to the realm of the institutionalized student experience: "the limitations of the relationship are generally understood and typically endure only during the students' tenure in an academic program."[150] The advising relationship at its best is symbiotic in that both the advisee and the advisor benefit from professional maturation and gained knowledge. Although the relationship forged through an institutionalized advising process may continue beyond its normal duration, it is usually a significantly changed relationship that no longer has recognized, formalized status.

Mentoring involves a greater intensity, a longer but less formally defined duration, and a more expansive interpersonal relationship than advising. It is "a serendipitous occurrence that can be fostered, but not dictated."[151] Van Fleet identified two primary models for understanding the relationship between mentors and their protégés: the market economy model and the gift exchange model. In the market economy model, which is typical of the corporate world, mentoring is a highly pragmatic process "employed for career progression and organizational effectiveness."[152] The relationship is largely impersonal and the primary benefits accrue to the organization and to the mentor. An altruistic approach to supporting the career advancement of junior members of the organization is rarely a motive for the mentor or a role recognized by the organization.

In the gift exchange model of mentoring, "the giver and receiver are bound by rules that transcend exchange of career-oriented benefits."[153] In this process, a "gift" bestowed by the mentor brings about a transformation within the receiver in a sustained process of substantial and meaningful duration. An essential aspect of the gift exchange model is that the gift is ultimately passed onto a new recipient as the protégé becomes the mentor of a member of the next generation. The major benefits—"knowledge, prestige, and power"—are similar to those of the market economy model, but the major focus of the gift exchange model is "the relationship itself, rather than . . . career progression or recognition."[154] Gift exchange mentoring relationships tend to be highly personal in character and generally involve some degree of the private and professional lives of the mentor and protégé. Although market economy mentor situations can to some extent be formally sponsored by an organization, gift exchange relationships are almost always spontaneous and serendipitous.

A major distinction between the apprenticeship paradigm and the mentoring paradigm lies in the nature of the risks associated with the relationship. In an apprenticeship, the risks accrue primarily to the apprentice and the organization; risks to the master are indirect and are to a considerable extent under the master's control. The master is free to choose an apprentice, has absolute control over the learning process, and can dismiss an apprentice at will as a means of reducing risk to the master or the organization. Although those principles apply to some extent in the market economy mentoring model, there is a heightened risk for the mentor in that the mentor's personal advancement is a major goal and benefit of the process. In this model, the overarching goal of benefit to the organization frequently means that a failed mentor-protégé relationship will have negative ramifications for both mentor and protégé. The risk factor is greatly increased for both parties in the gift exchange relationship in that such relationships "are distinguished . . . by their comprehensiveness (not confined to one aspect or dimension of life) and mutuality, as well as informality, intense level of interaction, and time of endurance."[155]

STEPS TOWARD A THEORY

Situated Learning does not quite succeed in formulating a theory that encompasses legitimate peripheral participation and situated learning. The book asks far more questions than it answers. The authors' reticence with regard to defining terms and their reluctance to address head-on the relationship between apprenticeship learning and formal learning limit both the reach and breadth of the discussion. Poorly grounded in the knowledge base of learning, the discussion ignores the thoughts and influences of important forebears such as Dewey.

Fuller, Hodkinson, Hodkinson, and Unwin related Lave and Wenger's model of legitimate peripheral participation to empirical studies of workplace learning and identified a number of limitations to Lave and Wenger's model in practice:

1. The concept of legitimate peripheral participation is applied too broadly, limiting its usefulness by attempting to "cover all workplace learning."
2. "Lave and Wenger are overly dismissive of the role 'teaching' plays in the workplace learning process and of learning in off-the-job settings."
3. In dismissing formal education, Lave and Wenger pit their views in a dualistic counterpoint to what they view as the standard view of learning, ignoring the more holistic thinking about learning that was emerging at the time.
4. The role of influences on individual learning other than that of the community of practice is essentially ignored; the authors overlook the knowledge, abilities, motives, and identity the individual brings to the workplace from outside.
5. The roles of conflict and power inequality are mentioned but are not given sufficient attention.

In conclusion, Fuller, Hodkinson, Hodkinson, and Unwin say, "We would argue that the concepts of legitimate peripheral participation and communities of practice provide important insights in to the nature of apprenticeship and workplace learning more generally. However, our case study research into complex institutional settings suggests that patterns and forms of participation are highly diverse. Further in-depth studies of workplace learning in a wide range of contexts are required if all the issues affecting learning and their inter-relationships are to be fully understood and theorised."[156]

NOTES

1. "Episcopal and Quaker," *Independent,* 1864 (March 3): 4.

2. "A French Critic on Goethe," *Littell's Living Age* 136 (February 23, 1878): 451.

3. Howard N. Brown, "The Liberal Movement and Religious Institutions," *Unitarian Review and Religious Magazine,* March 1882.

4. John Paterson, "Divorce and Desertion in the Old Testament," *Journal of Biblical Literature* 51 (June 1932): 162.

5. "The California Malpractice Controversy," *Stanford Law Review* 9 (July 1957): 736.

6. Donald J. Dawidoff, "The Malpractice of Psychiatrists," *Duke Law Journal* 1966, no. 3 (Summer 1966): 707.

7. *Oxford English Dictionary,* s.v. "Community" (New York: Oxford University Press, 1980).

8. Liana Nan Graves, "Cooperative Learning Communities: Context for a New Vision of Education and Society," *Journal of Education* 174, no. 2 (1992): 64.

9. Jean Lave and Etienne Wenger, *Situated Learning: Legitimate Peripheral Participation* (Cambridge: Cambridge University Press, 1991), 98.

10. *Oxford English Dictionary,* s.v. "Society" (New York: Oxford University Press, 1980).

11. Robert K. Merton, "Selected Problems of Field Work in the Planned Community," *American Sociological Review* 12 (June 1947): 304.

12. Dan W. Dodson, "Toward Community-Centered Professional Training," *Journal of Educational Psychology* 27 (February 1954): 242–48.

13. William J. Goode, "Community within a Community: The Professions," *American Sociological Review* 22 (April 1957): 194.

14. Ibid., 195.

15. Robert K. Merton, "The Functions of the Professional Association," *American Journal of Nursing* 58 (January 1958): 50.

16. Ibid.

17. Ibid., 51.

18. Harold L. Wilensky, "Orderly Careers and Social Participation: The Impact of Work History on Social Integration in the Middle Mass," *American Sociological Review* 26 (August 1961): 521–39.

19. Robert Hagedorn and Sanford Labovitz, "An Analysis of Community and Professional Participation among Occupations," *Social Forces* 45 (June 1967): 483–91.

20 Malcolm Knowles, "The Professional Organization as a Learning Community," *Training and Development Journal* 33 (May 1979): 40.

21. Kate Ronald, "On the Outside Looking In: Students' Analyses of Professional Discourse Communities," *Rhetoric Review* 7 (Autumn 1988): 130.

22. James E. Porter, "Intertextuality and the Discourse Community," *Rhetoric Review* 5 (Autumn 1986): 38–39.

23. Richard C. Freed and Glenn J. Broadhead, "Discourse Communities, Sacred Texts, and Institutional Norms," *College Composition and Communication* 38 (May 1987): 154–65.

24. Ibid.

25. Kelly Belanger and Elizabeth Black Brockman, "Writing Our Way into a Discourse Community," *Bulletin of the Association for Business Communication* 57, no. 1 (1994): 55–57; Karen Griggs, "A Legal Discourse Community," *Journal of Business & Technical Communication* 10, no. 2 (1996): 251–69; Larry R. Smeltzer, "Emerging Questions and Research Paradigms in Business Communication Research," *Journal of Business Communication* 30 (April 1993): 181–98.

26. Robert Burroughs, Tammy A. Schwartz, and Martha Hendricks-Lee, "Communities of Practice and Discourse Communities: Negotiating Boundaries in NBPTS Certification," *Teachers College Record* 102 (February 2000): 344–74.

27. M. Jimmie Killingsworth, "Discourse Communities, Local and Global," *Rhetoric Review* 11 (Autumn 1992): 110.

28. Arabella Lyon, "Re-presenting Communities: Teaching Turbulence," *Rhetoric Review* 10 (Spring 1992): 279–90.

29. Thomas Kent, "On the Very Idea of a Discourse Community," *College Composition and Communication* 42 (December 1991): 425.

30. Paul A. Miller, "In Anticipation of the Learning Community," *Adult Leadership* 17 (January 1969): 306–8, 327–28, 335.

31. Richard A. Graham, "The School as a Learning Community," *Theory into Practice* 11 (February 1972): 7.

32. Ibid., 8.

33. Maxwell Jones and Gene Stanford, "Transforming Schools into Learning Communities," *Phi Delta Kappan* 55 (November 1973): 201–3, 23–24.

34. Graves, "Cooperative Learning Communities," 60.

35. Ibid., 68–77.

36. Hugh Busher, "The Project of the Other: Developing Inclusive Learning Communities in Schools," *Oxford Review of Education* 31 (December 2005): 459–77.

37. Jean MacGregor and Barbara Leigh Smith, "Where Are Learning Communities Now?" *About Campus* 10 (May/June 2005): 2–8.

38. Teresa Secules, Carolyn Cottom, Melinda Bray, and Linda Miller, "Creating Schools for Thought," *Educational Leadership* 54 (March 1997): 58.

39. Ann Lieberman, "Creating Intentional Learning Communities," *Educational Leadership* 54 (November 1996): 51.

40. Vrasidas Charalambos, Zembylas Michalinos, and Richard Chamberlain, "The Design of Online Learning Communities: Critical Issues," *Educational Media International* 41, no. 2 (2004): 135–43.

41. J. D. Slocum, *The New Departure, or, a Natural System of Learning Writing, Spelling, English Grammar, and Punctuation at the Same Time* (New York: E. R. Pelton, 1883).

42. Guy Montrose Whipple, "Needed Investigations in the Field of the Textbook," *Elementary School Journal* 35 (April 1935): 575.

43. Grace Fisher Ramsey, "An Unusual Book on Visual Aids," *Journal of Educational Psychology* 11 (November 1937): 185.

44. Tara J. Fenwick, "Expanding Conceptions of Experiential Learning: A Review of the Five Contemporary Perspectives on Cognition," *Adult Education Quarterly* 50 (August 2000): 248.

45. Harry Daniels, "Cultural Historical Activity Theory and Professional Learning," *International Journal of Disability, Development and Education* 51 (June 2004): 189.

46. Bonnie A. Nardi, ed., *Context and Consciousness: Activity Theory and Human-Computer Interaction* (Cambridge, MA: MIT Press, 1996), 8.

47. Betty Collis and Anoush Margaryan, "Applying Activity Theory to Computer-Supported Collaborative Learning and Work-Based Activities in Corporate Settings," *ETR&D* 52, no. 4 (2004): 38–52; E. Scanlon and K. Issroff, "Activity Theory and Higher Education: Evaluating Learning Technologies," *Journal of Computer Assisted Learning* 21 (2005): 430–39.

48. Gregory Z. Bedny and Waldemar Karwowski, "Activity Theory as a Basis for the Study of Work," *Ergonomics* 47, no. 2 (2004): 124–53; Yrjo Engestrom, "Activity Theory as a Framework for Analyzing and Redesigning Work," *Ergonomics* 43, no. 7 (2000): 960–74.

49. Fenwick, "Expanding Conceptions," 248.

50. Ibid., 249–50.

51. Ibid., 251.

52. Ibid., 253.

53. Sarma R. Nidumolu, Mani Subramani, and Alan Aldrich, "Situated Learning and the Situated Knowledge Web: Exploring the Ground beneath Knowledge Management," *Journal of Management Information Systems* 18 (Summer 2001): 115.

54. John Seely Brown, Allan Collins, and Paul Duguid, "Situated Cognition and the Culture of Learning," *Educational Researcher* 18 (January/February 1989): 32.

55. Thomas Aastrup Romer, "Situated Learning and Assessment," *Assessment & Evaluation in Higher Education* 27, no. 3 (2002): 233.

56. John R. Anderson, Lynne M. Reder, and Herbert A. Simon, "Situated Learning and Education," *Educational Researcher* 25 (May 1996): 6–9.

57. Ibid., 10.

58. Cher C. Hendricks, "Teaching Causal Reasoning through Cognitive Apprenticeship: What Are the Results from Situated Learning?" *Journal of Educational Research* 94 (May/June 2001): 302–11.

59. Peter Pope, Philip Cuthbertson, and Bernadette Stoddart, "Situated Learning in the Practice Placement," *Journal of Advanced Nursing* 31, no. 4 (2000): 850–56.

60. Fenwick, "Expanding Conceptions," 254.

61. Anderson, Reder, and Simon, "Situated Learning and Education," 9.

62. Fenwick, "Expanding Conceptions," 256.

63. Ibid., 257.

64. Ibid., 259.

65. Paul Gray, "Required Reading," *Time,* June 8, 1998, 111; Craig. Kridel, "Books of the Century," *Educational Leadership* 57 (March 2000): 86.

66. John Dewey, *Democracy and Education: An Introduction to the Philosophy of Education* (New York: Macmillan, 1928), 1.

67. Ibid., 15.

68. Ibid., 3.

69. Ibid., 65.

70. Ibid., 49.

71. Ibid.

72. Ibid., 50.

73. Ibid., 53.

74. Ibid., 61.

75. Ibid., 7.

76. Ibid.

77. Ibid., 9.

78. Ibid., 11.

79. Ibid., 13.

80. Ibid., 14.

81. Ibid., 19.

82. Ibid., 26.

83. Ibid., 28.

84. Ibid.

85. Ibid., 47.

86. Ibid., 94.

87. Ibid., 95.

88. Ibid., 163.

89. Ibid., 164.

90. Ibid.

91. Ibid.

92. Ibid., 165.

93. Ibid.

94. Ibid., 167.

95. John Dewey and Arthur F. Bentley, *Knowing and the Known* (Boston: Beacon Press, 1949).

96. Dewey, *Democracy and Education,* 168.

97. Ibid., 169.

98. Ibid.

99. Ibid., 170.

100. Ibid., 172.

101. Ibid., 173.

102. Claude Shannon, *The Mathematical Theory of Communication* (Urbana: University of Illinois Press, 1949).

103. Dewey, *Democracy and Education,* 173.

104. Ibid., 174.

105. Ibid., 176.

106. Ibid., 180.

107. Ibid., 181.

108. Ibid., 186.

109. Ibid., 185.

110. Ibid., 358–59.

111. Ibid., 359.

112. Ibid.

113. Ibid., 372.

114. Ibid., 362.

115. Ibid. 361.

116. John Dewey, *Essays in Experimental Logic* (Chicago: University of Chicago Press, 1920), 331.

117. Ibid., 334.

118. Dewey, *Democracy and Education,* 368–69.

119. Ibid., 369.

120. Ibid., 370.

121. Lave and Wenger, *Situated Learning,* 121.

122. Maurice Block, "Situated Learning: Legitimate Peripheral Participation," *Man* 29 (June 1994): 487.

123. Lave and Wenger, *Situated Learning,* 33, 35.

124. Ibid., 47.

125. Ibid.

126. Ibid., 38.

127. Ibid., 33.

128. Ibid., 39.

129. Ibid., 39–40.

130. Ibid., 40.

131. Ibid., 41.

132. Ibid., 42.

133. Ibid., 98.

134. Ibid., 84.

135. Ibid., 91.

136. Ibid., 93.

137. Ibid., 95.

138. Ibid., 97.

139. Ibid., 105.

140. Ibid.

141. Ibid.

142. Ibid., 108.

143. Ibid., 113.

144. Ibid.

145. Ibid., 114.

146. Ibid., 116.

147. Ibid., 117.

148. Connie Van Fleet, "Advising and Mentoring: Complementary and Essential Roles," in *A Service Profession, a Service Commitment: A Festschrift in Honor of Charles D. Patterson,* edited by Connie Van Fleet and Danny P. Wallace (Metuchen, NJ: Scarecrow, 1992), 156.

149. Ibid.

150. Ibid., 157.

151. Ibid., 159.

152. Ibid., 163.

153. Ibid., 166.

154. Ibid., 168.

155. Ibid., 169.

156. Alison Fuller, Heather Hodkinson, Phil Hodkinson, and Lorna Unwin, "Learning as Peripheral Participation in Communities of Practice: A Reassessment of Key Concepts in Workplace Learning," *British Educational Research Journal* 31 (February 2005): 63–67.

3

Organizational Learning and Learning Organizations

organization, *n.* An organized body of people with a particular purpose, as a business, government department, charity, etc.

1793 *D. RAMSAY* Hist. Amer. Revolution (new ed.) I. p. vi (advt.) Some of these additions we have ourselves received, as in the case of the words "organize, and organization," when applied to political bodies.

IN THIS CHAPTER

KEY CONCEPTS

Origins of Organizational Learning and Learning Organizations
Organizational Learning vs. Learning Organization
Characteristics of the Learning Organization
Origins of Failure in Continuous Improvement

KEY PAPERS

Vincent E. Cangelosi and William R. Dill, "Organizational Learning: Observations toward a Theory"
C. West Churchman, *The Systems Approach*
Chris Argyris and Donald A. Schön, *Organizational Learning: A Theory of Action Perspective*
Peter Senge, *The Fifth Discipline: The Art and Practice of the Learning Organization*

ORIGINS OF ORGANIZATIONAL LEARNING AND LEARNING ORGANIZATIONS

Although some authors trace the notion of organizational learning and the learning organization to the late 1960s and early 1970s, Garratt expressed the belief "that all the necessary conditions to create both the intellectual and practical basis of a learning organisation were in place by 1947."[1] The expression "organizational learning" first appeared in 1950 as a subject heading in *Psychological Abstracts*. In 1955 Krulee referred to organizational learning in a very modern sense.[2] Simon is frequently credited with calling attention to organizational learning in his 1953 article in the *Public Administration Review*.[3] Jones and Hendry suggested that the term "learning organization" was introduced simultaneously in 1988 by Hayes and by Pedler, but the term was actually used as early as 1976 by Gardner, who attributed the expression to Schön's *Beyond the Stable State* (1970).[4] Lieberman, however, explored both organizational learning and the concept of the learning organization in his 1972 report on a series of experiments sponsored by the Rand Corporation.[5]

ORGANIZATIONAL LEARNING VS. LEARNING ORGANIZATION

Many authors tacitly define organizational learning as what happens in a learning organization. Huysman, however, suggested that the two concepts are quite distinct, and that there is in fact a gap between them that needs to be bridged if the general principles of organizational learning are to be incorporated into the practical specifics of the learning organization. "The ideas concerning the learning organization more often than not lack solid theoretical as well as empirical foundation."[6] Huysman proposed the descriptive theoretical orientation of the literature of organizational learning as the appropriate underpinning for the prescriptive, interventive arena of the learning organization: "A descriptive perspective on organizational learning leads to almost opposite insights than does the prescriptive perspective on the learning organization."[7] Lahteen-maki, Toivonen, and Mattila, however, found significant gaps and inconsistencies in the theoretical base for organizational learning that make it difficult even to verify the existence of learning organizations as a functional reality.[8]

CHARACTERISTICS OF THE LEARNING ORGANIZATION

Pedler suggested that there are two fundamental characteristics of a learning organization:

1. All the people who are associated with the organization must operate in a mode of continuous learning and development.
2. The organization as a whole must operate in a mode that incorporates and integrates the learning and development of individuals and leads to the "self-development" of the organization.[9]

According to Pedler, "given the resources and will, the first of these is not so difficult—the technologies and methods for encouraging all staff in continuous learning and development exist—but the second remains much more mysterious and challenging."[10] "No amount of individual development will alone produce an organization able to change itself as a whole. The learning company is *not* the training company."[11]

Elkjaer echoed Pedler's concern in a case study examination of a failed attempt to create a learning organization in which "the emphasis was placed on changing individual employees while the organization itself—its managerial structures and work practices—remained fairly constant."[12] Elkjaer attributed the failure in part to a "quick fix" approach to managing the transformation into a learning organization.[13] Elkjaer described the focus on individual learning within the organizational context as an acquisition metaphor for organizational learning, which has dominated the organizational learning literature, and contrasted that focus with a participation metaphor that emphasizes communities of practice rather than structured learning.[14]

ORIGINS OF FAILURE IN CONTINUOUS IMPROVEMENT

Garvin noted that failures in continuous improvement initiatives "far outnumber successes. Why? Because most companies have failed to grasp a basic truth. Continuous improvement requires a commitment to learning."[15] Garvin lamented that discussions of learning observations "have often been reverential and utopian, filled with near mystical terminology."[16] Garvin was particularly critical of the works of Senge and Nonaka, noting that while the scenarios they present are "idyllic" and their outcomes desirable, they fail to "provide a framework for action. The recommendations are far too abstract, and too many questions remain unanswered."[17] To Garvin, there are three unresolved critical issues that need to be addressed to make the idea of the learning organization accessible and practical: (1) the expression "learning organization" needs to be precisely defined in terms that are "actionable and easy to apply," (2) incorporation of the learning organization idea into management requires "clearer guidelines for practice, filled with operational advice rather than high aspirations," and (3) there needs to be a specific approach to measurement of "an organization's rate and level of learning to ensure that gains have in fact been made."[18] Unless these "three Ms"—meaning, management, and measurement—are addressed, Garvin predicted, it is unlikely that there will be meaningful progress toward realizing the promise of the learning organization.

Garvin contended that while there are many workable definitions of organizational learning, there is no useful definition of learning organization. He proposed the following working definition: "A learning organization is an organization skilled at creating, acquiring, and transferring knowledge, and at modifying its behavior to reflect new knowledge and insights."[19] The management problem can be addressed by understanding those things that a learning organization does well, which include "systematic problem solving, experimentation with new approaches, learning from their own experience and past history, learning from the experiences and best practices of others, and transferring knowledge quickly and efficiently throughout the organization."[20] It is through the systematic application of these "building blocks" that an organization manages its learning activities.

With regard to measurement, Garvin viewed the measures used in most organizations as "incomplete" in that they "focus on a single measure of output (cost or price) and ignore learning that affects other competitive variables, like quality, delivery, or new product introductions," while telling "us little about the sources of learning or the levers of change."[21] He saw a need to measure not just results, but also the processes that yield those results, which can be done through the use of surveys, questionnaires, interviews, and direct observation of behavior within the organization. Ultimately, the efforts to build a learning organization will pay off if they are accompanied by "a subtle shift of focus, away from continuous improvement and toward a commitment to learning. Coupled with a better understanding of the 'three Ms,' the meaning, management, and measurement of learning, this shift provides a solid foundation for building learning organizations."[22]

Vincent E. Cangelosi and William R. Dill, "Organizational Learning: Observations toward a Theory," *Administrative Science Quarterly* 10 (September 1965): 175–203.

Vincent E. Cangelosi (1928–88) earned bachelor's and master's degrees from Louisiana State University and a doctorate from the University of Arkansas. He held faculty positions at the University of Arkansas, the University of Texas, and Louisiana State University, where he was chair of the Department of Quantitative Methods and dean of the junior division of the university. William R. Dill received a bachelor's degree from Bates College, a master's degree from the Carnegie Institute of Technology, and a doctorate from the University of Oslo. He has held faculty positions at Carnegie-Mellon University, the Carnegie Institute of Technology, and New York University and was program director of education for IBM's research and development division. From 1981 to 1989 he was president of Babson College. "Organizational Learning: Observations toward a Theory" is a minor citation classic, with 59 entries in the *Social Sciences Citation Index* between 1974 and 2005.

AN ORGANIZATIONAL LEARNING GAME

Cangelosi and Dill describe a pseudoexperiment conducted in the form of a game at the University of Texas. Such games have been used extensively in business administration education. Seven students in a graduate administration program engaged in a highly structured and closely monitored semester-long simulation of a corporate management environment. "The tasks that management had to perform were sufficiently complex to induce the team to organize on a hierarchical, functionally specialized basis."[23] The simulated environment involved responsibility to a board of directors and competition with two parallel teams in the same industrial domain and three teams in a closely related industrial domain. Efforts were made to make the simulation sufficiently realistic to ensure that the learning processes necessary for team success were representative of those that would take place in the real world.

The game was structured in the form of "moves," each of which represented a month in the life of the simulated company, although the time frame was substantially condensed for purposes of the exercise. A typical move required a week at the beginning of the semester, but by the end of the semester, as the team developed higher comfort and confidence levels, up to three months of simulated action could be accomplished in a single week. The game was controlled and monitored by a sophisticated computer program.

FOUR PHASES OF ORGANIZATIONAL LEARNING

The main objective of the researchers was to observe and categorize the ways in which the team learned to accomplish the tasks necessary for team success in the simulated company environment. From those observations, Cangelosi and Dill identify four phases of organizational learning: (1) the initial phase, (2) the searching phase, (3) the comprehending phase, and (4) the consolidating phase.

In the initial phase, which accounted for the first three "game-months" of the simulation, decisions were relatively tentative, with each decision accounting for a single move. During this phase, team members were not fully in agreement with company objectives and were uncertain how to work together or with the board of directors. Submitting objectives to the board of directors for approval was viewed as a necessity rather than an active strategy for improvement. Most decisions and actions were short-term tactical moves with no long-term strategic value; many decisions were poorly structured and essentially ad hoc. During the initial phase awareness of competitors was focused primarily on learning what the competitors were doing and deciding which competitor characteristics to emulate. Information seeking, gathering, and use during the initial phase were disorganized and largely ineffective.

The searching phase was characterized by the transition from single moves to multiple moves as the team gained knowledge, experience, and confidence. The tentative nature of the initial phase was overcome as the team began to detect and search for patterns related to the simulated "history" of the company, which had been losing money prior to the beginning of the simulation, and their own actions and decisions. Objectives were strengthened and finalized, and a central goal of improving the product line, increasing market share, and making a profit emerged. During this phase the team recognized the need to divide responsibility into subteams or "departments" and to entrust responsibility and authority to the departments. The management team became more engaged with the board of directors. During the searching phase the team began to view the company's impact on competitors as being more important than competitors' impact on the company. Information seeking, gathering, and utilization processes began to improve as they became more structured, with the emphasis primarily on seeking and gathering. Although the team was coalescing and gaining the ability to understand the company, during the searching phase "it was difficult for management to feel any significant sense of accomplishment."[24]

The comprehending phase was "a period of more rapid and positive learning."[25] The overall team and departments began to make effective use of established objectives and the overall goal shifted from a focus on market share to a focus on profitability. Immediate and long-term objectives, decisions, and actions took on the characteristics of an integrated whole. Information processes shifted from a focus on seeking and gathering to an emphasis on assessment and utilization. More sophisticated decision-making tools and processes were employed as the team began to look outside the company for input from "economics, marketing, statistics, and operations research."[26] These processes were used to shape critical information into explicit models, which could then be tested to provide input into decisions. During this phase the team began to experience concrete signs of success, increasing the company's market share and improving production, although the company was initially still losing money. New products were explored and developed as an approach to enhancing market share and profitability. Interactions with competitors were increasingly driven by the desire to control competition rather than simply monitoring or being influenced by competition. As those actions began to pay off, the management team developed stronger relationships among themselves and with the board of directors. Toward the end of the comprehending phase, the company became truly profitable.

The consolidating phase was characterized by concentrated systematic actions designed to stabilize the company. Experimentation essentially stopped as processes and activities became established routines. At the same time, though, decision making became more creative and more flexible as the management team gained confidence in decision models and became more assured of the success of the company. The roles of the departments became less important and the team began to act as a cohesive whole. The board of directors, gaining confidence in the management team, assumed a supportive but more distant role.

Ultimately, Cangelosi and Dill conclude that the team learned a great deal but "it was not a clearly drawn and easy kind of learning."[27] Ultimately, although the authors feel confident that what was observed truly constitutes organizational learning, they are less sure of how it was that the organization learned. It is clear, however, that organizational learning was more a byproduct of the company simulation than a goal or activity deliberately addressed by the management team.

A THEORETICAL MODEL OF ORGANIZATIONAL LEARNING

Cangelosi and Dill assess their pseudoexperiment within the context of three "theories of organizational learning" as a means of attempting to provide insight into the learning process they observed: the Air Defense experiments carried out during the late 1950s, Cyert and March's "Behavioral Theory of the Firm," and Hirschman and Lindblom's exploration of imbalance and convergence.[28] From this assessment, the authors synthesize the theoretical model of organization learning visualized in figure 3.1

Cangelosi and Dill define the model in the following terms: "The basic concept of the model is that organizational learning must be viewed as a series of interactions between adaptation at the individual or subgroup level and adaptation at the organizational level."[29] The authors identify three key sources of stress in the organizational learning process. Discomfort stress and performance stress both affect individuals and groups. Discomfort stress is the pressure exerted on individuals and subgroups by "the complexity of the environment relative to the time, energy, and ability that groups can expend understanding it and of the uncertainty in the environment relative to a group's ability to forecast the future."[30] Performance stress "allows for the possibility that organizations may be highly sensitized either to success or to failure, or to some mixture of the two."[31] "Performance stress is affected by the outcomes of previous decisions, by changes in preferences or aspiration levels, by incentives existing within the organization and manipulated by its leaders, and by the degree to which management is challenged with the newness of its task."[32] Performance stress affects the organization as a whole as well as individuals and subgroups, but both discomfort stress and individual stress are experienced primarily by individuals.

Figure 3.1
Cangelosi and Dill's Model of Organizational Learning Sources of Stress

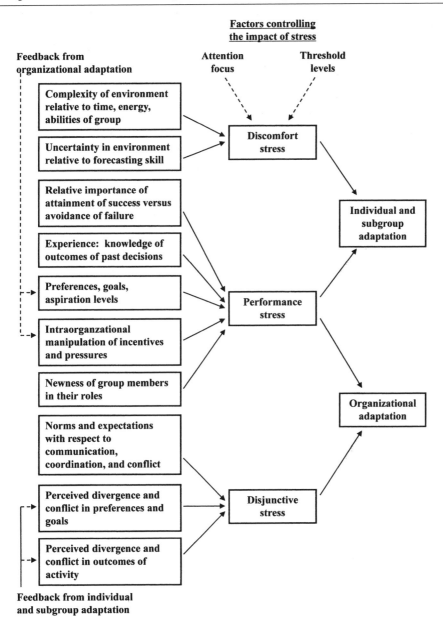

The third form of stress in organizational learning "results from increasing degrees of divergence and conflict in the ways in which individuals and subgroups behave" and is known as disjunctive stress.[33] According to Cangelosi and Dill, organizational learning is primarily a reaction to the disjunctive stress that is produced by individual and group adaptation to discomfort stress and performance stress. In other words, as individuals and groups learn and adapt, the organization as a whole is forced to learn and adapt.

Although discomfort stress is experienced entirely by individuals and groups, and performance stress is experienced mostly by individuals and groups, disjunctive stress is experienced only by the organization. "Thus, individual and subgroup adaptation control learning at the organizational level primarily by producing divergent and conflicting patterns of behavior."[34] Organizational growth and development are furthered as organizational adaptation influences individuals and groups and as individual and group adaptation influences the organization.

The impact of stress on individuals, groups, and the organization is tempered by two forces. Attention focus has to do with the extent to which individuals, groups, or organizations are aware of and responsive to sources of stress. Attention to stress is selective and variable: it is possible at any given time to pay attention to a limited number of influences, and the attention given to any particular influence varies over time. At any given point in time, each source of stress is associated with a threshold level that determines the extent to which the source of stress can exert an influence. Threshold levels are also variable over time. The influence of attention focus and threshold level for any given source of stress diminishes as attention shifts from the individual to the group or from the group to the organization, but the potential magnitude of a reaction to a source of stress increases. "Adaptation will occur more frequently and in smaller increments if an individual rather than a group is involved, if ideas for adaptation are readily available, if the persons involved are not under great time pressure to maintain current programs and activities, if the adaptation can be implemented routinely and without stress, and if it can be reversed or retracted after undesirable outcomes result."[35]

C. West Churchman, *The Systems Approach* (New York: Delta, 1968).

C. West Churchman (1913–2004) was a philosopher and professor of philosophy at the University of California, Berkeley. He was instrumental in the development of operations research and the expansion of systems analysis from a focus primarily on time and motion studies and computer science to a generalized approach to management and organizational analysis. *The Systems Approach* is one of the classic works in the field of general systems theory. It was generally well received, although it did not attract many reviews, and is represented by 320 citation entries in the *Social Sciences Citation Index.*

The Systems Approach is an attempt to make the fundamental nature and benefits of scientific systems thinking accessible to a general readership. Although it succeeds to a considerable degree, it is hardly surprising that the book did not emerge as a best seller. The topic is necessarily somewhat esoteric, and the phenomenon of the immensely popular business-world nonfiction book was not as widespread during the 1960s as it has been in more recent decades.

Argyris and Schön placed Churchman's approach to organizations as systems and organizational learning in the category of cyberneticists, who "have concentrated on organizations as systems of decision and control, seeking to apply the principles of control and communications theory to organizational phenomena."[36] "For systems theorists, organizational learning consists of the self-regulating process of error-detection and error-correction itself, whether or not maintenance of the organizational steady state is mediated by the self-conscious efforts of individual members of the organization."[37]

THE INFLUENCE OF SCIENCE

Churchman traces the origin of the systems approach to "the success of scientific teams in the military in World War II," particularly in the United States and Britain.[38] This unprecedented relationship between scientists and decision makers was mutually beneficial: as the expertise of the scientists expanded the decision-making toolkit, scientists themselves were transformed by their involvement in management processes.

As the scientist's perspective widened, he began to think of this approach as the "systems approach." He saw that what he was chiefly interested in was characterizing the nature of the system in such a way that decision making could take place in a logical and coherent fashion and that none of the fallacies characteristically resulting from narrow-minded thinking would occur. Furthermore, he expected that using his scientific knowledge would allow him to develop measures that would give as accurate information as possible about the performance of the system.[39]

TARGETS FOR SYSTEMS THINKING

Churchman describes five fundamental targets for systems thinking that characterize the systems approach:

1. *The objectives and performance measures of the system.* An important contribution of Churchman's thinking is the recognition that there are many sets of objectives associated with any system, only some of which can be directly linked to assessment of system performance. Some objectives are official in nature and are explicitly stated and codified, but even these objectives may not be amenable to assessment of the system's performance. "The inhabitants of systems dearly love to state what their objectives are, and the statements they issue have a number of purposes that are quite independent of the performance of the system."[40] Other objectives are personal in nature and are generally tacit; such objectives are rarely incorporated into performance assessment. Ultimately, there is a tension between the system's *stated* objectives and the *real* objectives that drive human behavior. Systems analysis requires exploration of both kinds of objectives. "The scientist's test of the objective of the system is the determination of whether the system will knowingly sacrifice other goals in order to achieve the objective."[41]

2. *The system environment, which includes everything external to the system that has an impact on the system.* Examining the system's environment and its impact on the system is substantially more complex than separating that which is internal to the system from that which is external. "The scientist has to have a way of thinking about the environment of a system that is richer and more subtle than a mere looking for boundaries."[42] From this point of view the environment entails all those entities that are not subject to the system's control and that "determine in part how the system performs."[43] The environment therefore acts to impose constraints on the system and its performance. A difficulty in separating the system from its environment lies in the principle that "the system is always embedded in a larger system."[44] Understanding the system of interest therefore always requires at least some understanding of other systems as well.

3. *The resources available for achieving system objectives.* System resources are internal to the system and are "the means that the system uses to do its jobs."[45] Within the context of the constraints imposed by the environment, system resources determine the system's performance capacity. "Resources are the general reservoir out of which the specific actions of the system can be shaped."[46]

4. *The fundamental components of the system.* "The specific actions [of a system] are taken by the components, or parts, or subsystems."[47] Churchman notes that the official subdivisions of the system (departments, divisions, teams, etc.) "are not the real components of the system even though they carry labels that seem to indicate that they are."[48] "In thinking about systems the management scientist ignores the traditional lines of division and turns instead to basic 'missions' or 'jobs' or 'activities,' all of these labels being used to describe the same kind of thing, namely, the rational breakdown of the tasks the system must perform."[49] "The ultimate aim of component thinking is to discover those components (missions) whose measures of performance are truly related to the measure of performance of the overall system."[50]

5. *The management, planning, and control mechanisms that influence the system.* "The management of a system has to deal with the generation of the plans for the system, i.e., consideration of . . . the overall goals, the environment, the utilization of resources, and the components. The management sets the component goals, allocates the resources, and controls the system performance."[51] Although by "management" Churchman means something more expansive than simply the individuals or teams of individuals who possess formal managerial control, he also recognizes that management is the one aspect of the systems process that is beyond the control of the management scientist. It is at the stage of system management that the system designer or analyst yields control to the management process.

Systems analysis has sometimes been criticized for overemphasizing the sequential nature of these planning targets, but Churchman actually emphasizes that "these steps are by no means steps that must be taken in sequence. Rather, as one proceeds in thinking about the system, in all likelihood it will be necessary to reexamine the thoughts one has already had in some previous steps. Logic is essentially a process of checking and rechecking one's reasoning."[52]

Churchman's book takes the form of a dialectic in which the author takes a neutral approach to a debate on the principles and benefits of the systems approach as represented by management scientists. Starting from an emphasis on the "old-fashioned" premise that "the dispassionate and yet clear mind of the scientist can aid in decision-making," Churchman creates a compare-and-contrast set of scenarios in which systems analysis is explored primarily from the point of view of management science, but also from the potential conflicting points of view of efficiency experts, humanists, and "anti-planners."[53]

EFFICIENCY

The efficiency expert's "approach to systems is based on the idea of 'the one best way' to carry out a specified task."[54] This is the approach of the scientific management explored by Frederick W. Taylor and others in the late nineteenth century. The author counterposes the management science of the late twentieth century with the scientific management movement of the nineteenth century, asserting that "the two philosophies are poles apart."[55] Churchman contends that although efficiency may be an appropriate approach to managing some components of a system, "concentration on efficiency *per se* may be a very inefficient way to manage a system" as a whole.[56] Furthermore, the emphasis on cost that defines the efficiency approach to systems entails what Churchman terms a "lie." "If the cost data have been collected in terms of direct expenditures and the manager tries to reduce these expenditures, he will find that what he considers to be real costs are illusory. Without a measure of the total system performance against which he can compare costs, his cost data mean nothing whatsoever."[57] Despite such fundamental disadvantages, the seemingly intuitive appeal of cost control dictates that the "spirit of the efficiency approach . . . does not die."[58]

HUMANISM

The humanist approach to systems adds to the delineation of system objectives the simple but fundamental question of "*whose* objectives are to be served."[59] Where the management scientist may attempt to approach the system with objectivity and neutrality, the humanist consciously approaches systems subjectively and from the point of view of human factors. Where the efficiency expert is focused on the value of the system, the humanist is interested in the values that are embedded in and reflected by the system. The humanist approach to systems is closely tied to human behavior.

Churchman contrasts the views and interests of the humanist with those of the behavioral scientist and additionally contrasts the behavioral scientist and the management scientist. "The management scientist sees the nature of the whole system as a determinant of individual behavior. For the behavioral scientist, on the other hand, the 'whole system' is made up of the behaviors of the individual persons."[60] In turn, the humanist tends to discount the dispassionate, disengaged approach of the behavioral scientist, who attempts to observe human behavior but not to influence it or be part of that which is observed. The humanist's view of the management scientist may be even more negative. "In the straight-faced seriousness of his approach, he forgets many things: basic human values and his own inability to understand all aspects of the system, and especially its politics."[61]

ANTI-PLANNING

Churchman describes two prominent approaches to systems and management that fall into the category of "anti-planning." The first is the tried and true pattern of most management environments, which Churchman defines as "experience coupled with intuition, leadership, and brilliance."[62] In this model, "the manager examines various aspects of the system, receives some data and reports from the staff, and then makes up his own mind what should be done."[63] The fundamental limitation of this approach to management is that it is not systematic. "The manager in most cases cannot make explicit what steps he has taken and he feels no need to do so."[64] "The management scientist would argue that the greatness of a manager can be determined only after one has studied the system by building a model of it and comparing what the manager did with the optimal."[65]

The other form of anti-planning exists in the combined forces of "the sceptic and the determinist. The sceptic firmly believes that we can never understand even minor aspects of a system."[66] Unlike the experienced manager, the skeptic is openly derisive of and opposed to the precepts of the systems approach. The determinist "believes that major human decisions are not in the hands of human decision makers but in uncontrolled sociological forces."[67] Although there are many manifestations of the determinist approach to systems, Churchman addresses two as particularly worthy of consideration: "the religious view of the world" and "the view of the world as a reflection of the self."[68]

THE SYSTEMS APPROACH

Ultimately, and not unexpectedly, Churchman's dialectic leads to the conclusion that the solution to seeking solutions and understanding systems lies in science, "which has been the main topic of conversation in the entire book" and "itself is a system subject to considerable change."[69]

A fundamental precept of Churchman's definition of the systems approach is that systems exist and must be analyzed in a holistic manner—that a system must be managed *"from the overall point of view."*[70] Just as understanding the system requires understanding the component parts of the system, understanding the component parts requires understanding the system as a whole. Senge restates this as: "You can only understand the system . . . by contemplating the whole, not any individual part of the pattern."[71] As essential as holistic thinking is, though, Churchman cautions against the "arrogance" of any one person who believes that he or she is capable of perceiving the entirety of any system.[72] At the same time, Churchman's dialectic is founded in the recurring theme "that when one is considering systems it's always wise to raise questions about the most obvious and simple assumptions."[73] Furthermore, meaningful problems "are interconnected and overlapping. The solution of one clearly has a great deal to do with the solution of another."[74]

An important aspect of systems thinking is recognition of the potential for error or failure and the development of plans, strategies, and tactics for coping with failure. "We need to set down the explicit steps that we will be willing to take and capable of taking when the plans fail."[75] "If the management system is acting correctly, it is never caught in a situation in which prior thinking could have saved it."[76] In fact, even "anti-planning must essentially be regarded as a fundamental part of the systems approach. No approach to systems can stand by itself. Its only method of standing is to face its most severe opposition."[77]

The Systems Approach concludes with four brief maxims related to the scientific approach to systems:

1. The systems approach begins when you first see the world from the eyes of another.
2. The systems approach goes on to discovering that every world view [sic] is terribly restricted.
3. There are no experts in the systems approach.
4. The systems approach is not a bad idea.[78]

Chris Argyris and Donald A. Schön, *Organizational Learning: A Theory of Action Perspective* (Reading, MA: Addison-Wesley, 1978).

Chris Argyris (1923–) earned a bachelor's degree from Clark University in 1947, a master's degree in psychology and economics from the University of Kansas in 1949, and a doctorate in the fledgling discipline of organizational behavior from Cornell University in 1951. He was a faculty member in the Department of Administrative Sciences at Yale University from 1951 to 1970, at which time he was named James Bryant Conant Professor in the graduate schools of business and education at Harvard University. Argyris is the author of *Personality and Organization* (1957), *Interpersonal Competence and Organizational Effectiveness* (1962), *Integrating the Individual and the Organization* (1964), *Intervention Theory and Method* (1970), *Overcoming Organizational Defenses* (1990), and *Knowledge for Action* (1993). Donald A. Schön (1931–97) was born in Boston and received a bachelor's degree from Yale University in 1951. After studying clarinet at the Sorbonne, he earned master's and doctoral degrees in philosophy from Harvard University. Over the course of his professional career, he spent time at the University of California, Los Angeles; Arthur D. Little Inc.; the National Bureau of Standards; and the Organization for Social and Technological Innovation, a nonprofit social research and development firm that he founded. In 1972 he joined the faculty of the Department of Urban Studies and Planning at the Massachusetts Institute of Technology; he remained there until his retirement in 1992. Schön is the author of *Beyond the Stable State* (1970), *The Reflective Practitioner* (1983), and *Educating the Reflective Practitioner* (1987). Argyris and Schön also collaborated on *Theory in Practice: Increasing Professional Effectiveness* (1974) and *Organizational Learning II: Theory, Method, and Practice* (1996). *Organizational Learning: A Theory of Action Perspective* was hardly a best seller and garnered few reviews at the time it was published but has generated nearly 1,500 entries in the *Social Sciences Citation Index*.

The preface to *Organizational Learning* provides a clear statement of the purpose of the work: "In the present work, we argue that organizations are not collections of individuals which can be understood solely in terms of the social psychology of group behavior. Neither are they understandable only as structures of authority and information-flow, or as instruments for the achievement of social purposes, or as systems for communication and control, or as cultures, or as theaters for the play of conflicts of interest."[79]

THE NATURE OF ORGANIZATION LEARNING

Chapter 1 of *Organizational Learning*, "What Is an Organization That It May Learn?" establishes a framework for exploring the nature of organizational learning. Echoing Cangelosi and Dill, Argyris and Schön emphasize early on that "it is not at all clear what it means for an organization to learn. Nor is it clear how we can enhance the capacity of organizations to learn."[80] Building on the common call for learning that accompanies perceptions of failure or stress in organizations of all kinds, the authors emphasize that learning is generally associated with the desire for or the actuality of change, but that neither change nor learning is inherently positive. "We need to spell out both the kinds of change we have in mind when we speak of learning, and the kinds of learning we have in mind when we call for more it."[81]

Again echoing Cangelosi and Dill, Argyris and Schön express the understanding that organizational learning and individual learning are different phenomena, and that there is no reliable reason to expect that what an organization knows will be in any way more than what is known by even one of the individuals who make up the organization. "There is something paradoxical here. Organizations are not merely collections of individuals, yet there is no organization without such collections. Similarly, organizational learning is not merely individual learning, yet organizations learn only through the experience and actions of individuals."[82]

The primary theoretical base for *Organizational Learning* is drawn from Argyris and Schön's 1974 book *Theory in Practice,* in which they proposed the construct of theories of action to describe "a theory of deliberate human behavior which is for the agent a theory of control but which, when attributed to the agent, also serves to explain or predict his behavior."[83] They further distinguish "espoused theory"—the terms in which an individual is inclined to predict his or her behavior—from "theory-in-use"—the actions that actually define that individual's behavior. From that theoretical base the authors undertake to define those circumstances that underlie organizational theories of action.

THE NATURE OF THE ORGANIZATION

Argyris and Schön define the nature of organizations from three points of view:

1. An organization is a *government* in that it possesses rule-defining and decision-making structures, delegates authority for individuals to act on behalf of the organization, and establishes boundaries that define the organization. Only as a political entity can the organization take action as an organization.
2. An organization is an *agency* if its existence has a continuous nature in which individuals act on behalf of the organization on an ongoing basis. An agency addresses a complex problem by subdividing the problem and assigning responsibility for subproblems to individuals or subgroups.
3. An organization is a *task system* in which the organization as agency addresses problems by defining and assigning roles to individuals and subgroups so that they can address subproblems.

THEORIES OF ACTION

Within the context of these points of view, "the norms, strategies, and assumptions embedded in the [organization's] practices constitute its *theory of action.*"[84] Each component activity or program area of the organization is represented by its own theory of action. The authors refer to the organization's global theories of action—those that span component activities and program areas—as the organization's instrumental theory of action. An instrumental theory of action encompasses (1) norms for organizational performance, (2) strategies for conforming to those norms, and (3) assumptions that link norms and strategies. This instrumental theory of action need not be—and frequently is not—officially adopted or recognized or encoded in the form of a document. In fact, "formal corporate documents such as organization charts, policy statements, and job descriptions often reflect a theory of action (the *espoused theory*) which conflicts with the organization's *theory-in-use* (the theory of action constructed from observation of actual behavior)—and the theory in-in-use is often tacit."[85] The tacit nature of the organization's instrumental theory of action may be a result of reluctance or refusal to recognize the conflict between espoused theory and theory-in-use or may occur because the instrumental theory of action is itself tacit rather than explicit organizational knowledge.

The argument for the existence of organizational theories of action is supported by the fact that an organization can exist for an extended period of time, during which it experiences multiple complete overturns of membership but still retains its essential character and identity. Studying the history of such an organization will reveal evolutionary changes of greater or lesser scope but will typically also demonstrate that the essential norms, strategies, and assumptions of the organization—those characteristics that define the organization's theory of action—have remained essentially constant. Such an external study of organizational history is unlikely to yield a complete picture of the organization's fundamental approach to theory-in-use. Furthermore, "each member of the organization constructs his or her own representation, or image, of the theory-in-use of the whole. That picture is always incomplete."[86] Argyris and Schön contend that individual members of an organization are constantly trying to complete their individual pictures of theory-in-use as they attempt to effectively place themselves within the organization. The individual's picture of the organization, then, is constantly being redrawn. It is through the collective revisioning of individual pictures of the organization that the organization's knowledge of its own theory-in-use is developed and through which organizational learning occurs. This is the process not of defining the organization but of organizing. "Hence, our inquiry into organizational learning must concern itself not with static entities called organizations, but with an active process of organizing which is, at root, a cognitive enterprise."[87]

SINGLE-LOOP AND DOUBLE-LOOP LEARNING

Argyris and Schön borrow Bateson's terminology to describe learning in organizations as conforming to two major patterns.[88] Learning is defined in terms of detection and correction of error. For learning to take place, there must be a feedback loop process through which detection of an error or a problem results in action designed to produce a correction or a solution.

In single-loop learning, "members of the organization respond to changes in the internal and external environments of the organization by detecting errors which they can correct so as to maintain the central features of organizational theory-in-use."[89] Although strategies for action may be changed as part of the process of correcting the error, the fundamental norms of the organization remain constant. There is a single feedback loop that connects detection of the error or problem to selection and identification of action strategies to address the error or problem.

The individual learning that characterizes the single-loop model is not sufficient for true organizational learning because the outcomes of such individual learning are not likely to become effectively embedded in the organization's collective memory. "It follows that there is no organizational learning without individual learning, and that individual learning is a necessary but insufficient condition for organizational learning."[90] That insufficiency is overcome when the organization is capable of double-loop learning.

In single-loop learning, when all possible strategies for action have been exhausted and found not to solve the problem or correct the error, the problem necessarily remains unsolved, because fundamental organizational norms preclude implementation of any additional strategies. In double-loop learning, the need for error correction generates reconsideration of the fundamental norms of the organization as well as strategies for action. There are two feedback loops, one of which links the error or problem to selection and implementation of action and strategies, and one of which links the error or problem to reconsideration of organizational norms. The relationship between single-loop learning and double-loop learning is presented graphically in figure 3.2.

Single-loop learning is a primarily individual process that may have definitive organizational benefits. Because the organization's fundamental norms remain constant, single-loop learning is rarely associated with any meaningful intraorganizational conflict. Double-loop learning, on the other hand, challenges fundamental norms and is frequently associated with intraorganizational conflict. Some individuals or groups within the organization may, for example, be extremely unwilling to alter or abandon a preexisting norm, while others may welcome the change and challenge that arise from shifting norms. "In this sense, the organization is a medium for translating incompatible requirements into interpersonal and intergroup conflict."[91] Such conflict is an inherent component of organizational learning and can be addressed through two major courses of action: battle and inquiry.

In the battle scenario, "the members may treat the conflict as a fight in which choices are to be made among competing requirements, and weightings and priorities are to be set on the basis of prevailing power."[92] The fight will end when either one faction prevails or the competing factions agree to a compromise that "reflects nothing more than the inability of either faction to prevail over the other."[93] In neither instance is the conflict completely resolved, and no meaningful learning takes place.

Alternatively, the conflicting factions may choose to pursue the conflict through some sort of structured inquiry that explores new organizational norms of performance, employs an explicit trade-off analysis to systematically compare norms and action strategies, or probes the individual values and perceptions that underlie the conflict. Such inquiry generally results in significant organizational change and can be termed true organizational learning.

Argyris and Schön recognize that the distinctions between single-loop and double-loop learning are not necessarily simple and that exploiting them in practice is complex and difficult. The opportunity for structured inquiry, for instance, is almost always tempered by individual or group power. The role of power is one of many factors that can influence the quality of inquiry either positively or negatively. To become a learning organization, the organization must engage in what Bateson termed "deutero-learning," or the process of "learning to learn."[94] Ultimately, "organizational learning occurs when

Figure 3.2
Single-Loop and Double-Loop Learning

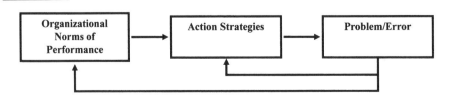

members of the organization act as learning agents for the organization, responding to changes in the internal and external environments of the organization by detecting and correcting errors in organizational theory-in-use, and embedding the results in their inquiry in private images and shared maps of organization."[95] Although a form of organizational learning takes place in the single-loop learning experiences that improve organizational effectiveness, the learning that occurs through double-loop experiences that lead to reexamination of organizational norms and conflict resolution is of both deeper and broader value in that it results in a restructuring of the organization's theory of action. When the organization further engages in deutero-learning, its capacity for learning is expanded and the role of double-loop learning naturally increases.

Peter Senge, *The Fifth Discipline: The Art and Practice of the Learning Organization* (New York: Doubleday, 1990).

Peter Senge (1947–) is senior lecturer in the Department of Behavioral and Policy Sciences of the Sloan School of Management at the Massachusetts Institute of Technology. He is founding chair of the Society for Organizational Learning. He holds a bachelor's degree from Stanford University, a master's degree in social systems modeling from MIT, and a doctorate in management, also from MIT. Senge is coauthor of *The Fifth Discipline Fieldbook: Strategies and Tools for Building a Learning Organization* (1994), *The Dance of Change: The Challenges to Sustaining Momentum in Learning Organizations* (1999), *Schools That Learn: A Fifth Discipline Fieldbook for Educators, Parents, and Everyone Who Cares about Education* (2000), and *Presence: Human Purpose and the Field of the Future* (2005). The best-selling *The Fifth Discipline* is probably the most influential work on all of the literature on learning organizations and organizational learning. The *Social Sciences Citation Index* shows nearly 1,100 citations to *The Fifth Discipline*. A revised and expanded edition of *The Fifth Discipline* was published in 2006.

The Fifth Discipline is not necessarily an easy read; reviews of the book were mixed. Micklethwait and Wooldridge termed it "completely impenetrable."[96] Paul Eldrenkamp, CEO of Byggmeister, noted that "people find *The Fifth Discipline* a bit abstract," a challenge that Eldrenkamp's undergraduate degrees in medieval philosophy and theology enabled him to overcome.[97] Stuttaford termed it "esoteric."[98] Larson lamented that "what the book provides in guidance, it lacks in practical insight."[99] Stubrich categorized the book as a fad and complained that it had completely missed the main problem of organizational dynamics, which Stubrich defined as "the real crisis in education."[100]

This is not to suggest that all reviews of the book were negative, although few were overwhelmingly positive. However, it is impressive and unusual that the first edition was still generating reviews seven years after its publication.

ORGANIZATIONAL "LEARNING DISABILITIES"

The key messages of *The Fifth Discipline* are (1) that many organizations are characterized by what Senge terms "learning disabilities" and (2) the need for organizations to develop holistic approaches to problem solving in response to such "learning disabilities." Senge introduces the term "metanoia" to define the "shift of mind" that is requisite to effective organizational learning and suggests that the concept of learning has "lost its central meaning in contemporary usage."[101]

FIVE DISCIPLINES

Like Churchman, Senge adopts a primary point of view that focuses on the organization as a system. In *The Fifth Discipline,* Senge describes five disciplines essential to organizational success, the fifth of which he considers the key to the learning organization:

1. *Personal mastery* entails "continually clarifying and deepening our personal vision, . . . focusing our energies, . . . developing patience, and . . . seeing reality objectively."[102]
2. *Mental models* are "deeply ingrained assumptions, generalizations, or even pictures and images that influence how we understand the world and how we take action."[103]
3. The importance of a *shared organizational vision* defines the third discipline, which Senge suggests has historically been the central theme of organizational leadership.
4. *Team learning* is "the process of aligning and developing the capacities of a team to create the results its members truly desire."[104]
5. *Systems thinking* is the "fifth discipline," the mortar that holds the learning organization together and the factor that facilitates the success of personal mastery, mental models, shared vision, and team learning as elements of organizational learning. Although a chapter is devoted to each of the first four disciplines, most of *The Fifth Discipline* focuses on the principles and applications of systems thinking.

Somewhat curiously, Senge pays no homage to Churchman's *The Systems Approach,* which is widely recognized as one of the seminal classic works on systems theory and systems thinking. This is probably in part because Senge is a disciple of Jay Forrester, who is credited with pioneering the field of system dynamics and whom Senge does cite; but the failure to recognize Churchman's contribution is nonetheless a significant oversight. Senge's exposition on systems thinking is largely anecdotal and has few ties to the extensive literature on systems analysis and operations research. The book identifies systems thinking and the other four disciplines as "new 'component technologies'" that "are gradually converging to innovate learning organizations."[105] It is very difficult to understand how any of these component technologies or their convergence could be defined as new in 1990, although there is certainly an appealing novelty in Senge's presentation.

THE LAWS OF THE FIFTH DISCIPLINE

Chapter 4 of *The Fifth Discipline* presents a collection of aphorisms termed "The Laws of the Fifth Discipline":

1. Today's problems come from yesterday's "solutions."
2. The harder you push, the harder the system pushes back.
3. Behavior grows better before it grows worse.
4. The easy way out usually leads back in.
5. The cure can be worse than the disease.
6. Faster is slower.
7. Cause and effect are not closely related in time and space.

8. Small changes can produce big results—but the areas of highest leverage are often the least obvious.
9. You can have your cake and eat it too—but not at once.
10. Dividing an elephant in half does not produce two small elephants.
11. There is no blame.

Many of the laws are adaptations of well-known expressions: "Faster is slower" is a rephrasing of Aesop's "Slow and steady wins the race." "The easy way out usually leads back in" reiterates Mencken's statement that "For every complex problem, there is a solution that is simple, neat, and wrong." Senge makes effective use of colorful metaphors to explicate and illustrate the applicability of the "laws" to both societal and business problems, but in the end they remain no more than aphorisms and as such are somewhat less than compelling. Many of the metaphors and examples are extremely limited in durability and breadth of applicability. In fact, the use of examples and metaphors frequently gets in the way of the message: the definition or description of systems thinking provided early in the book is stated entirely in terms of metaphor, leaving the reader struggling to understand what the author really means.[106]

LIMITS TO THE "LEARNING DISABILITIES" METAPHOR

The fundamental validity of any metaphor is defined by the relationship between the tenor of the metaphor—the fundamental idea or message the metaphor is intended to convey—and the metaphorical vehicle—the image through which the tenor is represented and the idea or message is communicated.[107] One of the central metaphors of *The Fifth Discipline* is the notion of the organizational "learning disability," which is the focus of chapter 2, "Does Your Organization Have a Learning Disability?" as well as a recurring theme throughout the book. This is an imaginative and expressive metaphor to the extent to which the inability of an organization to effectively learn and adapt can be likened to a human learning disability. Unfortunately, the metaphor breaks down very quickly, as Senge suggests very early in chapter 2 that the goal in addressing organizational learning disabilities is to "cur[e] them."[108] Even a cursory knowledge of human learning disabilities suggests that while there are effective treatments for some disabilities, there are only less effective means or no means of addressing others. Many of the available effective treatments are frankly palliative. There are competing treatments for many learning disabilities; the specific ways in which most of them operate are unknown, and in many cases no treatment is clearly superior. Treatment programs for individuals with learning disabilities are often admittedly and opening processes of trial and error in which treatments are induced serially until something seems to work.

An enlightened society therefore adopts not the goal of curing learning disabilities but the tripartite goals of treating those disabilities for which treatments currently exist; searching for new and more effective treatments, especially in areas where there is no current treatment modality; and incorporating, regulating, and enforcing societal accommodations for all forms of disability. Even though *The Fifth Discipline* was published prior to the passage of the Americans with Disabilities Act of 1992, the principles of accommodation encapsulated in the act are to a considerable extent extensions of the provisions of the Rehabilitation Act of 1973, as well as earlier laws, and should have been familiar to any expert in the management field writing in the late 1980s.

The learning disabilities metaphor breaks down further in Senge's enunciation of "the seven learning disabilities," which are so distant from the nature of human learning disabilities as to be insulting to individuals with true learning disabilities. Ultimately, Senge's metaphor collapses, as even a rather casual exercise in relating Senge's seven learning disabilities to the nature of common human learning disabilities reveals.

1. *"I am my position."* Senge correctly identifies as an organizational learning challenge the tendency for dedicated employees to over-associate with their jobs and therefore become incapable of seeing the organizational forest as a result of the influence of the position-centric trees. The parallel characteristic of many human learning disabilities, however, is exactly the opposite: a critically underdeveloped sense of self and a tendency to blur the boundaries between the individual and the environment.

2. *"The enemy is out there."* This is the tendency to externalize blame for failures and is defined by Senge as an extension from the "I am my position" problem. Although this characteristic does exist in some human learning disabilities, Senge has missed the mark in terms of its implications for learning organizations. In the human situation, the tendency to blame some external source for a problem is frequently—and in the case of many learning disabilities, typically—a function of frustration with not being able to control the problem. In many cases the individual exploiting the "the enemy is out there" tactic does not really believe that the cause is external in origin.

3. *"The illusion of taking charge."* Senge essentially rejects the principle of proactively addressing problems by posing the question, "Is taking aggressive action against an external enemy really synonymous with being proactive?" This begs the question, since there are probably very few advocates of proactivity who have ever defined proactive behavior in terms of either an "enemy" or "aggressive" action. A very common coping strategy for individuals with human learning disabilities is the development of explicit tactics for proactively taking charge of their own behaviors.

4. *"The fixation of events."* Senge asserts that "we are conditioned to see life as a series of events, and for every event, we think there is one obvious cause."[109] The author's premise is sound: focusing on a series of short-term events limits thinking and tends to impede rather than advance the search for solutions. The more common human learning disability, however, and one that is undoubtedly experienced in the organizational setting as well, is an inability to associate events with causes. For many individuals with learning disabilities, all experience is a series of seemingly random, unrelated events for which no cause can be discerned.

5. *"The parable of the boiled frog."* This is one of *The Fifth Discipline*'s most trite and most strained metaphors. The fable of the boiled frog suggests that a frog placed in boiling water will immediately attempt to jump out to save itself, but that a frog placed in water that is then heated to boiling will adjust its body temperature accordingly and, thus, not realize that it is being boiled to death. The fact that the parable is factually incorrect doesn't distract from its attractiveness.[110] It is undoubtedly the case that people are more prone to respond to suddenly emerging crisis situations than to problem situations that evolve over time. One of the most common problems facing individuals with learning disabilities, however, is the inability to recognize situations that present an immediate threat and a resulting inability to cope with emergencies.

6. *"The delusion of learning from experience."* This is actually a sound principle that is undermined by the choice of the word "delusion." Senge acknowledges that "the most

powerful learning comes from direct experience" and also correctly discusses the problem of consequences that are so distantly linked to the actions that precede them that the individuals responsible for those actions have no opportunity to experience the consequences. To Senge, "when our actions have consequences beyond our learning horizon, it becomes possible to learn from direct experience."[111] As previously discussed, many individuals with learning disabilities have difficulty associating cause and effect: just as they do not understand that events have causes, they do not understand that their own actions have consequences. An extremely important part of experiential learning for such individuals is developing an understanding that actions can have delayed or deferred consequences. Anticipating possible and probable long-term consequences is not only a possible component of learning from experience; it is a fundamentally essential outcome of the process.

7. *"The myth of the management team."* Team-based management has for some time been fact, fad, and fable in organizations of all kinds. Senge expresses grave concern about whether "typical management teams can surmount" organizational learning disabilities.[112] While there can be no doubt that the problems of team-based management the author describes are real and problematic, the metaphor of learning disabilities breaks down in the face of the widespread success of team-based case management for individuals with disabilities. A team approach is generally recognized as being essential to meeting the needs of individuals with learning disabilities.

The divergence of Senge's organizational "learning disabilities" from the realities of human learning disabilities is not necessarily a fatal flaw in *The Fifth Discipline*. The metaphor would have been richer and more meaningful, however, if the author had analyzed and adopted knowledge about human learning disabilities and had couched his argument in terms of a deeper, more systematic understanding of the nature of individual learning disabilities, rather than merely adapting and essentially misappropriating the term "learning disability."

Unfortunately, Senge doesn't really provide any meaningful guidance on how the 11 "laws" can or should be used or how to overcome the "learning disabilities." To his credit, the author makes no attempt to present simple solutions, but at the same time the book leaves a definite sense of unresolved complexity. Pedler has noted that *The Fifth Discipline* is "strong on ideas, less so on practical applications."[113]

THE APPEAL OF *THE FIFTH DISCIPLINE*

Jackson described the book as "neither novel or original" and emphasized that at the time of its publication it was one among several competing visions of the learning organization.[114] Jackson set about to explore the question of why *The Fifth Discipline* assumed the prominence that it did. Working from Cragan and Shields's delineation of the "master analogues" that define "rhetorical visions," Jackson's detailed analysis of the rhetorical vision of *The Fifth Discipline* suggests that the power of the work lies in its "underlying social master analogue."[115] "A rhetorical vision with a social master analogue reflects primary human relations, as it keys on friendship, trust, caring, comradeship, compatibility, family ties, brotherhood, sisterhood, and humaneness."[116] Senge's vision of the learning organization, then, is based not on what is pragmatically necessary or what is morally right, but on what is intrinsically good. The value and appeal of Senge's work reside not so much in the persuasiveness of the content of *The Fifth Discipline* as in the "dramatic qualities of his socially rooted vision, that is, its ability to inspire followers to see themselves actively engaged in building a learning organization."[117]

NOTES

1. Bob Garratt, "An Old Idea That Has Come of Age," *People Management,* September 21, 1995, 25.

2. Gilbert K. Krulee, "The Scanlon Plan: Co-operation through Participation," *Journal of Business* 28 (April 1955): 101.

3. Herbert A. Simon, "Birth of an Organization: The Economic Cooperation Administration," *Public Administration Review* 13 (Autumn 1953): 236.

4. Alan M. Jones and Chris Hendry, "The Learning Organization: Adult Learning and Organizational Transformation," *British Journal of Management* 5 (1994): 153–62; Neely Gardner, "The Non-hierarchical Organization of the Future: Theory vs. Reality," *Public Administration Review* 36 (September/October 1976): 591–98.

5. Arnold J. Lieberman, *Organizational Learning Environments: Effects and Perceptions of Learning Constraints* (Santa Monica, CA: Rand Corporation, 1972).

6. Marleen Huysman, "An Organizational Learning Approach to the Learning Organization," *European Journal of Work and Organizational Psychology* 9, no. 2 (2000): 133.

7. Ibid., 140.

8. Satu Lahteenmaki, Jouko Toivonen, and Merja Mattila, "Critical Aspects of Organizational Learning Research and Proposals for Its Measurement," *British Journal of Management* 12 (2001): 113–29.

9. Mike Pedler, "A Guide to the Learning Organization," *Industrial and Commercial Training* 27, no. 4 (1995): 21.

10. Ibid.

11. Ibid., 22.

12. Bente Elkjaer, "The Learning Organization: An Undelivered Promise," *Management Learning* 32 (December 2001): 437.

13. Ibid., 450.

14. Bente Elkjaer, "Organizational Learning: The 'Third Way,'" *Management Learning* 35 (December 2004): 419–20.

15. David A. Garvin, "Building a Learning Organization," *Harvard Business Review* 71 (July/August 1993): 78.

16. Ibid.

17. Ibid., 79.

18. Ibid.

19. Ibid., 80.

20. Ibid., 81.

21. Ibid., 89.

22. Ibid., 91.

23. Vincent E. Cangelosi and William R. Dill, "Organizational Learning: Observations toward a Theory," *Administrative Science Quarterly* 10 (September 1965): 176–77.

24. Ibid., 180.

25. Ibid.

26. Ibid.

27. Ibid., 189.

28. Robert L. Chapman, John L. Kennedy, Allen Newell, and William C. Biel, "The Systems Research Laboratory's Air Defense Experiments," *Management Science* 5 (April 1959): 250–69; Richard M. Cyert and James G. March, *A Behavioral Theory of the Firm* (Englewood Cliffs, NJ: Prentice-Hall, 1963); Albert O. Hirschman and Charles E. Lindblom, "Economic Development, Research and Development, Policy Making: Some Converging Views," *Behavioral Science* 7, no. 2 (1962): 211–22.

29. Cangelosi and Dill, "Organizational Learning," 200.

30. Ibid.

31. Ibid.

32. Ibid.

33. Ibid., 200–201.

34. Ibid., 202.

35. Ibid.

36. Chris Argyris and Donald A. Schön, *Organizational Learning: A Theory of Action Perspective* (Reading, MA: Addison-Wesley, 1978), 326.

37. Ibid.

38. C. West Churchman, *The Systems Approach* (New York: Dell, 1968), ix.

39. Ibid., x.

40. Ibid., 30.

41. Ibid., 31.

42. Ibid., 35.

43. Ibid., 36.

44. Ibid., 75.

45. Ibid., 37.

46. Ibid., 39.

47. Ibid.

48. Ibid.

49. Ibid., 40.

50. Ibid., 43.

51. Ibid., 44.

52. Ibid., 29.

53. Ibid., 13–14.

54. Ibid.

55. Ibid., 18.

56. Ibid., 18.

57. Ibid., 26.

58. Ibid.

59. Ibid., 184.

60. Ibid., 200.

61. Ibid., 228.

62. Ibid., 216.

63. Ibid., 215.

64. Ibid., 215–16.

65. Ibid., 216.

66. Ibid., 217.

67. Ibid., 218.

68. Ibid., 219.

69. Ibid., 229.

70. Ibid., 18.

71. Peter Senge, *The Fifth Discipline: The Art and Practice of the Learning Organization* (New York: Doubleday, 1990), 7.

72. Churchman, *The Systems Approach,* 28.

73. Ibid., ix.

74. Ibid., 4.

75. Ibid., 8.

76. Ibid., 9.

77. Ibid., 226.

78. Ibid., 231–32.

79. Argyris and Schön, *Organizational Learning,* iii.

80. Ibid., 9.

81. Ibid.

82. Ibid.

83. Ibid., 11.

84. Ibid., 14.

85. Ibid., 15.

86. Ibid., 16.

87. Ibid.

88. Gregory Bateson, "Physical Thinking and Social Problems," *Science* 103 (June 21, 1946): 717–18.

89. Argyris and Schön, *Organizational Learning,* 18.

90. Ibid., 20.

91. Ibid., 23.

92. Ibid.

93. Ibid.

94. Bateson, 718.

95. Argyris and Schön, *Organizational Learning,* 29.

96. "The Good, the Bad, and the Silly: A Guide to Management Books," *Psychology Today,* March/April 1997, 61.

97. George Gendron, "What CEOs Are Reading," *Inc.,* April 1995, 16.

98. Genevieve Stuttaford, "The Fifth Discipline: The Art and Practice of the Learning Organization," *Publishers Weekly,* June 22, 1990, 43.

99. Peter Larson, "The Learning Organization," *Canadian Business Review* 18 (Autumn 1991): 43.

100. Gustavo Stubrich, "The Fifth Discipline: The Art and Practice of the Learning Organization," *Columbia Journal of World Business* 28 (Summer 1998): 108–9.

101. Senge, *The Fifth Discipline,* 13.

102. Ibid., 7.

103. Ibid., 8.

104. Ibid., 236.

105. Senge, *The Fifth Discipline,* 6.

106. Ibid., 6–7.

107. William Flint Thrall and Addison Hubbard, *A Handbook to Literature,* revised and enlarged by C. Hugh Holman (New York: Odyssey, 1960), 281–82.

108. Senge, *The Fifth Discipline,* 18.

109. Ibid., 21.

110. Whit Gibbons, "The Legend of the Boiling Frog Is Just a Legend," *Ecoviews,* November 18, 2002, http://www.uga.edu/srel/ecoview11–18–02.htm (accessed November 22, 2006).

111. Senge, *The Fifth Discipline,* 23.

112. Ibid., 24.

113. Mike Pedler, "A Guide to the Learning Organization," *Industrial and Commercial Training* 27, no. 4 (1995): 24.

114. Bradley G. Jackson, "A Fantasy Theme Analysis of Peter Senge's Learning Organization," *Journal of Applied Behavioral Science* 36 (June 2000): 194.

115. Ibid., 203.

116. John F. Cragan and Donald C. Shields, "The Use of Symbolic Theory in Corporate Strategic Planning," *Journal of Applied Communication Research* 20 (May 1992): 202.

117. Jackson, "A Fantasy Theme Analysis," 207.

4

Intellectual Capital and the Knowledge Economy

knowledge economy *n. Econ.* and *Business* an economy in which growth is thought to be dependent on the effective acquisition, dissemination, and use of information, rather than the traditional means of production; cf. knowledge management n.

1967 T. J. WATSON in *Sat. Rev.* 14 Jan. 95/1 From an industrial economy, . . . we shall . . . more and more become . . . a *knowledge economy, with 50 per cent or more of our work force involved in the production of information.

IN THIS CHAPTER

KEY CONCEPTS

The Nature of Intellectual Capital
Property and Divine Right
Labor and Value
The Economics of Knowledge
Knowledge Industries
Discontinuity
The Knowledge Economy
Knowledge Market Roles
The Knowledge Price System

KEY PAPERS

John Locke, "Of Property"
Fritz Machlup, *The Production and Distribution of Knowledge in the United States*

Fritz Machlup, *Information through the Printed Word: The Dissemination of Scholarly, Scientific, and Intellectual Knowledge*

Fritz Machlup, *Knowledge: Its Creation, Distribution, and Economic Significance*

Peter F. Drucker, "The Knowledge Economy"

Thomas H. Davenport and Laurence Prusak, *Working Knowledge: How Organizations Manage What They Know*

THE NATURE OF INTELLECTUAL CAPITAL

The concept of intellectual capital is fundamental to most views of knowledge management. Although some authors distinguish between information capital and knowledge capital, both notions are clearly variations on the broader concept of intellectual capital. Intellectual capital is the dominant form of human capital and is closely related to social capital. The primary theme of all these terms is that the contributions of human beings have value that may both differ from and exceed the value of things. Intellectual capital and its cousins have historically been elusive elements in business and economics because they are intangible and inherently difficult to measure.

Concern for intellectual capital is not a new phenomenon, nor is it limited to the domain of knowledge management. Bontis cited Taylor's scientific management as an early attempt "to formalize workers' experiences and tacit skills into objective rules and formulae."[1] Sullivan traced the origin of the concept to 1980.[2] The term was in use, however, at least as early as 1836 in a context very similar to that of its current usage and has been used continuously ever since.[3] In 1925 Judd wrote: "The essence of social existence is not to be found in the instincts of isolated individuals but in those accumulations of intellectual capital which make it impossible for the individual to live except as he becomes a part of the cooperating group which has brought this intellectual capital into being and is now devoting a vast amount of its energy to solidifying its holdings."[4] This is a remarkably modern view and is also extremely congruent with current views of the fusion of intellectual capital and social capital. Galbraith used the expression "intellectual capital" in a 1969 letter to economist Michal Kalecki; the phrase appeared prominently in the title of a 1975 book about Kalecki.[5]

There is not—and perhaps cannot be—a universal definition of intellectual capital nor a definitive approach to distinguishing among intellectual capital and related terms such as "human capital," "social capital," and "cultural capital." Short directly relates knowledge capital to the nature of knowledge, stating that "knowledge capital includes all the firm's tacit and explicit knowledge."[6] Edvinsson and Malone developed an assessment model for intellectual capital based on the formula

Market Value = Financial Capital + Intellectual Capital[7]

Intellectual capital in this model consists of two components. Human capital is the capital that lies in people themselves, in their knowledge, abilities, and achievements. Structural capital is "all of those intangibles left behind, when people go home, and in that I include internal processes and structures, databases, customer relationships, and things like that."[8]

As early as 1889 an article in the *Nassau Literary Magazine* drew a distinction between intellectual capital and the capital of culture.[9] Seemann, De Long, Stucky, and Guthrie added to Edvinsson and Malone's equation their own definition of social capital, which is "reflected in the ability of groups to collaborate and work together and is a function of trust."[10] Short expanded on this definition: "Social capital is multidimensional and includes some familiar attributes such as culture, trust, anticipated reciprocity, context, and informal networks."[11] McElroy categorized Edvinsson and Malone's failure to include social capital in their model as a flaw and described two forms of social capital: "The first is the so-called 'egocentric' perspective, in which social capital is seen as the value of an individual's relationships with other individuals in helping to get things done in a firm. The other is the 'sociocentric' model in which social capital is still held by individuals, but has more to do with the added value of their position in the structure of a firm than with their interpersonal relationships, *per se.*"[12] McElroy extended from this distinction to a definition of social innovation capital, which "refers to the collective manner in which whole social systems (i.e. firms) organize themselves around—and carry out—the production and integration of new knowledge."[13]

John Locke, "Of Property," in *The Second Treatise of Government: An Essay Concerning the True Original, Extent, and End of Civil Government,* student edition, edited with an introduction and notes by Peter Laslett (Cambridge: Cambridge University Press, 1968), 285–302. First published 1690.

John Locke (1632–1704), an English philosopher closely associated with the Enlightenment and the rise of empiricism, has been credited with providing inspiration for the U.S. Constitution. Locke's view of epistemology is encapsulated in his *Essay Concerning Human Understanding,* in which he posits the notion of the human mind at birth as a tabula rasa, a blank slate to which knowledge is added through the use of the senses. It is his views on property, however, that are of most direct interest to the field of knowledge management.

Chapter 5 of Locke's *Second Treatise of Government* is titled "Of Property" and constitutes a definitive analysis of the origin and nature of property as a human resource and, most importantly, as an individual, personal resource. Exactly when "Of Property" was written is unknown; Laslett speculates that it was produced between 1679 and 1681.[14] According to Damstedt, the importance of Locke's work cannot be overstated: "Focusing a discussion of intellectual property on a 300-year-old text may seem unusual, but John Locke's Two Treatises of Government has an uncommon place in American intellectual property theory."[15]

PROPERTY AND DIVINE RIGHT

In keeping with the character of the age during which he lived, Locke grounds his approach to understanding and justifying personal property rights in the premise that the ultimate origin of all things is divine. His argument raises the possibility of—but quickly rejects—the notion of a sort of divine communism in which all things are collectively owned by all people, primarily on the grounds that such a scheme is functionally impractical. Locke contends that although all things are in some sense owned by all people, there must be some things that are inherently owned by individuals. "Though the Earth, and all inferior Creatures be common to all Men, yet every Man has a

Property in his own *Person.* This no Body has any Right to but himself. The *Labour* of his Body, and the *Work* of his hands, we may say, are properly his."[16] The premise that every person belongs exclusively to himself or herself was in its own right relatively radical in an era during which slavery was widespread around the globe, but the most important component of Locke's argument, and the central theme of the remainder of the essay, is that the things that any individual produces through interacting with the environment inherently belong to that individual. In other words, both the individual's labor and the products of that labor belong to the individual, and it is the investment of labor that defines the distinction between nature, which is owned by everyone, and property, which is owned by individuals.

Locke's views on ownership are couched in a primarily agrarian context and focus almost exclusively on property as the transformation of nature through labor. Locke subscribed to Hobbes's view that there is an inherent social contract that binds individuals and groups and dictates the limits and boundaries of behavior. There is a distinct moral element in his views on property that assigns property rights "to the use of the Industrious and Rational, . . . not to the Fancy or Covetousness of the Quarrelsome and Contentious."[17] There are moral limits that apply to the extent to which any person can claim ownership, the most fundamental of which are that no one can claim ownership of everything and that ownership should not interfere with the welfare of others. "As much as any one can make use of to any advantage of life before it spoils; so much he may by his labor fix a Property in. Whatever is beyond this, is more than his share, and belongs to others."[18] In this statement, Locke both outlines the boundaries of the social contract and sets the stage for the concept that some forms of property constitute a public good that is properly reflected in shared ownership.

LABOR AND VALUE

The most important statement in Locke's "On Property" is probably this: "For 'tis *Labour* that *puts the difference of value* on every thing."[19] Locke estimates that the labor invested in any product constitutes 99 percent of the value of the product in that "Nature and the Earth furnished only the almost worthless Materials."[20] If, as he contends, labor inherently belongs to the person who exerts it, then clearly the product belongs to that person as well. "Locke is perhaps the quintessential theorist of property as right. Property right according to Locke, as are all rights, are derived from natural law."[21]

Although Locke did not directly address the subject of intellectual capital, the emphasis in his argument on the role of labor rather than raw materials in determining value is a key underpinning of the concept of capital in general and intellectual capital in particular. Although labor in Locke's argument may be most closely associated with physical effort, it is clear that physical effort is of no value unless it is guided by knowledge and analysis. In a very true sense, the physical component of labor is no more than a byproduct of the intellectual activity that precedes and guides the physical component. It is possible, then, to extend from Locke's contention that labor provides the essential defining quality of property to the premise that the only real form of property is intellectual property and that intellectual capital is the backbone of all capital. In

Easterbrook's words, intellectual property is "no less the fruit of one's labor than is physical property."[22]

Most importantly, Locke's definition of property as a personal process with limits determined by the social contract allows for both the identification of ideas and their expression, which are clearly the outcomes of labor, to be considered property and for the allowance of public ownership for some ideas and expressions. It is this combination of personal and shared ownership that forms the foundation for modern thinking about intellectual property and intellectual capital.

The most obvious manifestations of intellectual property that derive from Locke's ideas are patents, copyright, and related statements of ownership such as trademarks and trade secrets. "Scholars find in Locke's theory of property, and the limits he sets on what a laborer can come to exclusively own and control, a solid argument with which to solve contemporary problems in copyright."[23] The alignment of Locke's thinking with current scholarship on intellectual property and intellectual capital is not perfect, but "despite the breakdown in some analogies between the kinds of labor used in producing physical vs. intellectual objects, Locke's theory nonetheless is applicable to the current debate."[24]

Fritz Machlup, *The Production and Distribution of Knowledge in the United States* (Princeton, NJ: Princeton University Press, 1962).

Fritz Machlup, *Information through the Printed Word: The Dissemination of Scholarly, Scientific, and Intellectual Knowledge* (New York: Praeger, 1978–80).

Fritz Machlup, *Knowledge: Its Creation, Distribution, and Economic Significance* (Princeton, NJ: Princeton University Press, 1980–83).

Fritz Machlup (1902–83) was, like Peter F. Drucker, born in Austria. He studied economics at the University of Vienna, where he earned a doctorate in 1923. Although he initially went into industry, he retained his academic interest in economics. After immigrating to the United States in 1993, he served until 1947 on the faculty of the University of Buffalo. In 1947 he moved to the Department of Political Economy at Johns Hopkins University, after which he pursued a number of visiting professorships and research fellowships until 1960, when he was named Walker Professor of International Finance and director of the International Finance Division at Princeton University, a position he held until 1971. He continued to be in demand as a visiting professor throughout his academic career and served in several government consultancies, with appointments to the U.S. Department of Labor and the Treasury.

THE ECONOMICS OF KNOWLEDGE

Although Machlup was a contributor to many aspects of economics, his most significant and most recognized contribution is in the area of the economics of knowledge. Drucker explicitly refers to Machlup's term "knowledge industries" in his chapter on "The Knowledge Economy."[25] No one before or since Machlup has undertaken such a massive categorization of the knowledge industries, which was very much Machlup's life's work. Machlup merits more than two thousand citation entries in the *Social Sciences Citation Index,* of which nearly six hundred are to his three major monographs on the economics of knowledge.

Machlup's 1963 *The Production and Distribution of Knowledge in the United States* provided in 416 pages and 85 tables a comprehensive economic analysis of knowledge industries, knowledge products, and knowledge tools in the first six decades of the twentieth century, with a liberal dusting of speculation about the future. By 1978 the same basic task required the three volumes of *Information through the Printed Word: The Dissemination of Scholarly, Scientific, and Intellectual Knowledge,* which was published over a five-year period. *Knowledge: Its Creation, Distribution, and Economic Significance,* begun in 1980 and planned as a 10-volume collection, was still a work in progress at the time of Machlup's death in 1983, at which time the first three volumes had been completed and published.

ELEVEN POINTS OF CURIOSITY

The Production and Distribution of Knowledge in the United States grew out of a lecture series Machlup delivered at Cornell University and Fordham University in 1959 and 1960. This monumental effort was inspired by 11 points of curiosity:

1. It is a fact that increasing shares of the nation's budget have been allocated to the production of knowledge.
2. It can also be shown that a large portion of the nation's expenditures on knowledge has been financed by government, so that much of the production of knowledge depends on governmental appropriations.
3. One may strongly support the judgment that the production of knowledge yields social benefits in excess of the private benefits accruing to the recipients of knowledge.
4. It is probable that the production of certain kinds of knowledge is limited by inelasticities in the supply of qualified labor, which raises questions of policy, especially concerning this allocation of public funds.
5. The facts that the production of knowledge of several types is paid for by others than the users of the knowledge, and that these types of knowledge have no market prices, raise questions of their valuation for national-income accounting as well as for welfare-economic considerations.
6. The production of one type of knowledge—namely, technology—results in continuing changes in the conditions of production of many goods and services.
7. One may advance the hypothesis that new technological knowledge tends to result in shifts of demand from physical labor to "brain workers."
8. There is evidence of a change in the composition of the labor force employed in the United States, in particular of an increase in the share of "knowledge-producing" labor in total employment.
9. There is ground for suspicion that some branches of the production of knowledge are quite inefficient, although it is difficult to ascertain input-output ratios and to make valid comparisons, especially since the very wastefulness is held to be productive of psychic incomes and social benefits.
10. It has been suggested that some of the growth in the production of knowledge may be an instance of "Parkinson's Law," which implies that administrators tend to create more work for more administrators.

11. There is probably more validity in the hypothesis that the increase in the ratio of knowledge-producing labor to physical labor is strongly associated with the increase in productivity and thus with the rate of economic growth.[26]

In these 11 points, formulated in the first years of the 1960s, Machlup adroitly summarizes all the core issues and questions of the knowledge economy. As Machlup simply points out, "An economic analysis of the production of knowledge is not only justified but overdue."[27] *The Production and Distribution of Knowledge in the United States* is a landmark attempt to carry out such an analysis.

THE INTRINSIC NATURE OF KNOWLEDGE

One of the key concepts of Machlup's exposition is "the 'promotion' of knowledge from the rank of an exogenous independent variable to that of an endogenous variable dependent on input."[28] In other words, the economic nature and value of knowledge are not derived from outside what is known but instead have their origin within the specific knowledge itself and, by extension, within the total corpus of actual or potential knowledge. Furthermore, there is a clear difference between the traditional view of knowledge as primarily of future value and what Machlup describes as knowledge that has an immediate payoff, such as those "types of knowledge that give immediate pleasure to the recipients."[29] He also calls attention to the supposed distinction between "productive" and "unproductive" knowledge, essentially rejecting that distinction and suggesting that the two are so closely tied as to be inseparable.

A fundamental opposition of perspectives on the economics of knowledge that Machlup appears to have originated is the distinction between knowledge as a *product* and knowledge as a *cost*. The view of knowledge as a product places the focus of production on the knowledge itself, either for consumption or for investment. The view of knowledge as a cost assigns value to knowledge primarily as overhead, as one of the costs of producing some other product. This distinction is a guiding force throughout the book and a fundamental element in understanding the economics of knowledge.

KNOWLEDGE INDUSTRIES

The Production and Distribution of Knowledge in the United States takes what Machlup defines as a *knowledge industries* rather than a *knowledge occupations* approach to the categorization of the knowledge economy, dividing the knowledge industries into five major groupings: (1) education, (2) research and development, (3) communications media, (4) information machines, and (5) information services. The emphasis on industries rather than occupations recognizes that there are knowledge workers in non-knowledge industries and that knowledge industries necessarily have employees who are not knowledge workers. The five chapters that address these concept areas provide detailed economic analyses of the contributions of each area to the knowledge economy, a term Machlup does not actually use but that is implied throughout the book. The final two chapters of the book bring the entire picture together. Ultimately, Machlup finds that the knowledge economy of 1958 has this composition:

Education	44.1 percent of total knowledge expenditures
Media of communication	28.1 percent
Information services	13.2 percent
Research and development	8.1 percent
Information machines	6.5 percent[30]

Taken together, Machlup estimates that knowledge production in 1958 accounted for 29 percent of the gross national product of the United States. By 1980, that percentage had grown to 34 percent.[31]

Curiously, although Machlup's ideas were clearly recognized by Drucker and other pioneers of knowledge management, they are rarely explicitly referenced in the current knowledge management literature. To the extent that Machlup is linked to knowledge management in the literature, it is exclusively through the academic literature, not the literature that could reasonably be expected to be linked to practice.

Peter F. Drucker, "The Knowledge Economy," in *The Age of Discontinuity: Guidelines to Our Changing Society* (New York: Harper and Row, 1969), 263–86.

Peter F. Drucker (1907–2005) was unquestionably one of the most influential leaders, authors, and thinkers in the realm of management. Born in Vienna and educated at the University of Frankfurt, he immigrated to the United States in 1937 and pursued a career as a freelance writer. He later joined the faculty of the Graduate Business School at New York University, where he spent more than 20 years before moving to Claremont Graduate University; the university's graduate school of management was named for him in 1987.

Although Drucker's contributions can hardly be overestimated, his legendary status has frequently caused other authors to attribute to Drucker achievements that he himself would not have claimed. For instance, Drucker is frequently credited with coining the terms "knowledge economy" and "knowledge worker" in his 1969 book *The Age of Discontinuity*. In fact, a 1968 book review attributed "knowledge economy" to Thomas S. Watson Jr.[32] Drucker may indeed have coined "knowledge worker," but he had used the term at least as early as 1962, seven years before the publication of *The Age of Discontinuity*.[33] Addleson suggests that Drucker "coined the phrase 'knowledge revolution'" in 1995, but that expression had been used at least as early as 1964.[34] At the other chronological extreme, Davenport and Prusak indicate that sometime after 1994, "Drucker . . . identified knowledge as the new basis of competition in postcapitalist society," although Drucker clearly postulated just that in 1969.[35]

The Age of Discontinuity has been published in several editions, including a Japanese translation, and has earned more than two hundred entries in the *Social Sciences Citation Index*. Interestingly, the book doesn't seem to have garnered a great deal of attention at the time it was published, and it generated almost no book reviews.

FOUR AREAS OF DISCONTINUITY

The basic theme of *The Age of Discontinuity* is social forecasting related to four areas of "discontinuity" that Drucker anticipates will have a significant impact on global society:

1. New technology
2. Economic transformation
3. The increasing focus of society on organizations
4. The emergence of a knowledge society

In attempting this sort of prognostication, Drucker anticipated the social forecasting books that became popular in the 1970s, such as Toffler's *Future Shock,* Bell's *The Coming of Post-industrial Society,* and Naisbitt's *Megatrends.*[36] Drucker eschews such explicit forecasting: "This book does not project trends; it examines discontinuities. It does not forecast tomorrow; it looks at today."[37] It is impossible, however, to read *The Age of Discontinuity,* particularly through the lens of the passage of 35 years, without interpreting its nature as being largely predictive; Drucker's choice of the subtitle *Guidelines to Our Changing Society* adds substantially to the impression that Drucker was protesting a bit too much in his insistence that the book was not intended to forecast the future.

THE KNOWLEDGE ECONOMY

Chapter 12 of *The Age of Discontinuity,* "The Knowledge Economy," provides the book's most direct approach to the core concepts of intellectual capital and is probably the most influential and enduring section of the book. The theme of the chapter is revealed in its single-sentence second paragraph: "From an economy of goods, which America was as recently as World War II, we have changed into a knowledge economy."[38] This relatively straightforward assessment, which many—perhaps most— observers now would accept with little or no question, was surely revolutionary in 1969. Drucker's use of statistical data regarding arenas of employment presents an excellent case for his core contention that knowledge itself constitutes the "central 'factor of production' in an advanced, developed economy."[39] Drucker also notes that economists have traditionally categorized those areas of the economy he attributes to knowledge as "services" and have treated them as "'secondary' industries."[40] In the course of the discussion Drucker refers to the "'brain drain,' which pulls educated people from countries of relative knowledge backwardness toward countries of advanced knowledge status," and the "'technology gap' that is supposed to open up between the United States and Western Europe," both of which were emergent concerns at the time of Drucker's writing.[41]

One of Drucker's most startling statements is his assertion that "'knowledge' rather than 'science' has become the foundation of the modern economy."[42] Although he does not by any means denigrate science or scientists, he draws explicit attention to the growing role for consultants who are scholars from all disciplines, including business, the arts, the humanities, and the social sciences.

It should be noted that Drucker draws no attention to any potential distinction between the definition of knowledge and the definition of information, using the two terms virtually synonymously, as in this paragraph:

> This demand, in turn, reflects the basic fact that knowledge has become productive. The systematic and purposeful acquisition of information and its systematic application, rather than "science" or "technology," are emerging as the new foundation for work, productivity, and effort throughout the world.[43]

Drucker does not ascribe this transformation exclusively to the United States, which he suggests "only started moving a few years earlier than the others."[44] The clear anticipation is that the dominance of the knowledge economy will sweep the world, carrying with it a seemingly insatiable demand for knowledge workers.

From these comments, Drucker formulates four "fundamentals of the knowledge economy":

1. "Knowledge work does not lead to a 'disappearance of work.'"[45] Drucker was remarkably ahead of his time in anticipating that the knowledge workers of the twentieth century would actually spend more time in work-related activities than did the workers of previous eras, whose tasks were primarily physical. Most notably, knowledge workers can and do work outside the formal workplace, while other workers do not and cannot do so. "Knowledge work, like all productive work, creates its own demand. And the demand is apparently unlimited."[46]

2. "Knowledge does not eliminate skill."[47] Whereas earlier analysts tended to contrast knowledge-based work and skill-based work, Drucker's view is that skill is directly dependent on knowledge and is a fixed prerequisite to the acquisition of skill. Ultimately, knowledge is of little use without skill, and skill is of no use if it is not grounded in knowledge. The changing relationship between knowledge and skill, however, has profound results, including the demise of apprenticeship as a form of skill acquisition, the rise of technical education, and the need for continuous knowledge and skill acquisition.

3. "While knowledge eliminates neither work nor skill, its introduction does constitute a real revolution both in the productivity of work and in the life of the worker."[48] Drucker also foretells the shift from a society in which an individual is likely to work throughout his or her life in an occupation that is "predetermined" rather than chosen to one in which individuals are capable of making proactive career choices and have the ability to change careers at will.[49] Not only will opportunities to choose specific areas of the knowledge economy as career avenues expand, but the range of possible careers within each area will be vastly varied and changing. In fact, the real problem may become an overabundance of choice that makes effective career selection difficult. Drucker also anticipates, if only in passing, the potential for the differences in choice that constitute major societal divides.

4. "Knowledge opportunities exist primarily in large organizations."[50] The eighth through eleventh chapters of *The Age of Discontinuity* are collectively named "A Society of Organizations." In this section Drucker expands on the increasing prominence and dominance of larger organizations, to which he returns in chapter 12,"The Knowledge Economy." Echoing Price's *Little Science, Big Science,* Drucker notes the transition from a past in which knowledge workers were primarily independent professionals to a present in which they are increasingly associated with expansive organizations and have subsequently lost substantial professional autonomy.[51] This pervasive change is

as present in the university and the hospital as it is the corporation. To Drucker, "The knowledge worker of today is . . . the successor to the employee of yesterday, the manual worker, skilled or unskilled."[52]

As Drucker recognizes, each of these four fundamental principles presents substantial potential for conflict. A society accustomed to collectively thinking of itself as being primarily engaged in the production of goods, with service industries playing a distinctly secondary role, must necessarily be challenged by the transition not only to service industries as the primary economic base but to a specific, hitherto unnamed component of those service industries as the primary base.

The final section of "The Knowledge Economy" addresses the question, "How did this shift to the knowledge society and knowledge economy come about?"[53] Drucker answers this question primarily in terms of the increased human life span rather than the increasing complexity of work. In fact, that perceived complexity is primarily an artifact of life span that reflects the accompanying increased working life of the typical worker. This produces a society in which it is possible to impose increased educational requirements. At the same time, society accepts and even expects that a given individual will sequentially pursue multiple seemingly unrelated career paths. Ultimately, the increase in individual and collective knowledge produces a situation in which the production of an increasing number and expanding variety of knowledge-related jobs is inevitable and essential.

Thomas H. Davenport and Laurence Prusak, *Working Knowledge: How Organizations Manage What They Know* (Boston: Harvard Business School Press, 1998).

Thomas H. Davenport is President's Distinguished Professor of Information and Technology in the Technology, Operations, and Information Management Division of Babson College, and co-director of Babson's Process Management Research Center. Laurence Prusak is an independent researcher and consultant. Davenport and Prusak are co-directors of Babson College's Working Knowledge Research Center.

Working Knowledge: How Organizations Manage What They Know provides an introduction to knowledge management that comprises an overview of the nature of knowledge, the role of knowledge in organizations, the processes and technologies of knowledge management, and practical advice on implementing knowledge management programs. The book is not explicitly either a textbook or a guide to action, although it has been used as both. Generally well received at the time of its publication, *Working Knowledge* has received more than 450 citation entries in the *Social Sciences Citation Index*.

In "The Promise and Challenge of Knowledge Markets," chapter 2 of *Working Knowledge,* Davenport and Prusak address the knowledge economy at the microeconomic level, primarily addressing the nature and implications of knowledge markets from the point of view of the individual corporation. The authors proceed from the assumption that knowledge is a dynamic market force in all organizations but is poorly understood. The chapter's goals are to provide a description of knowledge markets in organizations and "develop a preliminary taxonomy" of the knowledge marketplace.

KNOWLEDGE MARKET ROLES

As a preliminary step toward achieving those goals, the authors identify the "players in the knowledge market."[54] As in any market environment, these are buyers, sellers, and brokers. There are, however, real differences in the ways in which the roles of buyers, sellers, and brokers function in a knowledge market. Most importantly, any individual may not only take on the roles of buyer, seller, and broker many times in a day but may conceivably assume all three roles in a single transaction.

Buyers "are usually people trying to resolve an issue whose complexity and uncertainty precludes an easy answer."[55] Although buying knowledge may in some cases have a deliberate investment purpose, it is more frequently the case that the buyer has a direct consumption purpose in mind. Acquired knowledge is typically of immediate rather than deferred value. Sellers "are people in an organization with an internal market reputation for having substantial knowledge about a process or subject."[56] Knowledge transactions are typically "bundled" rather than piece by piece: the reward to the seller is, as a result, typically aggregate rather than transaction based. Davenport and Prusak note the phenomenon of knowledge hoarding and its generally negative impact on the knowledge market and emphasize encouragement of knowledge sharing as a knowledge management challenge.

Davenport and Prusak place particular attention on the role of knowledge brokers, who they equate with the gatekeeper phenomenon. The characteristics of knowledge brokers are explored, and the specific role of librarians as brokers is explored at some length. The central challenge to effective knowledge brokering is the tendency of organizations to undervalue the role of the broker and consequentially to undercompensate individuals who work in roles that are primarily focused on brokering, such as librarians. The authors indicate that organizations tend to incorrectly identify brokering as an expense rather than as an investment or a service that is directly valuable to the organization. They also emphasize that the true knowledge entrepreneur is primarily a broker rather than a buyer or seller.

THE KNOWLEDGE PRICE SYSTEM

Davenport and Prusak conclude that the price system of the knowledge market is fundamentally different from other price systems, particularly in the context of the internal exchange of knowledge within an organization. Although external exchanges may involve cash, the internal organizational "medium of exchange is seldom money, but there are agreed-upon currencies."[57] The authors identify three primary "currencies" common within organizations—reciprocity, repute, and altruism—all of which are grounded in the overarching influence of trust.

Reciprocity is the reasonable expectation that knowledge shared (knowledge sold) will at some future time be rewarded in the form of knowledge received (knowledge bought). There is also, however, a synergistic form of reciprocity in which knowledge is shared for the mutual benefit of the organization rather than in the interest of a direct exchange at the individual level.

Repute has to do with respect and image. "A knowledge seller usually wants others to know him as a knowledgeable person with valuable expertise that he is willing to share with others."[58] Repute is closely tied to reciprocity and may actually be a prerequisite for establishing an environment amenable to reciprocity. In many environments individual and collective success are directly dependent on repute.

Davenport and Prusak define altruism as the core characteristic of "individuals who simply like helping."[59] Mentoring is mentioned as a specific, valuable form of altruism. Altruism as a form of currency, however, may be devalued in an organization that successfully hires people who are motivated by the desire to help others but fails to inculcate an environment that makes it possible for such people to succeed.

The currencies of reciprocity, repute, and altruism have value only within an environment that encourages trust. "Trust can trump the other factors that positively affect the efficiency of knowledge markets."[60] According to Davenport and Prusak, trust in an organization must be visible and ubiquitous and "trustworthiness must start at the top."[61] Trust is especially important in knowledge markets, in which agreements typically are not enforced by formal contracts. The essential role of trust in a knowledge market explains why attempts to impose structures to forcibly guarantee knowledge sharing rarely work.

Davenport and Prusak's definition of the key "players" and the fundamental "currencies" of the knowledge market is important as a conceptual base for understanding knowledge market thinking in an organizational context. That base provides the foundation on which the remainder of the chapter is built. From that foundation the chapter builds to a discussion of "knowledge market signals," which include the individual and collective characteristics that define the knowledge organization and access structures of an organization; key knowledge market inefficiencies such as incompleteness of information, intraorganizational knowledge asymmetry, and overreliance on purely local knowledge; and knowledge market "pathologies," which include knowledge monopolies, artificially induced scarcity of knowledge, and trade barriers such as knowledge hoarding and faulty knowledge infrastructure. The chapter concludes with sections on "Developing Effective Knowledge Markets," "The Peripheral Benefits of Knowledge Markets," and "Thinking in Market Terms." The "preliminary taxonomy" of the knowledge marketplace promised early in the chapter never actually emerges, but the conceptualization and contextualization of knowledge market players and knowledge market currencies are in and of themselves important contributions to the knowledge management literature, as is the book as a whole.

NOTES

1. Nick Bontis, "Managing Organizational Knowledge by Diagnosing Intellectual Capital: Framing and Advancing the State of the Field," in *Knowledge Management and Business Model Innovation,* edited by Yogesh Malhotra (Hershey, PA: Idea Group, 2000), 272.

2. Patrick H. Sullivan, *Value-Driven Intellectual Capital: How to Convert Intangible Corporate Assets into Market Value* (New York: Wiley, 2000), 238–44.

3. "Intellectual Capital," *New York Evangelist,* January 9, 1836, 8.

4. C. H. Judd, "The Psychology of Social Institutions," *Journal of Abnormal and Social Psychology* 20 (July 1925): 151–56.

5. George R. Feiwel, *The Intellectual Capital of Michal Kalecki: A Study in Economic Theory and Policy* (Knoxville: University of Tennessee, 1975).

6. Thomas Short, "Components of a Knowledge Strategy: Keys to Successful Knowledge Management," in *Knowledge Management for the Information Professional,* edited by T. Kanti Srikantaiah and Michael E. D. Koenig (Medford, NJ: Information Today, 2000), 354.

7. Leif Edvinsson and Michael S. Malone, *Intellectual Capital: Realizing Your Company's True Value by Finding Its Hidden Brainpower* (New York: HarperBusiness, 1997), 11.

8. "Interview with Leif Edvinsson: Intellectual Capital: The New Wealth of Corporations," *New Economy Analyst Report,* November 13, 2001, http://www.juergendaum.com/news/11_13_2001.htm (accessed October 25, 2006).

9. "The Higher Education," *Nassau Literary Magazine,* June 1889, 107.

10. Patricia Seemann, David De Long, Susan Stucky, and Edward Guthrie, "Building Intangible Assets: A Strategic Framework for Investing in Intellectual Capital," in *Knowledge Management: Classic and Contemporary Works,* edited by Daryl Morey, Mark Maybury, and Bhavani Thuraisingham (Cambridge, MA: MIT Press, 2000), 87.

11. Short, "Components," 355.

12. Mark W. McElroy, "Social Innovation Capital," *Journal of Intellectual Capital* 3, no. 1 (2002): 31.

13. Ibid., 32.

14. John Locke, "Of Property," in *The Second Treatise of Government: An Essay Concerning the True Original, Extent, and End of Civil Government,* student edition, edited with an introduction and notes by Peter Laslett (Cambridge: Cambridge University Press, 1968), 285.

15. Benjamin G. Damstedt, "Limiting Locke: A Natural Law Justification for the Fair Use Doctrine," *Yale Law Journal* 112 (March 2003): 1179.

16. Locke, "Of Property," 287–88.

17. Ibid., 291.

18. Ibid., 290.

19. Ibid., 296.

20. Ibid., 298.

21. Donald G. Richards, "The Right to a Living in the International Economy," *International Journal of Social Economics* 30, no. 1/2 (2003): 186.

22. Frank H. Easterbrook, "Intellectual Property Is Still Property," *Harvard Journal of Law & Public Policy* 13 (Winter 1990): 113.

23. Lior Zemer, "The Making of a New Copyright Lockean," *Harvard Journal of Law & Public Policy* 29 (Summer 2006): 892.

24. Herman T. Tavani, "Locke, Intellectual Property Rights, and the Information Commons," *Ethics and Information Technology* 7 (2005): 96.

25. Locke, "Of Property," 263.

26. Fritz Machlup, *The Production and Distribution of Knowledge in the United States* (Princeton, NJ: Princeton University Press, 1962), 9–10.

27. Ibid., 10.

28. Ibid., 5.

29. Ibid., 6.

30. Ibid., 361.

31. Fritz Machlup, *Knowledge and Knowledge Production,* vol. 1 of *Knowledge: Its Creation, Distribution, and Economic Significance* (Princeton, NJ: Princeton University Press, 1980), 24.

32. Charles R. Walker, review of *The Impact of Computers on Management* by Charles A. Myers, *Journal of Business* 41 (January 1968): 133.

33. Peter F. Drucker, "The Economic Race: A Forecast for 1980," *New York Times,* January 21, 1962, 66.

34. Mark Addleson, "Organizing to Know and to Learn: Reflections on Organization and Knowledge Management," in *Knowledge Management for the Information Professional,* edited

by T. Kanti Srikantaiah and Michael E. D. Koenig (Medford, NJ: Information Today, 2000), 141; Frank P. Zeidler, "Five Revolutions Affecting Municipal Government," *Michigan Municipal Review* 37 (October 1964): 235–37.

35. Thomas H. Davenport and Laurence Prusak, *Working Knowledge: How Organizations Manage What They Know* (Boston: Harvard Business School Press, 1998), xiii.

36. Alvin Toffler, *Future Shock* (New York: Random House, 1970); Daniel Bell, *The Coming of Post-industrial Society: A Venture in Social Forecasting* (New York: Basic Books, 1973); John Naisbitt, *Megatrends: Ten New Directions Transforming Our Lives* (New York: Warner Books, 1982).

37. Peter F. Drucker, *The Age of Discontinuity: Guidelines to Our Changing Society* (New York: Harper and Row, 1969), xiii.

38. Ibid., 263.

39. Ibid., 264.

40. Ibid.

41. Ibid., 265.

42. Ibid.

43. Ibid., 266.

44. Ibid.

45. Ibid., 267.

46. Ibid.

47. Ibid.

48. Ibid., 272.

49. Ibid.

50. Ibid., 274.

51. Derek J. de Solla Price, *Big Science, Little Science* (New York: Columbia University Press, 1963).

52. Drucker, *The Age of Discontinuity*, 276.

53. Ibid., 278.

54. Davenport and Prusak, *Working Knowledge*, 27.

55. Ibid., 28.

56. Ibid.

57. Ibid., 31.

58. Ibid., 32.

59. Ibid., 33.

60. Ibid., 34.

61. Ibid., 35.

5

Knowledge Sharing

share, *v, intr.* To have a share (in something); to participate in, to take part in.

1598 *SHAKES.* Merry W. II. ii. 14 Didst not thou share? hadst thou not fifteene pence?

IN THIS CHAPTER

KEY CONCEPTS

Knowledge Sharing and Shared Knowledge
Knowledge Sharing vs. Knowledge Hoarding
Knowledge Diffusion
Best Practices

KEY PAPERS

Diana Crane, *Invisible Colleges: Diffusion of Knowledge in Scientific Communities*
Dorothy Leonard-Barton, *Wellsprings of Knowledge: Building and Sustaining the Sources of Innovation*
Gabriel Szulanski, "Exploring Internal Stickiness: Impediments to the Transfer of Best Practice within the Firm"

KNOWLEDGE SHARING AND SHARED KNOWLEDGE

It is extremely difficult to assign a historical starting point to the notion of knowledge sharing. The expression "knowledge-sharing" has been in use at least since the middle of the twentieth century. A 1955 *New York Times* article referred to efforts among nuclear powers to move from an era of exclusive secrecy to one of inclusive knowledge sharing.[1] Reddaway used the expression "knowledge sharing" very much in its current sense in 1968.[2] The basic concept of sharing knowledge to further organizational goals, however, underlies the development of the earliest libraries as well as the entire history of the development and transformation of business information systems.

KNOWLEDGE SHARING VS. KNOWLEDGE HOARDING

Textbooks and popular management books on knowledge management consistently reference the necessity of sharing knowledge—particularly in contrast to hoarding knowledge. Unfortunately, sharing knowledge is frequently not a traditional—and in many cases not even an official—operating strategy in many organizations. The truism that "Knowledge is power" dictates that the power of knowledge may be greatest when knowledge is withheld. The goal of institutionalizing the process of knowledge sharing is not an easy one to meet.

Davenport and Prusak presented a primarily economic model of knowledge sharing in which separate but overlapping and transitory roles are assigned to knowledge buyers, knowledge sellers, and knowledge brokers.[3] Most writers, however, depict a more altruistic model in which knowledge is shared within an organization to benefit the common good. Concern for organizational knowledge sharing has its roots in the compartmentalization of knowledge that tends to accompany bureaucratic organizational structures. In many organizations, the historical role of departments, divisions, or teams—organizational units that were created primarily to separate responsibility and authority along functional lines—has in practice resulted in separation of knowledge along jealously guarded political lines. In some organizations competition among units has been demonstrably more fierce than competition with other organizations. The result is a fragmented knowledge environment in which the organization "doesn't know what it knows."

KNOWLEDGE DIFFUSION

The goal of knowledge sharing, then, is the systematic distribution and effective diffusion of knowledge throughout the organization. Knowledge sharing as it is discussed in the knowledge management literature is an activity distinct from innovation and the creation of new knowledge and is generally distinct from Nonaka and Takeuchi's notion of the knowledge-creating organization, although knowledge sharing is generally a precondition for the creation of new knowledge.[4] Knowledge sharing also has in part to do with the transformation of tacit knowledge into explicit knowledge and is closely linked to organizational learning. Furthermore, knowledge sharing "encompasses sharing of both tacit and explicit knowledge at the individual, group, and enterprise level."[5]

BEST PRACTICES

Knowledge sharing is frequently closely linked to the concept of best practices—the notion that in any organization there will be a variety of approaches to solving common problems or performing standard tasks, and that it should be possible to identify the best approaches and share them across the organization. According to Szulanski, best practice "has a concrete and fairly unambiguous meaning to practitioners."[6] Some organizations have even built best-practice databases, sometimes referred to as knowledge bases, to help foster the diffusion of best practices.

A central problem of the concept of best practices is that it is fundamentally a product of the kind of "anti-planning" Churchman associated with "experience coupled with intuition, leadership, and brilliance."[7] Although intraorganizational practices can be identified and compared, the organizational practice that emerges as "best" may be ineffective in comparison to practices in use in other organizations within the same domain or even in comparison to the practices of radically different organizations. The search for best practices also leaves open the approach taken by Churchman's efficiency expert, whose fundamental goal is to identify the "one best way" to perform a particular function.[8]

Diana Crane, *Invisible Colleges: Diffusion of Knowledge in Scientific Communities* (Chicago: University of Chicago Press, 1971).

Diana Crane, professor emerita in the Department of Sociology at the University of Pennsylvania, previously held faculty positions at Yale University and Johns Hopkins University. She holds a bachelor's degree from Radcliffe College and master's and doctoral degrees from Columbia University. In addition to *Invisible Colleges,* Crane is responsible for *The Sanctity of Social Life: Physician's Treatment of Critically Ill Patients* (1975), *The Transformation of the Avant-Garde: The New York Art World, 1940–1985* (1987), *Fashion and Its Social Agendas: Class, Gender, and Identity in Clothing* (2000), and *Global Culture: Media, Arts, Policy, and Globalization* (2002). One of the most significant works on the phenomenon of knowledge sharing as it applies to scientific and scholarly communities, *Invisible Colleges* is represented by more than seven hundred entries in the *Social Sciences Citation Index.*

INVISIBLE COLLEGES

The term "invisible college" was first used in 1645 by Robert Boyle, who is "often referred to as the father of modern chemistry," to describe the Philosophical College, one of the progenitors of the Royal Society, which is now the premier independent research and scientific academy of the United Kingdom and the British Commonwealth.[9] Centuries later, the expression "invisible college" was appropriated by Price in his 1961 masterwork, *Science since Babylon,* in which he described invisible colleges within the context of the "diseases of science" and suggested that invisible colleges "might well be the subject of an interesting sociological study."[10] Price expanded on the idea in his 1963 book *Little Science, Big Science,* in which a chapter is devoted to "Invisible Colleges and the Affluent Scientific Commuter."[11] Price's analysis reveals that although the formal communication methods of publication and professional associations continue to be valuable, they are insufficient to provide the knowledge-sharing networks required by scholars. As a result, groups with little or no recognized status naturally coalesce to share knowledge through more immediate means, frequently on a daily basis. To Price, these informal groups "constitute an invisible college, in the same sense as did those first unofficial pioneers who banded together to found the Royal Society in 1660."[12]

> In exactly the same way, they give each man status in the form of approbation from his peers, they confer prestige, and, above all, they effectively solve a communication crisis by reducing a large group to a small select one of the maximum size that can be handled by interpersonal relationships. Such groups are to be encouraged, for they give status pay-off without increasing the papers that would otherwise be written to this end. I think one must admit that high-grade scientific commuting has become an important channel of communication, and that we must ease its progress.[13]

Advancing the progress of such "scientific commuting" requires creating and fostering effective means of communication. In Price's experience, the major means were the sharing of preprints and other works-in-progress information and informal meetings. Since the birth of the Internet in 1969, a mere six years after the publication of *Little Science, Big Science,* invisible college activity has been increasingly characterized by electronic communication, although there is no reason to believe that the need to share pre-publication papers and to meet in person has diminished.

Supporting a network of invisible colleges is neither conceptually nor pragmatically simple. As Price points out, "If such groups were made legitimate, recognized, and given newspaperlike broadsheet journals circulating to a few hundred individuals, this would spoil them, make them objects of envy or of high-handed administration and formality."[14]

In the early 1970s, two especially important works related to invisible colleges appeared: Griffith and Mullins's article in *Science* and Crane's *Invisible Colleges: Diffusion of Knowledge in Scientific Communities.*[15] Griffith and Mullins took a historical perspective in examining how the scientific community reacts to pressing needs that are reflected in "major advances and changes of direction in science."[16] In examining the patterns that underlie such advances and changes, the authors observed that "an important feature of these patterns is their consistency throughout a variety of disciplines, periods of time, and types of research."[17]

Griffith and Mullins found that "normal" scientific activities are associated with relatively loose interactions among researchers characterized by low levels of both organization and communication. Real advances in scientific knowledge and changes in approaches to science, however, are characterized by high levels of both organization and communication. Their findings indicated that these highly effective groups are characterized by (1) "an acknowledged intellectual leader or leaders," (2) "a geographical center," and (3) "a brief period of comparatively intense activity."[18] An additional phenomenon observed by Griffith and Mullins is the necessity of the demise of the kind of collaborative group they described: "the penalty of success, whether success is measured in specific goals or in the conversion of a discipline to a new point of view, is the death of the group as a distinct social and intellectual entity."

Crane's *Invisible Colleges* represents the first and last comprehensive examination of the invisible college phenomenon. Crane was admittedly influenced by Price and consciously extended from his work. The motivation for Crane's exploration of invisible colleges is concern that although much "attention is being paid to how knowledge is stored, distributed, and used, relatively little attention has been paid to why and how knowledge grows."[19] The book was not universally well received when published. Mason felt that the book was characterized by "methodological pitfalls" and that Crane's work did not contribute "significant new theoretical or empirical insight into the process by which the social organization of scientific communities affects their intellectual products."[20] Although Hagstrom termed the book "excellent," he also stated that "the theory presented is simple, too simple in fact."[21] Vachon's review was generally positive, although he found that "the work involved in reading the book is inversely proportional to its small size."[22] Storer, on the other hand, correctly predicted that Crane's work "will stand for some time as a major landmark in the progressive explication of the extension of scientific knowledge," calling the book "sound, comprehensive, and thoroughly deserving of inclusion in the library of anyone concerned with the social nature of science."[23]

SOCIAL CIRCLES

Crane defines "the social organization of the entire set of members of a research area" as a "social circle."[24] The membership and boundaries of a social circle are normally undefined.

> Each member of a social circle is usually aware of some but not all other members. The members of a research area are geographically separated to such an extent that face-to-face contact never occurs between all members and occurs only periodically among some. Indirect interaction, interaction mediated through intervening parties, is an important aspect of the social circle. . . . There is no formal leadership in a social circle although there are usually central figures.[25]

Crane identifies two prominent models of the growth of knowledge. The first, which is termed the most widely accepted, characterizes the growth of knowledge

> as a cumulative progression of new ideas developing from antecedent ideas in a logical sequence. Hypotheses derived from theory are tested against empirical evidence and either accepted or rejected. There is no ambiguity in the evidence and consequently no disagreement among scientists about the extent to which an hypothesis has been verified.[26]

This is clearly the model of scientific progression that has dominated throughout history and that is represented in the understanding of science of most people who are not sociologists of science. Science and scientists are neutral, dispassionate, objective, and supremely logical, and the growth of knowledge follows from the nature of both science and scientists.

> An alternative model that has been applied most frequently to the growth of nonscientific knowledge states that the origins of new ideas come not from the most recent developments but from any previous development whatever in the history of the field. In this model, there is a kind of random selection across the entire history of a cultural area. . . . Price argues that this kind of highly unstructured growth is characteristic of the humanities.[27]

Crane argues that there may be a third pattern that "includes periods of continuous cumulative growth interspersed with periods of discontinuity."[28] This is also the model presented by Kuhn, who defined scientific change in terms of the growth, development, and replacement of central scientific viewpoints or paradigms.[29] Although Crane provides an extensive comparison and discussion of alternative models of the growth of knowledge, it is clear that Kuhn's model is the one that most directly drives her work. According to Crane, there are two ways of looking at the phenomenon of the paradigm: "as a way of seeing, a perspective, a pattern," or "as a special kind of tool or problem-solving device."[30]

DIFFUSION AND THE GROWTH OF KNOWLEDGE

Following the work of Rogers, Crane defines scientific growth and development as an explicit diffusion process.[31] Drawing from Kuhn's paradigmatic model of scientific change, Crane identifies four stages of the process of the social diffusion of scientific knowledge. In the first, a new paradigm is just appearing, and there is little or no social organization to support the paradigm. In the second stage, a defined area of specialization comes into existence to support and exploit the paradigm, resulting in rapid growth of the social structure that supports the paradigm. During the third stage, growth slows as the social organization begins to question the paradigm, resulting in conflict and controversy. In the fourth and final stage, the conflict and controversy of the third stage take on the dimensions of crisis, and there is a decline of interest in the paradigm that may persist until the paradigm is rejected and attracts no further interest.

Crane's data are based on study of two specific social circles made up of researchers in the areas of the diffusion of agricultural innovations, a sub-specialty within rural sociology, and finite group mathematics. These two groups were well characterized by Crane's four-stage model. The author also examined the results of three other studies, finding that the pattern of the model was repeated in Mullins's study of molecular biology, but not in Fisher's study of invariant theory or in Wilder's study of reading research.[32] The latter two are explained through anomalies in the research environments of the studies.

Crane uses these and other research findings to explore the social organization of research ideas, diffusion of ideas, variations in the growth of knowledge, interactions among communities, and the structure of science. The final chapter of *Invisible Colleges* proposes a sociology of culture to encompass and transcend the sociologies of knowledge, "art, ideology, literature, philosophy, political thought, religion, and science."[33] The author rejects, at least in part, Price's argument "that science is radically different from all other cultural activities" and points out that the personalities of notable contributors to knowledge have played an important role in all domains of knowledge. Crane's discussion and comparison of models of cultural growth makes it clear that there is no readily definable or generally acceptable definition of the characteristics that distinguish the development of knowledge in the world of art from the development of scientific knowledge, a dividing line that should seemingly be easily drawn. Crane also calls for the "sociological study of culture" to "be viewed as a single field using the same concepts and hypotheses to examine different types of cultural progress."[34] Without such an approach, she fears that there will be no progress in understanding the sociology of culture. Crane explored this area further in *The Sociology of Culture.*[35] As yet a comprehensive sociology of culture doesn't seem to have emerged, but Crane's exploration of the phenomenon of the invisible college endures.

Dorothy Leonard-Barton, *Wellsprings of Knowledge: Building and Sustaining the Sources of Innovation* (Boston: Harvard Business School Press, 1995).

Dorothy A. Leonard (formerly Dorothy Leonard-Barton) is William J. Abernathy Professor of Business Administration Emerita at the Harvard Business School. Her publications include *When Sparks Fly: Igniting Group Creativity* (1999), *Deep Smarts: How to Cultivate and Transfer Enduring Business Wisdom* (2005), and numerous journal articles. *Wellsprings of Knowledge* has received more than four hundred citations in the *Social Sciences Citation Index.*

Wellsprings of Knowledge focuses on managing knowledge assets within organizations, with a specific emphasis on corporate knowledge assets, "a process that sounds abstract and yet is concrete, practical, and profoundly important."[36] The book is explicitly about technology-based companies, reflecting the author's "preoccupation . . . with *behavioral* interaction with technology."[37] The research base for the book has its origins in the work on diffusion of innovations of Rogers and others. Although *Wellsprings of Knowledge* is intended to be practical, it is very far from being a technical manual or how-to book. Instead, the author's goal is to foster understanding of knowledge assets and the processes necessary for managing them.

CORE CAPABILITIES AND CORE RIGIDITIES

Leonard-Barton grounds her work in the concept of organizational core capabilities—those strengths and abilities that "constitute a competitive advantage" for an organization.[38] Core capabilities are distinguished from supplemental capabilities "that add value to core capabilities but that could be imitated," and enabling capabilities that "are necessary but not sufficient in themselves to competitively distinguish" the organization.[39] Core capabilities, then, are those characteristics of an organization that define its competitive nature. Supplemental capabilities are of limited strategic importance, and enabling capabilities are of moderate strategic importance, but core capabilities define the strategic capability of the organization. The success of the organization lies in its ability to innovate within the context of core organizational capabilities.

Pitted against the organization's core capabilities are what Leonard-Barton terms core rigidities, which, perhaps surprisingly, *are* the core capabilities: the organization's "strengths are also—*simultaneously*—its weaknesses."[40] Core capabilities are transformed into core rigidities by one or both of two processes: (1) insularity resulting from the natural tendency of management to be internally focused and (2) overshooting the target by overinvestment in successful activities or strategies. A core rigidity is characterized by four "knowledge-inhibiting activities":[41]

1. *Limitedproblem solving* is grounded in overreliance on decision-making and problem-solving approaches that were effective in the past and that can implemented only by a select few members of the organization who have been delegated problem-solving authority and responsibility.

2. *Inability to innovate with new tools and methods* results in organizational stagnation and an inability to introduce change even when the need for change is recognized.

3. *Limited experimentation* is an outgrowth of limited problem solving and inability to innovate. To the extent that the organization is capable of experimenting with new ways of doing things, it does so only within the confined domain of what is already known.

4. *Screening out external knowledge* is the process of refusing to recognize the value of knowledge derived outside the organization. Organizations, like individuals, develop filters through which knowledge is either accepted or rejected. "By virtue of being excellent in one knowledge domain, an organization is relatively unreceptive to ideas from others."[42]

The solution to the inhibitions to knowledge produced by these activities can be found in four "primary learning activities" essential to effective knowledge building and innovation: (1) shared problem solving, which focuses on the solution of problems in the present time; (2) integration of new technologies and tools, which is an internal process; (3) experimentation and prototyping, which focus on the solution of future problems; and (4) exploitation of external expertise.[43]

Chapters devoted to each of these activities constitute the core content of the book.

DIMENSIONS OF RESISTANCE TO CHANGE

Leonard-Barton further defines four interrelated "dimensions" of core rigidities and resistance to change. Innovation is dependent on the introduction of change in one or more—and frequently *all*—of these dimensions. "The four dimensions differ in the ease with which they may be changed and therefore in the amount of managerial attention required."[44]

1. *Physical systems* define the dimension most amenable to alteration. Any modification of the hardware, software, or physical environment employed by the organization constitutes change to the physical system, as does the introduction of new techniques or methodologies for carrying out organizational activities. These alterations are essentially technical in nature and are typically obvious to everyone in the organization. "The largest problem is that this dimension of a capability is almost never independent of the other three dimensions."[45]

2. *Managerial systems* are all those functions and activities, formal and informal, overt and tacit, that support the operation of the organization within its physical environment. Every organization, either by design or by tradition, assigns varying levels of status to the organization's essential functions and activities. "In every organization . . . the very system that attracts, nurtures, and reinforces the status of one function, discipline, or type of knowledge tends to downgrade others. . . . Informal management systems grow into implicit routines that systematically support status differentials and subtly undermine the credibility of some disciplines."[46] Managerial systems are inherently more difficult to change than physical systems and change within managerial systems is frequently difficult to control and direct.

3. *Skills and knowledge* are of three basic varieties: (1) the public or scientific knowledge that is external to the specific domain of the organization, (2) industry-specific knowledge that defines and explicates the organizational domain, and (3) organization-specific knowledge that is internal and in most cases proprietary and closely guarded. Leonard-Barton points out that "altering the skills and knowledge of a core capability is as simple

and as devastatingly difficult as hiring new people."[47] Although public and industry-specific knowledge can be imported from outside the organization, organization-specific knowledge "cannot be hired; it must grow up over time."[48]

4. *Values* are the ways of understanding and the norms of behavior that underlie the organization. "All organizations have . . . sets of values that determine the kinds of skilled people who are attracted to the company and rewarded by choice assignments and/or higher pay than their colleagues."[49] Leonard-Barton identifies two major categories of values: (1) generic values that "are associated with attitudes and beliefs about other people, including customers," and (2) "little" values that "are tied to prizing particular ways of carrying out activities, with specific disciplinary approaches or with certain ways of operating."[50] In most organizations there is some potential for changing "little" values through deliberate action, but only to the extent that such a change preserves generic values.

SIGNATURE SKILLS, CREATIVE ABRASION, AND KNOWLEDGE SHARING

To a considerable extent, the entirety of *Wellsprings of Knowledge* is about knowledge sharing. The section most directly related to knowledge sharing is chapter 3, "Shared Problem Solving." "Increasingly, the complexity of the problems, the proliferation of formally educated specialties, and the pace of globalization require that the problem-solving activities involved in new-product development be shared across disciplinary, cognitive, geographic and culture boundaries."[51] Leonard-Barton's discussion of shared problem solving focuses on "three sources of individual differences in problem solving—specialization, preferred cognitive style, and preferences in tools and methodologies."[52] These differences combine to define an individual's signature skills—those traits, mind-sets, biases, and abilities that define the individual professionally. The word "signature" is used deliberately to denote "the idiosyncratic nature of the skill—a personally defining characteristic, as much a part of someone's identity as the way the individual signs his or her name."[53] "In our technically advanced society, specialists are rewarded for pursuing their signature skills in depth—at least until and unless those skills are rendered obsolete. In consequence, our organizations have created and encouraged enclaves of specialized skills emotionally tied to people's egos and identities."[54]

Leonard-Barton borrows the term "creative abrasion" from Gerlad Hirshberg to describe the conflict of signature skills that occurs when diverse individuals are brought together to share responsibility for a task or problem. Her contention is that it is possible and productive to "channel" such conflict such that it emerges as a creative rather than a destructive force. The manager's goal is to create an environment in which "individuals are able to accept cognitive diversity without enthroning divisiveness."[55] To do this, management must recognize and effectively work with individual variations in specialized knowledge, preferred cognitive styles and approaches, and preferred approaches to the selection and use of tools and methodologies. "Abrasion is guaranteed; it is management's task to ensure that the friction is creative."[56] The alternative is the unproductive abrasion of personal battles and hoarded knowledge. Leonard-Barton describes a number of approaches to the process of managing creative abrasion, presenting most of them in the form of specific examples from industrial experiences.

BOUNDARY SPANNING AND CLARITY OF DESTINATION

Leonard-Barton emphasizes that creative abrasion does not occur naturally or automatically and presents two "managerial levers" for integrating and consolidating the diversity of signature skills necessary for effective shared decision making. The first is the development of models or prototypes to serve as boundary objects. Although the examples used are mostly from manufacturing and focus on physical models, the basic principle of exploiting prototypes or models as boundary-spanning devices is readily extensible to other endeavors as well. The use of the term "prototype" here is a very specialized one in that the prototype does not need to be fully or even partially functional: its primary purpose is to bring diverse signature skills together by providing a target or focal point for consideration, understanding, and problem solving. This is a substantial expansion of the notion of the prototype, as it is generally understood in a technical or engineering sense. "When prototypes are used only for testing technical concepts and not as communication vehicles for problem solving across boundaries, developers are overlooking enormous opportunities for creative abrasion—and integration."[57]

The second "lever" is establishment and maintenance of a clear sense of direction and a sharply defined destination, which are a "manager's most powerful ally in focusing creative energies."[58] Leonard-Barton suggests that the development of a new product has the potential for being accompanied by two prominent outcomes: the product itself and the process by which the product is developed and produced. The latter is a function of conceptualization and visualization of both the product and the process. Conceptualization ensures that the outcome will be appropriately aligned with the clientele the product is intended to serve. Visualization ensures that the outcome will be appropriately aligned with the organization responsible for the product. Both the concept and the vision should be arrived at through a shared decision-making process and explicitly stated.

Gabriel Szulanski, "Exploring Internal Stickiness: Impediments to the Transfer of Best Practice within the Firm," *Strategic Management Journal* 17 (Winter 1996): 27–43.

Gabriel Szulanski is a professor of strategy at INSEAD (Institut Européen d'Administration des Affaires), an internationally focused business school with campuses in Singapore and France, from which he received a doctorate in 1995. He was formerly a member of the faculty at the Wharton School of Business at the University of Pennsylvania. "Exploring Internal Stickiness" has been cited more than 350 times in the *Social Sciences Citation Index*. Szulanski's 2003 monographic exploration of stickiness, *Sticky Knowledge: Barriers to Knowledge in the Firm,* was cited 17 times in the first three years following its publication.

STICKINESS

The core theme of "Exploring Internal Stickiness" is at once simple and elegant: knowledge intrinsic to an organization is sometimes difficult to transfer effectively within the organization. Knowledge that is difficult to transfer is "sticky knowledge." The difficulty in transferring knowledge *within* an organization is internal stickiness.

The concept of sticky knowledge has its origin in von Hippel's exploration of "sticky information"—information that is "costly to acquire, transfer, and use."[59] While von Hippel was concerned exclusively with technical information, Szulanski's work is focused on the transfer of best practices within an organization and the difficulties inherent in the transfer process. In von Hippel's analysis, stickiness is reflected primarily in the "incremental expenditure" necessary to effect the transfer of information.[60] Szulanski suggests that cost alone is insufficient to explain the phenomenon of stickiness and that stickiness may be better understood in the context of "eventfulness"—"the extent to which problematic situations experienced during a transfer are worthy of remark."[61]

STAGES OF BEST PRACTICES TRANSFER

Although Szulanski draws heavily on the diffusion of innovation research of Everett Rogers, he very deliberately distinguishes between diffusion and knowledge transfer, using the word "transfer" "to emphasize that the movement of knowledge within the organization is a distinct experience, not a gradual process of dissemination, and depends on the characteristics of everyone involved."[62] The internal transfer of knowledge within an organization is characterized by four stages:

1. The *initiation* stage "comprises all events that lead to the decision to transfer," including the identification of a need for a transfer of best practices, the determination of what constitutes best practice, and the decision-making processes that ultimately lead to the transfer.[63]
2. The *implementation* stage involves the establishment of a relationship between the source of best-practices knowledge and the intended recipient (and sometimes other parties), adaptation of practice to meet specific recipient needs, and any other activities necessary to make it possible for knowledge to actually be used by the recipient.
3. During the *ramp-up* phase, which "begins when the recipient starts using the transferred knowledge," best-practices knowledge is fine tuned, unanticipated problems are addressed, and use of the knowledge gradually improves until it reaches an effective level.
4. In the *integration* stage, use of the transferred knowledge continues at an improved level and becomes a routine, ingrained, institutionalized process. The novelty of the transferred process fades from memory, and it becomes difficult to reconstruct or even to remember the transfer process.

Stickiness of the knowledge to be transferred can interfere with the transfer process at any stage.

CHARACTERISTICS OF STICKINESS

Szulanski identifies "four sets of factors . . . likely to influence the difficulty of knowledge transfer":

1. *Characteristics of the knowledge transferred* include a) causal ambiguity, which is the situation in which the underlying causes for the success of a transferable best practice are uncertain or unclear, and b) unprovenness, which is lack of an established track record for the knowledge to be transferred.

2. *Characteristics of the source of knowledge* include a) lack of motivation to share knowledge with the proposed recipient or even with any recipient and b) the situation in which the source is not perceived by the recipient to be reliable or trustworthy.

3. *Characteristics of the recipient* include a) lack of motivation to receive or use knowledge, b) lack of the absorptive capacity necessary for exploiting new knowledge, and c) lack of the retentive capacity necessary for making use of knowledge after it has been transferred.

4. *Characteristics of the context* include a) a "barren organizational context" in which the infrastructure to support transferred knowledge is lacking and b) an "arduous relationship" between the source of knowledge and the proposed recipient that impedes the development of a relationship conducive to knowledge transfer.[64]

RESEARCH AND RESULTS

Szulanski explores the impact of these characteristics and sub-characteristics through an empirical study of 122 transfers representing 38 practices in eight companies. A highly structured questionnaire was used to gather data from three categories of respondents: sources of transferred knowledge, recipients of transferred knowledge, and third parties. Results were analyzed to determine the relationship between stickiness, reflected in the overall outcome of the transfer and the four stages of transfer, and origins of stickiness, reflected in the nine sub-characteristics.

Both practitioners and previous research have tended to attribute stickiness "almost exclusively to motivational factors" such as "interdivisional jealousy, lack of incentives, lack of confidence, low priority, lack of buy-in, an inclination to reinvent the wheel or to plow the same fields twice, resistance to change, lack of commitment, turf protection, and of course the NIH [not-invented-here] syndrome."[65] The solution has typically been presented in terms of building into the organization those motivational factors and incentives that will encourage knowledge transfer.

Szulanzki found, however, that the factors most closely associated with stickiness were causal ambiguity, lack of absorptive capacity, and arduous relationships, only the third of which is in any way related to motivation. His results suggest that introducing motivational activities and incentives is unlikely to be either necessary to or sufficient for effective knowledge transfer. "The results suggest that it might be profitable instead to devote scarce resources and managerial attention to develop the learning capacities of organizational units, foster closer relationships between organizational units, and systematically understand and communicate practices."[66]

NOTES

1. William L. Laurence, "Secrecy Is Eased as Atomic Parley in Geneva Closes," *New York Times,* August 21, 1955, 1, 34.

2. W. B. Reddaway, *Effects of U.K. Direct Investment Overseas: Final Report* (Cambridge: Cambridge University Press, 1968).

3. Thomas H. Davenport and Laurence Prusak, *Working Knowledge: How Organizations Manage What They Know* (Boston: Harvard Business School Press, 1998), 28–30.

4. Ikujiro Nonaka and Hirotaka Takeuchi, *The Knowledge-Creating Company: How Japanese Companies Create the Dynamics of Innovation* (New York: Oxford University Press, 1995).

5. Cynthia T. Small and Andrew P. Sage, "Knowledge Management and Knowledge Sharing: A Review," *Information Knowledge Systems Management* 5, no. 3 (2005–6): 153–69.

6. Gabriel Szulanski, "Exploring Internal Stickiness: Impediments to the Transfer of Best Practice within the Firm," *Strategic Management Journal* 17 (Winter 1996): 28.

7. C. West Churchman, *The Systems Approach* (New York: Dell, 1968), 216.

8. Ibid., 18.

9. *Columbia Encyclopedia,* 6th ed., s.v. "Boyle, Robert."

10. Derek J. de Solla Price, *Science since Babylon* (New Haven, CT: Yale University Press, 1961), 99.

11. Derek J. de Solla Price, *Big Science, Little Science* (New York: Columbia University Press, 1963), 62–91.

12. Ibid., 85.

13. Ibid.

14. Ibid., 85–86.

15. Belver C. Griffith and Nicholas C. Mullins, "Coherent Social Groups in Scientific Change," *Science* 177, no. 4053 (September 1972): 959–64; Diana Crane, *Invisible Colleges: Diffusion of Knowledge in Scientific Communities* (Chicago: University of Chicago Press, 1971).

16. Griffith and Mullins, "Coherent Social Groups," 959.

17. Ibid.

18. Ibid., 960.

19. Crane, *Invisible Colleges,* 1.

20. Karen Oppenheim Mason, review of *Invisible Colleges: Diffusion of Knowledge in Scientific Communities* by Diana Crane, *Social Forces* 52 (September 1973): 136.

21. Warren O. Hagstrom, review of *Invisible Colleges: Diffusion of Knowledge in Scientific Communities* by Diana Crane, *Contemporary Sociology* 2 (July 1973): 381.

22. P. David Vachon, review of *Invisible Colleges: Diffusion of Knowledge in Scientific Communities* by Diana Crane, *Isis* 64 (September 1973): 402.

23. Norman W. Storer, review of *Invisible Colleges: Diffusion of Knowledge in Scientific Communities* by Diana Crane, *Technology and Culture* 15 (January 1974): 142.

24. Crane, *Invisible Colleges,* 13.

25. Ibid.

26. Ibid., 26.

27. Ibid., 26–27.

28. Ibid., 27.

29. Thomas Kuhn, *The Structure of Scientific Revolutions* (Chicago: University of Chicago Press, 1962).

30. Ibid., 30.

31. Everett M. Rogers, *Diffusion of Innovations* (New York: Free Press of Glencoe, 1962).

32. Crane, *Invisible Colleges,* 25.

33. Ibid., 129.

34. Ibid., 141.

35. Diana Crane, *The Sociology of Culture: Emerging Theoretical Perspectives* (Oxford: Blackwell, 1994).

36. Dorothy Leonard-Barton, *Wellsprings of Knowledge: Building and Sustaining the Sources of Innovation* (Boston: Harvard Business School Press, 1995), xi.

37. Ibid., ix.

38. Ibid., 4.

39. Ibid.

40. Ibid., 30.

41. Ibid., 35–41.

42. Ibid., 59.

43. Ibid., 8.

44. Ibid., 45.

45. Ibid., 47.

46. Ibid., 49.

47. Ibid., 50.

48. Ibid., 51.

49. Ibid., 26.

50. Ibid., 51.

51. Ibid., 61.

52. Ibid.

53. Ibid., 62.

54. Ibid., 62–63.

55. Ibid., 64.

56. Ibid., 74.

57. Ibid., 84.

58. Ibid., 86.

59. Eric von Hippel, "'Sticky Information' and the Locus of Problem Solving: Implications for Innovation," *Management Science* 40 (April 1994): 429.

60. Ibid., 430.

61. Szulanski, "Exploring Internal Stickiness," 30.

62. Ibid., 28.

63. Ibid.

64. Ibid., 30–32.

65. Ibid., 36–37.

66. Ibid., 37.

6

Knowledge Representation

representation The action or fact of exhibiting in some visible image or form.

1483 *CAXTON Cato* Aiijb, Thymages of sayntes . . . gyue us memorye and make representation of the sayntes that ben in heuen.

IN THIS CHAPTER

KEY CONCEPTS

Cognition, Artificial Intelligence, and Design
Representation and Cognition
Representation and Artificial Intelligence
Representation in Knowledge Bases
Representation and the World Wide Web: The Semantic Web

KEY PAPERS

Vannevar Bush, "As We May Think"
William A. Woods, "What's Important about Knowledge Representation?"
Terrence A. Brooks, "Where Is Meaning When Form Is Gone? Knowledge Representation on the Web"

COGNITION, ARTIFICIAL INTELLIGENCE, AND DESIGN

Knowledge representation is a concept primarily of concern in three areas: (1) cognitive science, (2) artificial intelligence, and (3) design for the World Wide Web. Although there are meaningful differences in the ways in which representation is understood in these three domains, there are also important similarities.

REPRESENTATION AND COGNITION

In cognitive science, knowledge representation has primarily to do with the ways in which people form and use mental representations of knowledge. The concept and nature of mental representation have been explored from many points of view, resulting in many approaches to and models for understanding mental representation of knowledge. There is no one model agreed upon by psychologists and cognitive scientists. Markman, in his extensive exploration of approaches to representing knowledge, contended that "mental representation is a critical part of psychological explanation" and identified four fundamental characteristics or components of a successful definition of mental representation:

1. *A represented world* that is described or explained through representation. The represented world presumably has some internal integrity, some sense of reality, that makes it an appropriate subject for representation. A key element of a mental or cognitive representation is that it exists in the mind of a human. The represented world may exist outside the mind or inside the mind, or it may be characterized by some combination of external and internal. The represented world may itself be a set of representations, as would be the case when the represented world is a collection of works of art or a library of publications.

2. *A representing world* that consists of the content of a system or set of representations. There are many possible approaches to representing any domain, including, but not limited to, images, sounds, words, and numbers. Some representations, such as images or sounds, are analogs of the representing world. Others, such as letters or numbers, are symbols that have no inherent relationship to the representing world. The expressiveness of a representation is in part a function of how the representing world reflects the represented world. The process of representation inevitably results in the loss of some information about the represented world—it is never possible for the representing world to completely encapsulate the represented world.

3. *Representing rules* that determine how representations can be used to connect the representing world and the represented world. The link between the represented world and the representing world is achieved primarily through the application of such rules. Just as there are many different possible approaches to defining the nature of the representing world, there are many possible rule sets and rule structures that can be used to link the representing world to the represented world. The meaning or interpretation of a representation is as much a function of the nature of the representing rules as of the nature of the represented world or the nature of the representing world.

4. *A process that uses the representation* to accomplish some goal or achieve some purpose. Knowledge representation doesn't occur in a vacuum or at random. A representation is formulated for some reason; the reason defines the process, which may to some extent define the rules and influence the nature of the representing world, thereby determining the extent to which the represented world is properly represented.[1]

It is the combination of these components that defines the knowledge representation, allows for its use, and defines its usefulness.

According to Markman, there are three essential ways in which representational formats differ: (1) "the duration of representational states," (2) "the presence of discrete symbols," and (3) "the abstractness of representations."[2] Markman examines six categories of knowledge representation addressed in the literature of cognition: (1) spatial representations, (2) featural representations, (3) associative representations, (4) structural representations, (5) conceptual relationships, and (6) scripts and schemata.

Cognitive science deals with the roles of meaning and interpretation in knowledge representation primarily by ignoring them. Elements of epistemology and semantics and the problems of variability in interpreting meaning are "avoided . . . by assuming that the cognitive system is a computational device."[3] Issues of meaning are basically assigned to philosophers. This is not to imply that meaning is unimportant. The relationship of knowledge representation to meaning is central to the arguments of Polanyi and Popper regarding the roles of perception and description in knowledge representation.

REPRESENTATION AND ARTIFICIAL INTELLIGENCE

From an artificial intelligence perspective, knowledge representation is closely linked to reasoning. According to Brachman and Levesque, artificial intelligence is "the stud of intelligent behavior achieved through computational means," and the combination of knowledge representation and reasoning "is the study of thinking as a computational process."[4] Drawing from epistemology, artificial intelligence defines knowledge in terms of propositions that can be either true or false, propositional attitudes that define "relationships between agents and propositions," and beliefs.[5] Overall, the specific nature of knowledge is of limited interest in artificial intelligence.

As is the case with cognitive science, artificial intelligence defines knowledge representation as being fundamentally about "a relationship between two domains, where the first is meant to 'stand for' or take the place of the second."[6] Brachman and Levesque used the term "representor" as an equivalent of Markman's "representing world." Propositions are stated in terms of symbols, which are the representors of central importance to artificial intelligence. Within this context, "knowledge representation . . . is the field of study concerned with using formal symbols to represent a collection of propositions believed by some putative agent."[7]

Smith presented the nature and importance of knowledge management for artificial intelligence in terms of a "knowledge representation hypothesis":

> Any mechanically embodied intelligent process will be comprised of structural ingredients that a) we as external observers naturally take to represent a propositional account of the knowledge that the overall process exhibits, and b) independent of such external semantic attribution, play a formal but causal and essential role in engendering the behavior that manifests the knowledge.[8]

Smith's hypothesis echoes cognitive science's avoidance of meaning, implying that derivation or interpretation of meaning is not an essential component in a "mechanically embodied intelligent process."

Knowledge representation is essential to developing knowledge-based systems, which is perhaps the most significant area of work in the field of artificial intelligence. Although the most obvious kind of knowledge-based system is the expert system, the principles of knowledge-based systems are also found in areas such as game playing, diagnostic systems, machine learning environments, robotics, and language analysis.

REPRESENTATION IN KNOWLEDGE BASES

A fundamental requirement for any knowledge-based system is the encapsulation of knowledge representations in a knowledge base. A knowledge base includes "diverse kinds of knowledge. These include, but are not limited to, knowledge about objects, knowledge about processes, and hard-to-represent *commonsense* knowledge about goals, motivation, causality, time, actions, etc."[9] A knowledge base differs from a database in that the knowledge base includes context as well as content. A knowledge-based system typically employs a much more complex logical model than a database system—rather than relying on the binary logic of Boolean operators, a knowledge-based system makes use of some sort of propositional logic that takes into account the propositional role of belief. A knowledge-based system is an attempt to create an environment in which action depends "on what the system *believes* about the world, as opposed to just what the system has *explicitly represented.*"[10] In other words, a knowledge-based system is designed to achieve or at least emulate reasoning.

Representing knowledge in a knowledge base requires generation of a specific environment that has four basic characteristics:

1. A *domain* of interest that is at least minimally understandable and can be described in terms of entities and relationships among entities
2. A *vocabulary* that can be used to describe the domain
3. A *syntax* that provides structure for application of the vocabulary to description of the domain and makes it possible to identify and manipulate relationships
4. A system for applying *pragmatic meaning* to the entities and relationships described by the vocabulary and syntax[11]

REPRESENTATION AND THE WORLD WIDE WEB: THE SEMANTIC WEB

The World Wide Web Consortium has defined the World Wide Web "as a freeform, decentralised knowledge representation system."[12] Berners-Lee, Hendler, and Lassila, however, noted that "knowledge representation . . . is currently in a state comparable to that of hypertext before the advent of the Web: it is clearly a good idea, and some very nice demonstrations exist, but it has not yet changed the world."[13] They described the current state of the World Wide Web as one in which "content is designed for humans to read, not for computers to manipulate meaningfully."[14] They proposed a new structure for Web content known as the Semantic Web, which "will bring structure to the meaningful content of Web pages, creating an environment where software agents roaming from page to page can readily carry out sophisticated tasks for users."[15] Berners-Lee, Hendler, and Lassila essentially rejected the potential of artificial intelligence and knowledge-based systems for providing semantic access to the Web, contending that it should be possible to provide access through relatively simple markup processes requiring no particular technical expertise.

Van Harmelen and Fensel surveyed the potential for applying existing and emerging Web technologies to semantic processing. They identified four fundamental problems related to the large bodies of semi-structured information that characterize the World Wide Web:

- *Searching information:* Existing keyword-based search retrieves irrelevant information that uses a certain word in a different meaning or it may miss information where different words about the desired content are used.
- *Extracting information:* Currently human browsing and reading is required to extract relevant information from information sources since automatic agents miss all common sense knowledge required to extract such information from textual representations, and they fail to integrate information spread over different sources.
- *Maintaining* weakly structured text sources [is a] difficult and time consuming activity when such sources become large. Keeping such collections consistent, correct, and up-to-date requires mechanized representation of semantics and constraints that help to detect anomalies.
- *Automatic document generation:* . . . Generating . . . semi-structured information presentations from semi-structured data requires a machine-accessible representation of the semantics of these information sources.[16]

Van Harmelen and Fensel described two categories of solutions to these problems: (1) a declarative process in which semantic markup is employed to enrich Web content and (2) a procedural process in which the semantic content of Web pages is automatically extracted. The Semantic Web, as envisioned by Berners-Lee, Hendler, and Lassila, is based on the principles of the first category and relies primarily on the Extensible Markup Language (XML) and the Resource Description Framework (RDF) to add semantic content to the markup of Web pages. Van Harmelen and Fensel's analysis, however, found that XML and RDF did not provide significant advantages over HTML with regard to semantic markup; they were particularly critical of RDF's poor representation of "basic lessons in language design."[17] None of the conventional approaches examined by Van Harmelen and Fensel supported any meaningful approach to inferential processing. They concluded that further artificial intelligence research is necessary to build a true semantic approach to using Web content.

Horrocks and Patel-Schneider were also critical of RDF as an approach to implementing the Semantic Web, writing that "more expressive power is clearly both necessary and desirable in order to describe resources in sufficient detail."[18] They suggested that a better solution could be found in the first-order logic approach of knowledge-based systems. McCool stated that "Because it's a complex format and requires users to sacrifice expressivity and pay enormous cost in translation and maintenance, the Semantic Web will never achieve widespread public adoption."[19] Singh's analysis suggested that "the best hope for the semantic web is to encourage the emergence of communities of interest and practice that develop their own consensus knowledge on the basis of which they will standardize their representations."[20] Schoop, De Moor, and Dietz presented a "manifesto" for the Pragmatic Web, a model that recognizes the problems of applying the tools of the Semantic Web in a universal manner and proposes an alternative model in which the basic principles of the Semantic Web are applied within specific contexts.[21]

Vannevar Bush, "As We May Think," *Atlantic Monthly,* July 1945, 101–8.

Vannevar Bush (1890–1974) was educated at Tufts University and in 1916 earned a joint PhD in engineering from Harvard University and the Massachusetts Institute of Technology. During World War I he taught at Tufts and independently developed a submarine detection device. Following the war, he joined the engineering faculty at MIT, where he remained for 20 years. During that time he worked to improve vacuum tubes, becoming a cofounder of the Raytheon corporation in 1922, and was the primary force behind the development of the Differential Analyzer, a protocomputer. In 1939 he became president of the Carnegie Institution, and during World War II he served as an advisor to President Roosevelt. After his retirement from the Carnegie Institution, he served as president of the Merck Corporation. His works include the 1945 presidential report "Science: The Endless Frontier," *Scientists Face the World of 1942* (1842), *Modern Arms and Free Men* (1949), and *Endless Horizons* (1975). Although "As We May Think" has only generated 750 citation entries in the *Social Sciences Citation Index* and *Science Citation Index,* the core concepts introduced in the work have fundamentally affected modern life. The editor of the *Atlantic Monthly* equated the importance of "As We May Think" to that of Emerson's "The American Scholar," describing Bush's essay as calling for "a new relationship between thinking man and the sum of our knowledge."[22]

MANAGING THE INFORMATION EXPLOSION

Writing at the conclusion of World War II, Bush was primarily concerned with the vast amounts of scientific information generated by the infusion of scientists into the war effort. He noted the advancing ability to communicate and preserve information but was concerned that "methods of transmitting and reviewing the results of research are generations old and by now are totally inadequate for their purpose."[23] Furthermore, Bush contends that the problems presented by the "growing mountain of research . . . [seem] to be, not so much that we publish unduly in view of the extent and variety of present-day interests, but rather that publication has been extended beyond our present ability to make real use of the record."[24] Citing the failure of historically important devices such as the Leibniz calculator and Babbage's Arithmetic Engine, Bush proposes that the solution lies in developing new technological approaches to managing recorded information.

In some ways the technological solutions that Bush explores seem quaint from the perspective of the 60 years that have passed since the publication of "As We May Think." He focuses on photography, mentioning dry photography, the core technology of present-day photocopiers, laser printers, and faxes, but concentrating on microphotography. He also mentions the potential for voice-input typewriters and predicts the computer revolution. Ultimately, Bush forecasts a future in which scientists will concentrate on higher-level reasoning and analytical processes and will entrust calculation and similar repetitive tasks to machines.

Bush anticipates that the future of scientific and business machines will require reexamination of the logic of data manipulation. "A new symbolism, probably positional, must apparently precede the reduction of mathematical transformations to machine processes."[25] Although Bush doesn't directly predict the binary logic that underlies digital media, he is confident that "we may some day click off arguments on a machine with the same assurance that we now enter sales on a cash register."[26]

RETHINKING INFORMATION RETRIEVAL

Although Bush is abundantly confident that machine-based approaches to information storage and manipulation will emerge and make it possible to "enormously extend the record," he also suggests that being able to do so not only does not fully solve the problem but in fact exacerbates it.[27] "This is a much larger matter than merely the extraction of data for the purposes of scientific research; it involves the entire process by which man profits by his inheritance of acquired knowledge. The prime action of use is selection, and here we are halting indeed."[28] Bush is critical of the "artificiality" of traditional systems in which data "are filed alphabetically or numerically, and information is found (when it is) by tracing it down from subclass to subclass."[29] Such systems are inherently inefficient in that an item "can be in only one place, unless duplicates are used; one has to have rules as to which path will locate it; and the rule are cumbersome. Having found one item, moreover, one has to emerge from the system and re-enter on a new path."[30]

To Bush, the structure of traditional retrieval systems is at odds with the basic function of the human mind, which, he asserts, "operates by association."[31] Although Bush recognizes that it is probably not possible to replicate human mental information processing, he asserts that it should be possible to learn from the associative model. "Selection by association, rather than by indexing, may yet be mechanized."[32] This notion of associative indexing is the foundation for a seemingly fanciful individualized information system, "a sort of mechanized private file and library," which Bush terms the memex.[33] Although Bush suggests that the term "memex" was chosen "at random," it is clear that he put substantial thought into the choice of the term.

THE MEMEX

"A memex is a device in which an individual stores all his books, records, and communications, and which is mechanized so that it may be consulted with exceeding speed and flexibility. It is an enlarged intimate supplement to his memory."[34] The memex is a desktop information environment that includes a display screen for viewing information, a keyboard and "sets of buttons and levers" for input and control, and a component "devoted to storage" that is sufficient in capacity that the user "can be profligate and enter material freely."[35] Books, journal articles, news, pictures, and other sources of information can be purchased and stored in the memex. Alternatively, the user has the ability to create new sources of information either by using the keyboard or by scanning materials not available for purchase. The scanner is capable of handling any kind of graphical information. Business correspondence and other forms of communication can be exchanged among memex users. The user can scan forward or backward through any document at whatever speed is suitable to the task at hand. The entire information store is indexed for retrieval, and commonly used search commands are abbreviated as mnemonics to facilitate the search process. It is possible to display multiple sources simultaneously and to add personal notes and comments to documents. According to Bush, "all of this is conventional, except for the projection forward of present-day mechanisms and gadgetry."[36]

In other words, the memex has all the characteristics of a sophisticated desktop personal computer and more. What makes Bush's vision of the memex phenomenal is that the capacity to build any machine remotely similar to the memex simply did not exist in 1945. Bush's primary storage mechanism was microfilm, not any kind of digital medium, and his primary input mechanism was a dry photographic process. Rather than sitting on top of a desk, the memex *is* the desk.

It may be difficult in an era in which computers are ubiquitous to fully appreciate Bush's vision of a desktop information system so directly predictive of the personal computer. Some perspective on the depth of that vision may be found by placing 1945 in the context of selected events:

- ENIAC, the Electronic Numerical Integrator and Calculator, which was introduced in February of 1945, weighed 27 tons, occupied 1,800 square feet of space, and was approximately as capable as the least functional handheld calculator currently available.
- In 1945, there were only nine airports worldwide equipped with instrument landing systems.
- Total sales of televisions had not yet reached 100,000 in 1945.
- The first practical transistor wasn't invented until 1947.
- The torque converter transmission, currently the dominant form of automotive automatic transmission, first appeared in 1948.
- The first commercially viable computer, the UNIVAC I, was introduced in 1951.
- The first jet airliner didn't enter service until 1952.
- The first commercially viable transistor radio entered the market in 1954.

Bush was an extremely well-informed visionary. He played the pivotal role in the development of the Differential Analyzer, a protocomputer introduced in 1931; received funding from the U.S. Navy in 1935 to support development of another protocomputer known as the Comparator; and later worked on the Rapid Selector, a protocomputer that incorporated elements of the memex. Although the Differential Analyzer was a definite success and contributed substantially to Bush's successful career, neither the Comparator nor the Rapid Selector was successful.[37] He was also, in his role as the president's science advisor, undoubtedly familiar with the Mark I project at Harvard University and the ENIAC project at the University of Pennsylvania, both of which were supported by federal funding as part of the war effort.

ASSOCIATIVE INDEXING

As intriguing and forward thinking as the notion of the memex as a device was, it was pragmatically a dead end. The technological environment of the mid-twentieth century was far from sufficient to allow even a distant approximation of the machine

Bush describes. It was not until the microprocessor appeared in the early 1970s that any resemblance of the memex became even a potentiality.

The most significant aspect of "As We May Think" is Bush's discussion of the essential retrieval philosophy that underlies the memex—associative indexing. In fact, Bush describes the concept of the memex primarily as "an immediate step . . . to associative indexing."[38] The most fundamental principle of associative indexing is that the links among like items in the database are defined by the user, not predefined by an indexer or cataloger. The user of the memex has two basic approaches to linking information sources: (1) identifying the existence of a link between two or more items and (2) naming that link. In practice, the second approach is optional as long as the link between the items is created. The user doesn't have to identify the nature of the link or even be able to articulate that nature—the link is a personal tool that serves as a permanent reminder of some thought process through which the user envisioned a useful connection between information sources. These links combine to form "trails" of connections among information sources: the user "builds a trail of his interest through the maze of materials available to him."[39] Importantly, these trails are durable. As long as the user can at some point in the future identify one of the linked information sources, the trail to all those sources linked to the entry source will be available. Furthermore, any one item may be linked via multiple trails to other items.

Although associative indexing is primarily a personal tool, Bush allows for the possibility that a given memex user may wish to share associations with other memex users. For this purpose, Bush posits a "reproducer" that can be used to make it possible to record a trail and distribute it for use. These networks of linked users sharing trails will lead to a situation in which "wholly new forms of encyclopedias will appear, ready-made with a mesh of associative trails running through them, ready to be dropped into the memex and there amplified. . . . There is a new profession of trail blazers, those who find delight in the task of establishing useful trails through the enormous mass of the common record."[40]

What Bush had actually invented, in a time when there was no possibility of implementing it in a practical manner, was hypertext—the principle of creating flexible links among information sources stored in a common format. Nelson, who is generally credited with coining the terms "hypertext" and "hypermedia," defined hypertext as "a body of written or pictorial material interconnected in such a complex way that it could not conveniently be presented or represented on paper."[41] Echoing Bush, whom he explicitly acknowledged, Nelson asserted that "the kinds of file structures required if we are to use the computer for personal files and as an adjunct to creativity are wholly different in character from those customary in business and scientific data processing. They need to provide the capacity for intricate and idiosyncratic arrangements, total modifiability, undecided alternatives, and thorough internal documentation."[42] Nelson proposed a system that, although addressing a complex problem, would do so by deliberately using a "very simple" file structure that he named the Evolutionary List File, or ELF. Paralleling Bush's motives for the memex, the purpose of ELF was "to create techniques for handling personal file systems and manuscripts in progress."[43] Nelson faced many of the obstacles that prevented the memex from being achievable: (1) the expense of the computing environment in the pre-microprocessor era (Nelson described a $37,000 computer by writing, "The costs are now down considerably"), (2) lack of a common sense of need for such a system, and (3) lack of a viable system design.[44] Nelson described a highly structured approach to implementing associative indexing in a computer system, based on the concepts of the list, "an ordered set of entries designated by the user," and the link, "a connector, designated by the user, between two particular entries which are in different lists."[45]

Nelson's paper on hypertext and hypermedia was followed by a number of experiments in building hypertext systems. The Hypertext Editing System was developed at Brown University in 1967 and followed in 1968 by FRESS, the File Retrieval and Editing System. NLS, the oN Line System, introduced at the Stanford Research Institute in 1968, linked more than 100,000 documents in a "shared journal." PROMIS, the first public release of a hypertext system, was developed at the University of Vermont in 1976 as a patient information management system. Hyperties, developed at the University of Maryland in 1983, introduced the use of embedded highlighted links. Apple's Hypercard was introduced in 1988 and, although not widely used, helped call some attention to the potential of hypertext systems.[46]

The hypertext concept didn't really achieve any meaningful popularity until it was adopted in 1990 as the guiding model for the World Wide Web.[47] Bush's legacy of associative indexing lives on in the billions of Web transactions that take place every day throughout the world.

William A. Woods, "What's Important about Knowledge Representation?" *Computer* 16 (October 1983): 22–27.

William A. Woods is principal scientist and distinguished engineer at Sun Microsystems. He holds a bachelor's degree in mathematics and physics from Ohio Wesleyan University and master's and doctoral degrees in applied mathematics from Harvard University. Over the course of his career, he has both been a faculty member and worked in the computer industry. He has published extensively in the areas of computer architecture, natural language processing, and knowledge representation.

KNOWLEDGE REPRESENTATION PROBLEMS

"What's Important about Knowledge Representation?" is primarily concerned with knowledge representation in the context of artificial intelligence system design and is framed in the context of a knowledge representation language known as KL-One. Woods begins his discussion of knowledge representation with a simple premise: "A good solution often depends on a good representation."[48] Woods identifies a number of essential problems in need of further research:

- How to structure a representational system that will be able, in principle, to make all the important distinctions
- How to remain noncommittal about details that cannot be resolved
- How to recognize efficiently what knowledge is relevant to the system in a particular situation
- How to acquire knowledge dynamically over the system's lifetime
- How to assimilate pieces of knowledge in the order in which they are encountered rather than in a specific order of presentation[49]

From these general problem areas, Woods distills two essential aspects of the core knowledge representation problem: (1) *"expressive adequacy,* which has to do with the expressive power of the representation," and (2) *"notational efficiency,"* which "concerns the actual shape and structure of the representation as well as the impact this structure has on the system's operations."[50] In other words, the essential challenge of knowledge representation is finding an appropriate, workable balance between describing the object of the representation thoroughly and describing it in an appropriately compact manner. The distinction between expressive adequacy and notational efficiency is extremely important, but Woods notes that drawing that distinction is not always easy. One of the goals of knowledge representation research is to develop the conventions and mechanisms that "simultaneously address expressive adequacy and notational efficiency," thereby building "reasonable foundations for the practical use of knowledge in reasoning, perception, and learning."[51]

THE NEED FOR DELIBERATE TAXONOMIES

Woods's work effectively provides a link between knowledge representation and taxonomies, contending that the decision rules that govern knowledge representation and interpretation can be "organized into a structured taxonomy of all the situations and objects" of a knowledge system.[52] Such taxonomies are hierarchical in nature, with each rule or parallel set of rules providing links both upward to more general concepts and downward to more specific concepts, much as a subject heading list provides broader and narrower cross-references. In the simplest of decision rule taxonomies, the process of analyzing rules and reaching a decision "entails testing each of the system's rules against the current state; however, as the number of rules increases, techniques are sought to avoid testing all of them."[53] In a taxonomy that includes a sufficiently large number of decision rules, the rules take on a role that is more advisory than mechanistically directive.

One of the problems of knowledge representation is that meaningful knowledge is inherently complex and necessarily difficult to describe. Knowledge representations entail "concepts of objects, substances, times, places, events, conditions, predicates, functions, individuals, etc. Each concept can be characterized as a configuration of attributes or parts, satisfying certain restrictions and standing in specified relationships to each other."[54] Woods defines those attributes or parts in terms of roles, which are generalizations that can be organized into structured taxonomies. One of the characteristics of such a taxonomy is that some of the characteristics of a specific concept are unique to that concept, but other characteristics are conferred by the broader concept that subsumes the specific concept: the concept of wire-haired terrier, for instance, possesses individual characteristics but is also characterized by the broader concept of terrier, which is in turn characterized in part by the still broader concept of dog. This downward transference of characteristics is known as inheritance.

SEMANTIC NETWORKS

Structured taxonomies can be expressed graphically in the form of semantic networks. A semantic network is a visualization in which concepts are presented in terms

Figure 6.1
Semantic Network: John Gives the Book to Mary

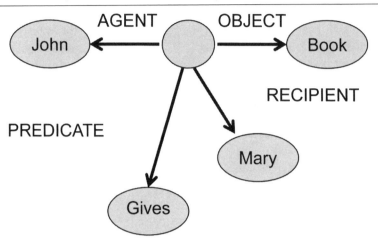

Source: Gordon McCalla and Nick Cercone, "Guest Editors' Introduction: Approaches to Knowledge Representation," *Computer* 16 (October 1983): 14.

of their links to other concepts in a hierarchical manner. Some semantic networks are reminiscent of the structures used to diagram sentences.

The term "semantic network" probably first appeared in M. Ross Quillian's 1967 doctoral dissertation.[55] Collins and Quillian later expanded on the idea, presenting the notion that knowledge can be understood in terms of hierarchical trees of interconnected nodes, each of which may inform and be informed by other nodes, and that connections can be defined by class-induction relationships.[56] Although the simplicity of the Collins and Quillian model has been questioned, the notion of mapping semantic networks has been the subject of substantial research. Steyvers and Tenenbaum, for instance, identified recurring growth patterns in semantic networks and proposed a model for understanding language acquisition and growth.[57]

PRODUCTION RULES

Systematic taxonomies and semantic networks combine to constitute a set of "'production rules,' a set of pattern-action rules characterizing the desired behavior of the system. Such a system operates by determining at every step what rules are satisfied by the current state of the system, then acting upon that state by executing one of those rules."[58]

Terrence A. Brooks, "Where Is Meaning When Form Is Gone? Knowledge Representation on the Web," *Information Research* 6 (January 2001), http://informationr.net/ir/6–2/paper93.html.

Terrence A. Brooks is an associate professor in the Information School at the University of Washington. He holds a bachelor's degree from the University of British Columbia, master's degrees in library science and business administration from McGill

University, and a PhD in library science from the University of Texas at Austin. He works in the area of cultural impacts on the use of Web technologies, markup languages, Web semantics, and information literacy.

LEGACY APPROACHES TO REPRESENTATION AND THE WORLD WIDE WEB

Brooks explores the fundamental question, "How shall knowledge be represented on the Web?"[59] His article explores the validity of "legacy" approaches to representing knowledge in the evolving context of the World Wide Web and particularly in the context of extensible Web technologies such as XML. Placing twentieth-century approaches to knowledge representation in their origin in "a historic transition from paper-based to digital systems," Brooks identifies four fundamental assumptions that are typical of the legacy approach in the library context:

- A single, multi-purpose record structure may be sufficient.
- Database records persist through time and will not disappear or transform into something else.
- There are information professionals who develop and employ subject terms and phrases.
- Aggregating information into a few large databases is useful and efficient.[60]

Brooks does not present these assumptions as an exhaustive list even within the library context, and he suggests that other twentieth-century information systems are undoubtedly couched in similar but not identical assumptions.

LOCALES OF MEANING

Noting that methods of knowledge representation are necessarily products of the eras in which they arise, Brooks proposes that the "locales of meaning" in extensible technologies may lie not within the traditional legacy approaches that have characterized library and database practice, but in

- The structure of the information resource itself, implicitly in the markup tags, and explicitly as meaning-bearing attribute qualifiers
- The relationships among information resources: implicitly in the links, and explicitly as meaning-bearing attribute qualifiers
- Situational expertise that orients information seekers to the semantic norms of a specific community of information users[61]

Limitations of legacy methods arise from assumptions such as

- A uniform catalog entry such as the MARC record can represent holdings.
- A single list of subject terms such as LCSH can provide subject access.
- A single database such as WorldCat can store information.

Although these assumptions are applicable only within the context of library catalogs and even then not universally applicable, they are illustrative of the potential need to explore new ways of representing knowledge for general use. Brooks is certainly on target in expressing concern that these assumptions may not apply in an environment dominated by the structures and principles of the World Wide Web. There are, however, serious problems with this list of assumptions, even within the library context.

- The limitations of the MARC (MAchine Readable Cataloging) record are well understood and were to a substantial degree predicted by the report that preceded the beginning of the MARC project.[62] MARC is best understood not as a uniform record structure but as a family of standards that truly qualify as an approach to knowledge representation for specific but varied and variable purposes. Emerging standards such as MARCXML, MODS (Metadata Object Description Schema), and METS (Metadata Encoding and Transmission Standards) are doing much to reshape the validity of the basic approach of MARC in a dynamic Web context.[63] Although MARC and its derivatives have primarily been used in libraries, they have also found usefulness in the museum, archive, and business worlds.

- It has never been realistic to expect that a single subject heading list could serve all purposes, and it would be difficult to identify any source of expertise that would support such a notion. Even within the library world, public libraries and school library media centers frequently employ the *Sears List of Subject Headings,* now in its eighteenth edition, while health sciences libraries typically use the National Library of Medicine's Medical Subject Headings (MeSH). Producers of structured database systems have typically developed individualized subject languages such as the BIOSIS subject headings used for *Biological Abstracts* and related sources and the INPSEC thesaurus used in the Engineering Information Village. All these languages have found application in representation of Web content.

- Cutter, in the first sentence of his *Rules for a Dictionary Catalog,* wrote, "No code of cataloging could be adopted in all points by every one."[64] WorldCat was never intended to constitute a single all-purpose database. It is explicitly a union catalog of library holdings in the tradition of the *National Union Catalog* and the statewide, regional, and consortium-sponsored union catalogs that were developed in the twentieth century to facilitate interlibrary cooperation. No such union catalog has ever successfully supplanted local library catalogs. The continued success of structured database services provides further evidence of the lack of feasibility of supporting all needs from a single database.

DYNAMIC CONTENT

One of the problems of the World Wide Web as a model for knowledge representation is the "extreme decentralization" that "permits anyone anywhere to post pages on any topic and in any language," resulting in "a large, heterogeneous, decentralized phenomenon with a high rate of growth."[65] The Web is fluid and amorphous—content appears and disappears constantly. An increasing but unmeasurable component of Web content is comprised of the "invisible Web" of pages produced by databases, which do not generate a permanent presence on the Web. The already great and rapidly expanding size of the Web results in multiple problems, including difficulty in evaluating Web content and impediments to "timely delivery of content."[66] Solutions employed to ensure speedy delivery, such as caching and housing content on distributed servers, exacerbate the problems of volume. The ultimate problem is, however, even more profound: although Web pages have the appearance of static documents, they frequently are "produced by a combination of dynamic scripts or programs, various database manipulations, with content possibly originating from caching and/or distributed processing."[67] The problems inherent in dynamic "documents" may be worsened by the ways in which browsers present Web content, which is largely influenced not by the content or its developer but by the browser and its designer.

From this discussion of the nature of the World Wide Web and its content, Brooks derives a fundamental conclusion: "The document paradigm ill suits many Web phenomena, and . . . the classic example of knowledge representation (i.e. *A librarian giving a subject heading to a book*) may no longer be applicable, or economical, in the Web environment."[68] The author ascribes attempts to apply the document model to the Web to the natural tendency to view new technologies as extensions of older technologies. Brooks describes the limited power of labor-intensive efforts such as the CORC and Net-First projects to address the enormous size and phenomenal rate of growth of the World Wide Web. He is pessimistic about the potential of manually applied metadata tagging.

Unfortunately, it is not clear that a librarian giving a subject heading to a book can be accepted as "the classic example of knowledge representation." Knowledge representation, as understood in the contexts of cognitive science and artificial intelligence, has to do with developing models for understanding and expressing meaning. Applying that definition of knowledge representation either to the description of documents in a more-or-less static environment or to dynamic Web content requires a much more robust view of representation than that allowed by Brooks's analysis.

TWO FALSE ASSUMPTIONS

Although Brooks agrees that "the idea of a particular user group customizing its data is a powerful one, as is the idea of a controlled set of terms and phrases used to advantage in Web resource discovery," he describes two "false assumptions [that] seem to block the success of current metadata efforts at this time."[69] The first he calls the "false community assumption," which posits that any given community of users can be characterized by disinterested, altruistic individuals willing to assume responsibility for applying the principles of subject cataloging to their domain within the Web. In reality, though, authors of Web content are frequently motivated more by the desire to promote use of their contributions than by the purpose of ensuring accurate or appropriate retrieval and are therefore prone to selecting metadata on the basis of decidedly less noble goals than supporting a user community. As a result, Web search engines are frequently programmed to ignore content-oriented metadata.

The second false assumption is termed the "false document assumption" and reiterates Brooks's earlier discussion of the ways in which Web content fails to resemble traditional notions of documents, particularly in terms of dynamic content and the potential for the "deconstruction" of portions of what would once have been indivisible documents. It is Brooks's prediction that "in the future, meaning might find a home as a part of extensible markup technologies" such as XML (Extensible Markup Language) and XLink (XML Linking Language).[70]

EXTENSIBLE TECHNOLOGIES AND COMMUNITIES

Application of extensible technologies to markup of dynamic Web content is not enough, however, to overcome both of the identified false assumptions. Brooks argues that "content-bearing metadata may most profitably be employed in a strongly normative community that does not rely on the legacy concept of the document."[71] Such communities, which are exemplified by electronic marketplaces, have the ability to share information efficiently and can provide the normative regulation of members necessary to create and preserve an environment of shared trust. These communities can also serve to build "situational expertise [that] can orient users to appropriate metadata, concepts and technical vocabulary."[72]

The fact is that such communities already exist and are active and have been for a great many years. The activities of the Chemical Abstracts Service, the American Psychological Association, the Online Library Computer Center, the National Library of Medicine, the Library of Congress, and countless other membership organizations, libraries, public institutions, and even commercial endeavors constitute exactly the environment of communities of practice that makes the application of extensible technologies in an environment of situational expertise and normative regulation possible.

NOTES

1. Arthur B. Markman, *Knowledge Representation* (Mahwah, NJ: Lawrence Erlbaum Associates, 1999), 5–11.

2. Ibid., 14.

3. Ibid., 15.

4. Ronald J. Brachman and Hector J. Levesque, *Knowledge Representation and Reasoning* (Amsterdam: Elsevier, 2004), 1.

5. Ibid.

6. Ibid., 3.

7. Ibid., 4.

8. Brian Cantwell Smith, "Reflection and Semantics in a Procedural Language" (Technical Report 272, MIT Laboratory for Computer Science, 1982), 35.

9. Gordon McCalla and Nick Cercone, "Guest Editors' Introduction: Approaches to Knowledge Representation," *Computer* 16 (October 1983): 12–18.

10. Brachman and Levesque, *Knowledge Representation and Reasoning,* 9.

11. Ibid., 18–32.

12. World Wide Web Consortium, "Collaboration, Knowledge Representation and Automatability," http://www.w3.org/Collaboration (accessed February 1, 2007).

13. Tim Berners-Lee, James Hendler, and Ora Lassila, "The Semantic Web," *Scientific American,* May 17, 2001, 37.

14. Ibid., 36.

15. Ibid.

16. Frank van Harmelen and Dieter Fensel, "Practical Knowledge Representation on the Web" (paper presented at the IJCAI 1999 Workshop on Intelligent Information Integration, Stockholm, 1999), 1.

17. Ibid., 6.

18. Ian Horrocks and Peter F. Patel-Schneider, "Three Theses of Representation in the Semantic Web" (paper presented at the WWW2004, Budapest, 2003).

19. Rob McCool, "Rethinking the Semantic Web, Part I," *IEEE Internet Computing* 9 (November/December 2005): 87.

20. Munindar P. Singh, "The Pragmatic Web: Preliminary Thoughts" (paper presented at the NSF-OntoWeb Workshop on Database and Information Systems Research for Semantic Web and Enterprise, Amicalola State Park, GA 2002).

21. Mareike Schoop, Aldo de Moor, and Jan L. G. Dietz, "The Pragmatic Web: A Manifesto," *Communications of the ACM* 49 (May 2006): 75–76.

22. Editor's introduction to "As We May Think," *Atlantic Monthly,* July 1945, 101.

23. Vannevar Bush, "As We May Think," *Atlantic Monthly,* July 1945, 101.

24. Ibid., 101–2.

25. Ibid., 105.

26. Ibid.

27. Ibid.

28. Ibid.

29. Ibid., 106.

30. Ibid.

31. Ibid.

32. Ibid.

33. Ibid.

34. Ibid., 106–7.

35. Ibid., 107.

36. Ibid.

37. Colin Burke, "The Other Memex: The Tangled Career of Vannevar Bush's Information Machine, the Rapid Selector," *Journal of the American Society for Information Science* 43, no. 10 (1992): 648–57.

38. Bush, "As We May Think," 107.

39. Ibid.

40. Ibid., 108.

41. T. H. Nelson, "Complex Information Processing: A File Structure for the Complex, the Changing, and the Indeterminate" (paper presented at the Proceedings of the ACM 20th National Conference 1965), 96.

42. Ibid., 84.

43. Ibid., 85.

44. Ibid.

45. Ibid., 90.

46. Brad A. Myers, "A Brief History of Human-Computer Interaction Technology," *Interactions* 5 (March 1988): 48–49.

47. Tom Standage, "Tim Berners-Lee," *Smithsonian,* November 2005, 76–78.

48. William A. Woods, "What's Important About Knowledge Representation?" *Computer* 16 (October 1983): 22.

49. Ibid.

50. Ibid., 22–23.

51. Ibid., 23.

52. Ibid.

53. Ibid.

54. Ibid., 24.

55. M. Ross Quillian, "Semantic Memory" (PhD thesis, Carnegie-Mellon University, 1967).

56. A. M. Collins and M. R. Quillian, "Retrieval Time from Semantic Memory," *Journal of Verbal Learning and Verbal Behavior* 8 (1969): 240–48.

57. Mark Steyvers and Joshua B. Tenenbaum, "The Large-Scale Structure of Semantic Networks: Statistical Analysis and a Model of Semantic Growth," *Cognitive Science* 29 (2005): 41–78.

58. Woods, "What's Important," 23.

59. Terrence A. Brooks, "Where Is Meaning When Form Is Gone? Knowledge Representation on the Web," *Information Research* 6 (January 2001), http://informationr.net/ir/6–2/paper93. html (accessed February 3, 2007).

60. Ibid.

61. Ibid.

62. Lawrence F. Buckland, *The Recording of Library of Congress Bibliographical Data in Machine Form; a Report Prepared for the Council on Library Resources, Inc.* (Washington, DC: Council on Library Resources, 1965).

63. Morgan V. Cundiff, "An Introduction to the Metadata Encoding Transmission Standard (METS)," *Library Hi Tech* 22, no. 1 (2004): 52–64; Sally H. McCallum, "An Introduction to the Metadata Object Description Schema (MODS)," *Library Hi Tech* 22, no. 1 (2004): 82–88; Sally H. McCallum, "Marc/Xml Sampler," *International Cataloging and Bibliographic Control* 35 (January/March 2006): 4–6.

64. Charles A. Cutter, *Rules for a Dictionary Catalog* (Washington, DC: Government Printing Office, 1904).

65. Brooks, "Where Is Meaning."

66. Ibid.

67. Ibid.

68. Ibid.

69. Ibid.

70. Ibid.

71. Ibid.

72. Ibid.

7

Content Management

content, *n*, spec. (pl.) The things contained or treated of in a writing or document; the various subdivisions of its subject-matter. Formerly also in sing.

1509 *Paternoster, Ave & Creed* (W. de W.) Cvj, Praye for your broder Thomas Betson which . . . drewe and made the contentes of this lytell quayer and exhortacion.

IN THIS CHAPTER

KEY CONCEPTS

Origins of Content Management
Data Management, Document Management, and Content Management
The Nature of Content Management
Enterprise Content Management
Global Content Management
Digital and Virtual Libraries
The World Wide Web as Universal Knowledge Repository

KEY PAPERS

Paul Otlet, "Something About Bibliography"
H. G. Wells, *World Brain*
Tim Berners-Lee, "Information Management: A Proposal"
John M. Budd and Bart Harloe, "Collection Development and Scholarly Communication in the 21st Century: From Collection Management to Content Management"

ORIGINS OF CONTENT MANAGEMENT

The term "content management" appears to have entered the business literature in the mid-1970s.[1] The term later entered the operations research vocabulary: Bryant discussed the balance between process management and content management in the operations research context in 1988.[2] The term was also in use in the geographic information systems literature by the late 1980s.[3] The term seems to have reached maturity in the early 1990s, when it became closely associated with the management of information for the Internet and with building organization-wide information systems based on the Internet model.

The history of content management is not remarkably clear. According to Feldstein, "the modern content management system was invented in 1996."[4] Kartchner traced the basics of content management to the publishing industry, suggesting that the emergence of the World Wide Web in the early 1990s led to a revolution in publishing that was accompanied by "a significant paradigm shift that has dramatically changed the publishing industry."[5] Arnold noted the influences of records management and the demands of the World Wide Web.[6] Boiko found the origins of content management in the combined influences of the publishing industry, document management, the multimedia industry, communication theory, library and information science, and the software development industry.[7] Although the term "content management" and the concept of content management systems are relatively new, content management "has been around as long as content."[8]

Content management as the term is currently understood has to do with "collecting, managing and publishing content."[9] The breadth of this definition certainly implies an expansive history, perhaps extending as far back as the invention of writing or of the primitive symbolic languages that may have preceded true writing. It certainly seems reasonable to ground the history of content management in the histories of libraries, archives, business information systems, and related endeavors.

DATA MANAGEMENT, DOCUMENT MANAGEMENT, AND CONTENT MANAGEMENT

Some commentators distinguish among data management, document management, and content management. The Data Management Association defines data management as "controlling, protecting, and facilitating access to data in order to provide information consumers with timely access to the data they need."[10] In this context, data are highly structured representations of content that can be readily decomposed into component parts (fields) that are easily linked as units (records). The underlying structure is consistent across records and can be implemented as a database management system that allows for flexible storage and retrieval of information.

Documents are structured containers for information that have a unitary identity and a unitary existence. A document cannot be readily decomposed into component parts and is typically stored and manipulated as a unit. Document management has to do with "the creation, revision, approval, and consumption" of documents.[11] Documents in a document management system are typically somewhat heterogeneous, but limited in nature and in format.

Document management is closely related to records management, which ARMA International defines as the "systematic control of records throughout their life cycle. ... Records are the evidence of what the organization does."[12] A record is typically a highly structured document; the records in a records management system are usually very homogeneous in nature and in format.

THE NATURE OF CONTENT MANAGEMENT

Content consists of various sources of information that are more-or-less unstructured and that have been stored such that they can be manipulated to generate new document-like products. Content in the context of content management is generally assumed to be extremely heterogeneous in nature and in format, including documents and records as they are traditionally understood, but also including e-mail, Web content, digital transaction archives, voice records, and any of the other recordable, preservable entities that reflect business practice and interpersonal interaction. Most discussions of content management emphasize digital content rather than print, microform, or other analog media. Asprey and Middleton explicitly viewed the distinction between content management and document management as trivial: "A document is a container for information that may be represented in multiple formats, which includes 'content' published as Web pages."[13] Gamble and Blackwell linked the purpose of content management to decision making, evoking the decision support systems of the 1960s.[14]

Arnold stated that a problem with content management is that "no one knows what content is" and suggested that content is not the sources or products of content management, but the process whereby documents and other products are generated.[15] Arnold defined four basic content management functions: (1) check-in/check-out, (2) editing, (3) storage (the "library" function), and (4) updating, a definition very close to that of document management.[16] Blair also identified four categories of content management functions: (1) capturing, (2) managing, (3) retaining and storing, and (4) delivering.[17] Leise reduced the functions to three: (1) the authoring system, (2) the document library, and (3) the publishing system.[18] Boiko also described three central functions: (1) collection, (2) management, and (3) publishing.[19]

ENTERPRISE CONTENT MANAGEMENT

Much of the literature of content management focuses explicitly on technological solutions made possible by enterprise content management. "Enterprise Content Management (ECM) is the technologies used to capture, manage, store, preserve, and deliver content and documents related to organizational processes."[20] The focus on ECM stems from the concept of enterprise management, which in turn has its origins in the increasing involvement of companies "in activities that are outside the boundaries of the traditional *company* (a single autonomous legal entity)," driven by forces that include "globalization, outsourcing, and virtualization."[21] Blair noted two motives for enterprise content management: (1) compliance with regulatory requirements such as those imposed by the Sarbannes-Oxley Act of 2002, and (2) "the need to make digital information assets accessible and usable to the business in a way that improves efficiency and contributes strategically."[22]

GLOBAL CONTENT MANAGEMENT

Creating a system that can somehow manage *all* of the world's recorded knowledge has been a dream since ancient times. Aristotle might have believed it possible and practical to experience directly all that could be known and record it for use by others; his collective works have been described as an attempt "at encompassing universal knowledge."[23] Early encyclopedias were attempts to encapsulate all knowledge in a reasonably compact form. Harris's 1704 *Lexicon Technicum,* for instance, has been described as "an encyclopedic exposition of all the arts and sciences known."[24] The Enlightenment promised to yield "an encyclopedia in which a universal science will be exemplified."[25] Diderot's *Encyclopédie* was intended not only to "expose the order and linkage of human knowledge" but also to "go back to the origin and generation of our ideas."[26] Although later encyclopedias were generally substantially less ambitious, the notion that an encyclopedia could act as a source of all knowledge even found its way into popular fiction, in such outlets as Burroughs's *Tarzan of the Apes* and Fleming's *Doctor No.*

The attractiveness of the universal source of knowledge did not go away with the failure of the dream of the encyclopedia as a universal knowledge source. Efforts shifted, though, to the goals of universal bibliography and global libraries. The Royal Society of London's *Catalogue of Scientific Papers* attempted to capture all science journal publications (within defined limits) between 1800 and 1900. In 1895, Goode described the "Ideal Index to Scientific Literature," which would have the following features:

1. It "should be international in scope."
2. "It should be exhaustive within its own limits, no latitude being given to the judgment and taste of its editors, in the matter of rejecting titles."
3. "It should be printed in annual installments."
4. It "should be in the form of a bibliographical catalogue" with an author arrangement.
5. "A subject-index of the most exhaustive character should be issued."
6. It should include
   a. "Publications of scientific academies and societies"
   b. "Scientific publications of universities, colleges, and technical schools"
   c. "Publications of scientific expeditions"
   d. "Scientific publications of national, municipal and other governments"
   e. "Independently published scientific books of reputable character"
   f. "All articles in journals and magazines devoted exclusively to the sciences"
   g. "Articles of scientific importance" in other journals and magazines
   h. "All bibliographical publications, relating wholly or in part to scientific literature"
   i. Festschriften
   j. "Scientific biography"

Goode also provided guidance on the subject organization of the catalog.[27] The *International Catalogue of Scientific Literature,* begun in 1896 and closely resembling Goode's model, was intended to "compile and publish a complete catalog of current scientific literature."[28] The Institut International de Bibliographie Sociologique was founded in 1895 by Otlet and La Fontaine with the goal of building a bibliography in card form of everything that had ever appeared in print.

Even a universal bibliography, however, was not as attractive as a universal library. In many ways, the earliest libraries were designed to be universal. Although not a great deal is known about the library of Assurbanipal at Nineveh, it is reasonable to assume that it was intended to encapsulate all recorded knowledge available to the Assyrians. One of the assumed goals of the Alexandrian Library was to gather books from around the known world to make it possible to effect better relationships with the far-flung subjects of the Greek Empire and its trade partners. The goal of many of the "librarians" who served early royal and private libraries was to gather as much published knowledge as was available and affordable.

Naudé viewed universality as the goal in building a library collection:

> And therefore I shall ever think it extreamly necessary, to collect for this purpose all sorts of books, (under such precautions, yet, as I shall establish) seeing a Library which is erected for the public benefit, ought to be universal; but which it can never be, unless it comprehend all the principal authors, that have written upon the great diversity of particular subjects, and chiefly upon all the arts and sciences; . . . For certainly there is nothing which renders a Library more recommendable, then when every man findes in it that which he is in search of.[29]

The universal library has found substantial attention in the world of popular culture, from Kurd Lasswitz's short story "The Universal Library" to Jorge Luis Borge's short story "The Library of Babel" to the *Star Trek* television and film series.

In 1911 Ostwald, Bührer, and Saager began work on the Institute for the Organization of Intellectual Work, an attempt to bring together "associations, societies, libraries, museums, companies, and individuals" to create a "comprehensive, illustrated world encyclopedia" that would contain not brief encyclopedia entries but primary sources.[30] Later efforts moved toward less centralized approaches, such as the interlibrary loan networks facilitated by the *National Union Catalog,* and even later were greatly expanded by statewide and consortial online union catalogs.

DIGITAL AND VIRTUAL LIBRARIES

One of the most immediate impacts of the introduction of the World Wide Web in 1990 was the movement toward digital libraries, also known as virtual libraries. Digitization in libraries was essentially a curiosity until the 1980s and was far from ubiquitous during the 1980s. "But just a decade later, by the end of the 1990s, research, practical developments, and general interest in digital libraries exploded globally."[31] Although there is no universal definition of the term "digital library," Borgman et al.'s definition is frequently cited:

1. Digital libraries are a set of electronic resources and associated technical capabilities for creating, searching, and using information. In this sense they are an extension and enhancement of information storage and retrieval systems that manipulate digital data in any medium (text, images, sounds; static or dynamic images) and exist in distributed networks. The content of digital libraries includes data, metadata that describe various aspects of the data (e.g., representation, creator, owner, reproduction rights), and metadata that consist of links or relationships to other data or metadata, whether internal or external to the digital library.
2. Digital libraries are constructed—collected and organized—by a community of users, and their functional capabilities support the information needs and uses of that community. They are a component of communities in which individuals and groups interact with each other, using data, information, and knowledge resources and systems.

In this sense they are an extension, enhancement, and integration of a variety of information institutions as physical places where resources are selected, collected, organized, preserved, and accessed in support of a user community. These information institutions include, among others, libraries, museums, archives, and schools, but digital libraries also extend and serve other community settings, including classrooms, offices, laboratories, homes, and public spaces.[32]

The Digital Library Federation supports a slightly different but parallel definition:

Digital libraries are organizations that provide the resources, including the specialized staff, to select, structure, offer intellectual access to, interpret, distribute, preserve the integrity of, and ensure the persistence over time of collections of digital works so that they are readily and economically available for use by a defined community or set of communities.[33]

Digital libraries can readily be understood as an approach to content management. One of the interesting aspects of digital libraries is that they have frequently defied traditional definitions of the concept of library in that digital libraries may be sponsored, created, and maintained by agencies that would not normally be associated with the notion of a library and for purposes greatly at variance with the established roles and functions of libraries. Projects such as Google Book Search and Google Library significantly blur the line between traditional and nontraditional libraries.

There are few libraries in the United States that do not provide significant access to digital content, although the balance of digital and nondigital content available in U.S. libraries varies dramatically. Digitization is a variable factor in libraries in other nations, where its influence ranges from domination of library activities to a completely unattainable dream.

THE WORLD WIDE WEB AS UNIVERSAL KNOWLEDGE REPOSITORY

The expression "worldwide" implies universal access, but the goal of the World Wide Web as a universal knowledge repository is far from being met. As of January 2007, Internet penetration as measured by the percentage of regional populations with Internet access was 69 percent for North America, 54 percent for Australia/Oceania, 39 percent for Europe, 16 percent for Asia, 10 percent for the Middle East, and less than 4 percent for Africa.[34] Although Web and digital library technologies have great promise for helping developing countries to leapfrog to new levels of information access, those developments are taking place slowly and sporadically.[35]

Paul Otlet, "Something About Bibliography," in *International Organization and Dissemination of Knowledge: Selected Essays of Paul Otlet*, translated and edited by W. Boyd Rayward (Amsterdam: Elsevier, 1990), 11–24. First published 1903.

Paul Otlet (1868–1944) was born in Brussels and educated at the Université Libre. In 1891 he embarked on a largely unsuccessful law career. However, Otlet had been fascinated with the classification and arrangement of knowledge since childhood. In 1895 he and Henri La Fontaine established the Institut International de Bibliographie Sociologique, which later became the Federation for Documentation and Information

(FID), the first of several significant collaborations between Otlet and La Fontaine. They were also cofounders of the Union of International Associations and co-creators of the Universal Decimal Classification. Otlet and La Fontaine coined the term "documentation" to describe the domains now known as information storage and retrieval and information science; they were the founders of the documentation movement in Europe. "Something About Bibliography" originally appeared as "Un Peu de Bibliographie" in *Palais* (1891–92): 254–71.

THE INFORMATION EXPLOSION AND DECOMPOSITION OF CONTENT

Otlet, like many authors since, is concerned about the proliferation of publications and the difficulty of retaining either knowledge of or control over everything being published. He is particularly concerned about the originality and duplication of ideas. Otlet finds the solution in the field of bibliography, and in particular in the notion of knowledge constituting not the summation of individual works but a sort of universal "collective work" that has the power to "direct individual efforts toward a single goal and to be careful not to waste anyone's time and money."[36]

Contending that bibliography as a science has not yet advanced sufficiently to solve the problems of the information explosion, Otlet outlines a process for decomposing literature into four essential categories: (1) facts, (2) interpretations of facts, (3) statistics, and (4) sources.[37] Otlet concludes that it is possible to derive from this analysis a compilation of all essential knowledge, free from unnecessary duplication. These synthetic, modular pieces of knowledge can be interconnected based on subject relationships. Otlet's contention is that the fundamental integrity of knowledge is retained even when the knowledge was separated from its immediate, planned context. He writes that "the external makeup of a book, its format, the personality of its author [are] unimportant provided that its substance, its sources and its conclusions" are valid.[38] In fact, Otlet sees the packaging of knowledge in the form of publications or other physical products as an artificial process essentially separate from the knowledge itself. He would later write, "Objectively there exist only distinct objects or separate ideas. Knowledge is not identical with the documents which make it available and preserve its elements."[39] "All links which we establish between objects or ideas bear the mark of subjectivity. This, in a certain sense, it would be exact to say that the sciences are simply collectivities of what is known that can be shaped in very different and varying ways into self-contained bodies of doctrine."[40]

Once the knowledge encapsulated in a body of publications has been decomposed to represent the facts, interpretations, statistics, and sources that are the knowledge content of the publications, those decomposed elements can be retained as discrete entities to form "a collective bibliographic work" that "permits the formation of the catalogue from contributions coming in from everywhere."[41] Otlet envisioned the physical format of this tool in terms of standardized paper cards, with each card representing a discrete idea or piece of knowledge, "thus allowing for all the manipulations of classification and continuous interfiling."[42] He envisions this model transforming the publishing industry as well as libraries, with publishers preparing texts in a manner that facilitates creation of the card system and libraries, particularly "the great public libraries" having primary responsibility for constructing the catalog.[43] The "reasonable goal proposed here is that any one person should be able rapidly to find out, not all about a subject, but all about the branches into which it has been divided and about the work already done relative to these branches. What must be avoided are repetition and duplication because of ignorance of previous work."[44] Underlying the catalog will be a "very systematic and very detailed synoptic outline of knowledge" that will "briefly mention all the aspects of a science, either in the form of a set of questions or according to a careful arrangement of its nomenclature."[45] This "synoptic outline" will have a hierarchical structure that makes it possible via a "gradation of five or six words" to "move from the more general, to the less general, to a particular fact. Each card of the catalogue [will] have its own argument, the basis of its classification, and the terms of the argument would be the same as those of the synoptic outline."[46] An essential aspect of the catalog is that it will be available "in every library or study."[47]

Otlet returned to this model frequently over the course of his career. He later envisioned an extension of the catalog called the Universal Knowledge Repertory and expanded on the central mission of the vision. "The aim of the Repertory is to detach what the book amalgamates, to reduce all that is complex to its elements and to devote a page to each."[48] Otlet named this decomposition of content the monographic principle.[49]

PREDICTING THE WORLD WIDE WEB

What Otlet proposes can be summarized as a system in which publications are represented in terms of their essential content, which is recorded in a universally accessible common format using a simple and easily understood standardized language, with defined links that establish sources of commonality and provisions for generating new synthetic publications. In other words, Otlet, within the technological limitations of the late nineteenth century, proposes the World Wide Web, enabled by linkages identifiable as the prototype for hypertext, and envisions the modern content management system.

Otlet's system was much more than a dream; Otlet and La Fontaine actually set about to implement it. Creating such a system in the context of the late nineteenth century would necessarily require strong organizational backing. In 1895, with support from the Belgian government, Otlet and La Fontaine established the International Institute of Bibliography (l'Institut International de Bibliographie [IIB]), and its administrative headquarters in the International Office of Bibliography (OIB). The International Office of Bibliography was the physical location of the Universal Bibliographic Repertory (RBU), which, in keeping with Otlet's 1892 plan, would be implemented as a gigantic card file. In preparation for the establishment of the International Institute of Bibliography and the International Office of Bibliography, Otlet and La Fontaine had actually built a card-file database with 400,000 entries to demonstrate the principle of the RBU. Otlet and La Fontaine adapted and revised the Dewey Decimal Classification as the means for providing a subject classification for the RBU; the result was the Universal Decimal Classification (UBC), the first edition of which was published between 1904 and 1907. By 1934 there were nearly sixteen million entries in the RBU, and other repertories had also been created, including the Universal Iconographic Repertory (an image database) and the Encyclopedic Repertory of Dossiers (a full-text extension from the RBU).[50]

H. G. Wells, *World Brain* (Garden City, NY: Doubleday, Doran, 1938).

Herbert George Wells (1866–1946) was originally apprenticed to a draper but was eventually able to complete a bachelor's degree at the University of London. Following graduation, he became a biology teacher, a career he pursued for five years before launching a successful career as a novelist. He is primarily known for his socially and politically charged novels, which include *The Time Machine, The Invisible Man,* and *The War of the Worlds,* all of which have been made into feature films. *World Brain* is a collection of essays, articles, and transcripts of public addresses revolving around the theme of social organization. *World Brain* has generated more than 50 citations in the *Social Sciences Citation Index* and has acted as a metaphoric inspiration to many authors. *World Brain* was reprinted in 1971 and again in 1994; the 1994 edition includes a bibliography of more than two hundred publications about or related to the core ideas presented in the book.

Two of the entries in *World Brain* are of particular interest. "World Encyclopaedia" is a transcript of a lecture presented to the Royal Institution of Great Britain on November 30, 1936. "The Brain Organization of the Modern World" is a transcript of a lecture delivered in America during a lecture tour in October and November of 1937.

THE WORLD ENCYCLOPAEDIA

"World Encyclopaedia" proceeds from the premise that "we want the intellectual worker to become a more definitely organized factor in the human scheme."[51] Wells recognizes that the nature of the world workforce is changing, and that the domination of manual labor is rapidly giving way to the rise of the "intellectual worker." Wells is concerned that the world's information systems and processes are not suited to supporting a workforce dominated by intellectual workers. He is also concerned that there is a growing gap between the specialized knowledge possessed by intellectual workers and the general knowledge of society at large. There is some reason to fear that these intellectual workers will attempt to control the world by forming an intellectual elite, a role for which they are poorly suited. In response to that fear, Wells asserts that "it is *science* and not *men of science* that we want to enlighten and animate our politics and rule the world."[52]

Wells's solution is the New Encyclopaedism and "a new social organ, an new institution," called the World Encyclopaedia.[53] His vision is of no ordinary encyclopedic work but of "a scheme for the reorganization and reorientation of education and information throughout the world."[54] Wells thoroughly recognizes the inertia of the world's existing institutions and traditions and the difficulty of replacing them with a new structure but voices the opinion that existing structures have "failed to participate in the general advance in power, scope and efficiency that has occurred in the past century."[55]

Wells forecasts a world in which "every ordinary citizen will be an educated citizen."[56] This "ordinary citizen" will experience the World Encyclopaedia much as anyone experiences a traditional encyclopedia, as a set of volumes in his or her home, in a neigh-bor's home, in a library, in a school, or in a college. The World Encyclopaedia will, however, be more definitive, more deliberative, and more up to date than a traditional encyclopedia. "It would not be a miscellany, but a concentration, a clarification and a synthesis."[57]

The impact of the World Encyclopaedia on "the specialist and the super-intellectual" will be different from its impact on the ordinary citizen.[58] The specialist will benefit from access to information about areas of interest parallel to his or her own expertise and will be able to observe and participate in the way in which his or her own field is expressed to the world. For the specialist, the World Encylopaedia will provide an opportunity to participate in a broad-based discussion of the field. "It would give the specialist just that contact with the world at large which at present is merely caricatured by more or less elementary class-teaching, amateurish examination work and college administrations."[59] The specialist will take on a new role of "enlightening the general mind" and "will broaden himself."[60]

Wells notes two prominent "obstructions" to what he views as "a perfectly sane, sound and practicable proposal."[61] The first is that "science is always contradicting itself." Wells contends that the basis for this argument "is largely mental laziness on the defensive."[62] The second obstruction is the contention that the model of the World Encyclopaedia is an attempt to make everyone think alike, to "stereotype people."[63] Wells counters that the true impact will be order, not uniformity or enforced conformity.

Achieving the World Encyclopaedia will require some new organization, "an Ency-clopaedia Society," to promote and eventually implement the model. Providing content for the Encyclopaedia is largely a matter of distilling and synthesizing, since "most of the material for a modern Encyclopaedia exists already—though in a state of impo-tent diffusion."[64] A first step toward the World Encyclopaedia is bringing together the expertise to compile "a sort of key bibliography to the thoughts and knowledge of the world."[65] Following the compilation of this bibliography, a general editorial board and subject-specific boards will be created as "permanent bodies" to ensure that the Ency-clopaedia has "a perennial life."[66] This will require physical facilities and a permanent staff. The primary role of the staff will be to "induce leading exponents of this or that field of science or criticism to co-operate in the selection, condensation, expansion or simplification of what they already said so well."[67] Wells feels that any potential financial challenges can be overcome by the inherent benefits of the World Encyclopaedia and by establishing the Encyclopaedia as a world monopoly.

THE WORLD BRAIN

In "The Brain Organization of the Modern World," Wells addresses "the World Problem, the universal world problem of adapting our life to its new scale and its new powers."[68] More specifically, Wells is concerned by the "problem of World Knowledge." The educated specialist "can increase knowledge, but without a modern organization backing him he cannot put it over. He can increase knowledge which ultimately is power, but he cannot at the same time control and spread this power that he creates. It has to be made generally available if it is not to be monopolized in the wrong hands."[69]

Wells reiterates his concern regarding the knowledge explosion: "An immense and ever-increasing wealth of knowledge is scattered about the world today, a wealth of knowledge and suggestion that—systematically ordered and generally disseminated—would probably give this giant vision and direction and suffice to solve all the mighty difficulties of our age, but that knowledge is still dispersed, unorganized, impotent in the face of adventurous violence and mass excitement."[70] The "knowledge apparatus" of the world, however, has been developed in an unsystematic, "unpremeditated" manner, "without a plan."[71] This apparatus "is not up to our necessities."[72] Wells sees a need for a more orderly solution, which he again finds in a "new encyclopaedism": "I put forward this new encyclopaedism as a possible method, the only possible method I can imagine, of bringing the universities and research institutions of the world into effective co-operation and creating an intellectual authority sufficient to control and direct our collective life. I imagine it as a permanent institution—Untrammeled by precedent, a new institution—something *added* to the world network of universities, linking and co-ordinating them with one another and with the general intelligence of the world."[73]

Wells's thinking about the structure of the World Encyclopaedia has evolved substantially since his 1936 address to the Royal Institution:

> A World Encyclopaedia no longer represents itself to a modern imagination as a row of volumes printed and published once for all, but as a sort of mental clearing house for the mind, a depot where knowledge and ideas are received, sorted, summarized, digested, clarified and compared. It would be in continual correspondence with every university, every research institution, every competent discussion, every survey, every statistical bureau in the world. It would develop a directorate and a staff of men of its own type, specialized editors and summarists. They would be very important and distinguished men in the new world. The Encyclopaedic organization need not be concentrated now in one place; it might have the form of a network. It would centralize mentally but not physically. Quite possibly it might to a large extent be duplicated. It is its files and its conference rooms which would be the core of its being, the essential Encyclopaedia. It would constitute the material beginning of a real World Brain.[74]

This World Brain is both a product and an institutional structure: "a double-faced organization, a perpetual digest and conference on the one hand and a system of publication and distribution on the other."[75] An important contribution of "The Brain Organization of the Modern World" is the suggestion that the best structure for the World Brain may be that of a network, although certainly a network with some sort of centralized organization and control. "While I believe that ultimately the knowledge systems of the world must be concentrated in this world brain, this permanent central Encyclopaedic organization with a local habitat and a world-wide range[,] . . . yet nevertheless I suggest that to begin with, the evocation of the World Encyclopaedia may begin at divergent points and will be all the better for beginning at divergent points."[76]

WORLD BRAIN = WORLD WIDE WEB

Like Otlet, Wells has assembled in his essays and addresses on the World Encyclopaedia and the World Brain a preview of the World Wide Web: a colossal, globally accessible compendium of everything knowable. Although the World Wide Web clearly lacks the authority and editorial consistency both Otlet and Wells favor, the notion of a practicable universal source of information preceded the realities of the Internet and the World Wide Web by several decades.

Tim Berners-Lee, "Information Management: A Proposal" (unpublished report, CERN, 1989).

Sir Tim Berners-Lee is director of the World Wide Web Consortium and senior research scientist in the Computer Science and Artificial Intelligence Lab at the Massachusetts Institute of Technology. He was educated at Oxford University. "Information Management: A Proposal" presents the original exposition of the idea that became the World Wide Web, which Berners-Lee developed while working for CERN, the European Organization for Nuclear Research. The proposal was an extension of work Berners-Lee had begun at CERN a decade earlier. Berners-Lee also wrote the original World Wide Web server, httpd, and the first Web client, WorldWideWeb, a combination hypertext editor and browser. Although the proposal is relatively unrecognized, Berners-Lee's 1999 *Weaving the Web* has received more than two hundred citation entries in the *Social Sciences Citation Index.*

THE MOTIVE FOR THE WORLD WIDE WEB

"Information Management: A Proposal" "was an attempt to persuade CERN management that a global hypertext system was in CERN's interests."[77] The goal of the proposal is very simply and directly stated: "This proposal concerns the management of general information about accelerators and experiments at CERN. It discusses the problems of loss of information about complex evolving systems and derives a solution based on a distributed hypertext system."[78]

Berners-Lee characterizes the environment at CERN as being made up of thousands of people who "are nominally organised into a hierarchical management structure," which "does not constrain the way people will communicate, and share information, equipment and software across groups." However, he notes that "the actual observed working structure of the organisation is a multiply connected 'web' whose interconnections evolve with time."[79] Although the working structure is "remarkably successful," "information is constantly being lost" due to the rapid rate of turnover; Berners-Lee indicates that the typical employee remains at CERN for about two years.[80] The dynamic nature of the organization demands a new approach to retaining and organizing information.

NODES AND LINKS

Berners-Lee's proposed information system is presented graphically in figure 7.1. The graphic model very closely resembles that of a semantic network. Berners-Lee uses the term "node" to describe the circles in the graphic and "link" to describe the arrows that connect nodes. Nodes can represent

- People
- Software modules
- Groups of people

Figure 7.1
Berners-Lee Information System Schematic

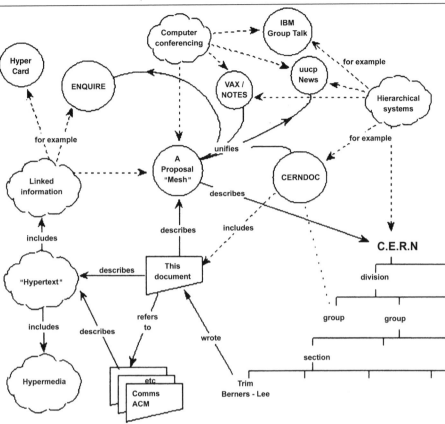

Source: Tim Berners-Lee, "The Original Proposal of the WWW, HTMLized," http://www.w3c.org/History/1989/proposal.html (accessed February 22, 2007).

- Projects
- Concepts
- Documents
- Types of hardware
- Specific hardware objects[81]

Similarly, there are various possible links between nodes. The link between node A and node B can include:

- A depends on B
- A is part of B
- A made B
- A refers to B
- A uses B
- A is an example of B[82]

Although Berners-Lee doesn't explicitly address reciprocity, it is clearly the case that if A is related in some way to B, B is also related to A.

LIMITATIONS OF HIERARCHICAL TREES AND KEYWORDS

Berners-Lee is specifically critical of hierarchical tree systems for organizing information, noting that, although a "tree has the practical advantage of giving every node a unique name . . . it does not allow the system to model the real world."[83] Hierarchical trees are both inefficient and inflexible.

Keyword systems suffer from semantic ambiguity. "The usual problem with keywords . . . is that two people never chose the same keywords. The keywords then become useful only to people who already know the application well." This can be solved by requiring that keywords be "registered" in a structured thesaurus, but that is only a partial solution.[84]

A HYPERTEXT SOLUTION

The solution proposed by Berners-Lee is to apply keywords to name nodes in a linked information system and to use keyword nodes as a mechanism for retrieving linked nodes. Berners-Lee describes the Enquire system, a hypertext system for organizing software that he developed in 1980. An important feature of Enquire is that it "ran on a multiuser system, and allowed many people to access the same data."[85] Although Berners-Lee developed Enquire while working elsewhere, he duplicated it on the system at CERN to serve as his own personal information management system.

SYSTEM REQUIREMENTS

One of the possible limitations of a hypertext system is that although a variety of hypertext and hypermedia systems are available, none has been tested with a truly large body of information. Berners-Lee is confident, however, that hypertext can be used to manage very large bodies of information, such as those in place at CERN. Berners-Lee presents a treatment of the qualities that an information system must possess to be usable at CERN:

1. It must provide remote access across networks.
2. It must be heterogeneous across platforms and operating systems.
3. It must be decentralized.
4. It must provide access to existing data.
5. It must be possible for users to create personal, private links.
6. It must at a minimum support ASCII text and standard displays; graphics are a nicety but not a necessity.
7. Some provision should be provided for data analysis.
8. Both permanent and temporary live links must be supported.[86]

Although Berners-Lee was not specifically thinking beyond the context of information management needs at CERN, in stating these qualities he implicitly identified the fundamental requirements of any broad-based distributed information system.

DEFINING THE SYSTEM

The system envisioned by Berners-Lee inherently requires a client-server structure in which the interface software for interacting with the system is separate from the software used to store and organize information. "Given the requirement for network access, it is natural to let this clean interface coincide with the physical division between the user and the remote database machine."[87] Defining and developing that interface is an essential challenge. "This will have been done well if many different information sources, past, present and future, can be mapped onto the definition, and if many different human interface programs can be written over the years to take advantage of new technology and standards."[88]

An additional challenge is that of making it possible for the system to provide access to existing data with no requirement that data be converted into a format unique to the system. Berners-Lee suggests that the need for data conversion is a key limitation to existing hypertext systems that must be overcome if the proposed system is to be successful. He proposes the introduction of a "gateway" server that will allow at least limited access to documents that have not been designed for hypertext access. This "dummy" server will make non-hypertext information viewable in a hypertext browser.

THE WORLD WIDE WEB: DREAM TO REALITY

In many ways, Berners-Lee's proposal is as revolutionary and as fanciful as those of Otlet and Wells. The goal is substantially less ambitious, however. Where Otlet and Wells aspired to solving the world's information problems, Berners-Lee is focused on solving the problems of a single organization. The emphasis on making it possible to use both the hardware and software already in place at CERN and provide access to documents in their native formats allows for a potentially very simple solution and ease of implementation.

John M. Budd and Bart Harloe, "Collection Development and Scholarly Communication in the 21st Century: From Collection Management to Content Management," in *Collection Management for the 21st Century: A Handbook for Librarians*, edited by G. E. Gorman and Ruth H. Miller (Westport, CT: Greenwood Press, 1997), 3–25.

John M. Budd is a professor in the School of Information Science and Learning Technologies at the University of Missouri–Columbia. He is a graduate of Louisiana State University and the University of North Carolina at Chapel Hill. Bart Harloe is university librarian at the University of Missouri–St. Louis. He holds degrees from San Francisco State University and the University of Pittsburgh.

COLLECTION, CONTENT, AND INTERPRETATION

"Collection Development and Scholarly Communication in the 21st Century" presents in the library context a problem common to organizations of all kinds: information has historically been managed primarily in a secondary manner by managing the containers that hold and convey information rather than by managing the content within the containers. Regardless of the ways in which collections of information containers are defined, described, formatted, organized, manipulated, and managed, the process is a step removed from providing access directly to content. "While it is true that artifacts (using the term a broadly as possible) allow for communication between a user of information, the package itself . . . is not the essential element in the communication process. The user is not so much interested in the information package as in the information itself."[89]

Information use requires interpretation, understanding, and synthesis. "When we use the word 'information,' it connotes much more than the available morass of data; it refers to both the collection and interpretation of those data into a meaningful and informing presentation. An active role is required to produce a presentation that informs; the passive acquisition of artifacts cannot achieve the user-based goal."[90] All too often, however, the passive acquisition and maintenance of information packages or containers is allowed to substitute for the active role described by Budd and Harloe: information is compiled and stored seemingly as if compilation and storage are the goals of the system. Part of the problem is the proliferation of information, the essential challenge that inspired Otlet in the late nineteenth century. "The bulk of data available mitigates against meaning."[91] That is only part of the problem, however. "Even with . . . an active posture, informing is not easy; the problem is not merely one of bulk of data, but of interpretation. Interpretation is not synonymous with awareness; the pressures on interpretation are exacerbated by an increasing inattention to the critical faculty that is necessary to reading."[92]

READING AND THE HYPERTEXT WORLD

"The pressures on an individual's critical faculty are made greater by the proliferation of information sources, including networked information."[93] Budd and Harloe note that "the structure of electronic media has altered the possibilities for writing and, so, for communication generally. As writing changes, either necessarily or not, the nature of reading must also change."[94] Traditional texts are at least to some extent designed to be read sequentially from a defined beginning to a carefully structured end. Hypertext is designed to be entered from any of a potentially large number of points defined by hyperlinks. Furthermore, the nature of hypertext is such that "the reader can be in a constant state of reinterpretation, since the text is mutable, since it is, in effect, versions of a metatext."[95] This may exacerbate the problem of interpretation and meaning. "One implication of hypertext and networked information is that meaning is even more individualized than it is with traditional texts."[96] Budd and Harloe suggest that there may be an emerging transformation of the ways in which people read and the ways in which they understand what is read. The resulting impacts on the management of information in systems are likely to be substantial.

INFORMATION RETRIEVAL AND SYSTEMS DESIGN

Budd and Harloe contend that the mechanisms traditionally employed for providing access to information are increasingly inadequate for addressing complex information needs. Most systems, particularly but not exclusively those found in libraries, are based in the technologies of the past and assume constraints that may no longer apply. "We have entered an era wherein the limitations of the past do not necessarily tie our hands, and we, as a profession, are making strides in the consideration of possibilities that, while perhaps not completely nondeterministic, present arrays of options that were not previously presented."[97] Interestingly, some of the ideas discussed by Budd and Harloe as "new" ways of providing access are not at all new. The inclusion of chapter titles in bibliographic records, presented by Budd and Harloe as a suggestion "that may have some potential," was considered essential by Otlet.[98] Despite the attractiveness of providing access to complete texts electronically, making full-text content searchable has not been found to significantly improve information retrieval.

Budd and Harloe move toward the suggestion that providing access to content requires some combination of traditional and nontraditional approaches. They quote Mann's principal goals of cataloging and classification, which can be paraphrased to provide a set of goals for all information retrieval operations: (1) making retrieval predictable, (2) encouraging serendipity in retrieval, and (3) providing depth of access to content.[99] It is not clear that "traditional" approaches to information retrieval can achieve these goals, but neither is it evident that emerging approaches to content management can do so.

THE CHANGING FORMAT ENVIRONMENT

> It must be admitted that the transformation from concentration on managing collections (physical objects, their placement and storage, and their economics) to managing content is not an easy one, either conceptually or practically. For one thing, it is much easier to manage things than ideas.[100]

Most of the history of information management has had to do with managing information containers, with the implicit assumption that managing the container is a direct substitute for managing the content of the container. This is, of course, deceptive, but at the same time the physical existence of content plays a more than negligible role, since it has a definitive influence on the ways in which content can be understood and used. "A focus on content does not ignore the physical; it embraces an awareness that the physical affects the content and its reception."[101]

A development that may have a profound influence on content management is the availability of user choice in physical formats. Throughout most of the history of recorded knowledge, there were few or no available choices in format and typically no need whatsoever for the user to consider or make a decision regarding format. Format was entirely a choice of content producers, and even then choices were severely restricted. As more content becomes available in alternative formats, particularly digital formats made possible by new technologies, user choice becomes a factor. Budd and Harloe point out, however, that "technological concerns are not the only ones to consider."[102] There are also considerations of financial, physical, and intellectual access. Any system "that makes a particular item less accessible, intellectually and physically, can ensure that there is little demand for that item."[103] Mooers, writing in 1960, stated that "an information retrieval system will tend not to be used whenever it is more painful and troublesome for a customer to have information than for him not to have it."[104] Although Budd and Harloe do not specifically invoke Mooers's Law, they imply it.

A limitation in forecasting the future is that "the entire infrastructure of networked information is less than stable at present."[105] It is unclear that any significant improvement in stability has taken place in the decade since the publication of Budd and Harloe's essay. There is certainly little stability in the information systems technologies marketplace. On the other hand, managers of information systems and the organizations those systems support are much more intimately acquainted with technological solutions than they were a decade ago. Budd and Harloe do not anticipate any future scenario in which digital formats completely replace other media, stating that "there are aspects intrinsic to the content that have an impact on the means of communication."[106] This is true regardless of the specific medium under consideration. Given the interactions among format, content, and reading, it is essential that information professionals develop "a deep understanding of the phenomenon of 'reading' (for lack of a better term) and of the essential character of content."[107]

MANAGEMENT AND MEDIATION

Any consideration of the move from managing collections of objects to truly managing content must focus on the essential nature of management. Budd and Harloe contend that the approach to what is being managed necessarily determines the approach taken to management itself. Past management philosophies have focused on "the physical packages of information, the buildings in which they are stored, the people who oversee them, the money to acquire them, and the technology to enhance access to them and, in some extreme visions, to replace them."[108] Budd and Harloe view the management function differently: "Management is an intellectual activity dependent on individuals' ability to comprehend what information producers are trying to communicate, to divine the needs and desires of information seekers, and to conjoin the two on the basis of what the mind endeavors to create."[109] To a considerable extent, then, the distinction between collection management and content management is a matter of point of view or vision.

A fundamental characteristic of content management is that it is a mediated process. The information or knowledge professional is an arbiter between content and the individuals who need content. Individuals approach information systems from varying experiential and knowledge backgrounds, influenced by a wide variety of motivational and capability factors. They "are attempting to apprehend content in personal contexts that are complex."[110] The ways in which content is relevant to user needs are therefore also complex and frequently difficult to understand. Content inherently has multiple contextual origins and aspects, some of which are inherent to the content and some of which are inherent to the user. The need to develop effective means of mediating the link between content and user is therefore paramount and implies that the development of content management systems that require no professional mediation is unlikely. The relationship is further complicated by the nature of the medium by which content is represented. "Access to content can be tenuous, not necessarily because of a property of the content itself, but because of a connection between content and medium."[111]

Budd and Harloe conclude that content management is a form of mediation and that "because users will be relying upon content managers to organize, select, and provide content for the information on the Net, there is likely to be a need for more . . . mediation, not less."[112] The authors identify seven "critical activities that content managers might be expected to engage in as they seek to meet the needs of users in a networked 21st-century world":

1. "Evaluating, selecting, and ranking content"
2. Maintaining "the content that is discovered and [making] it accessible by means of 'logical gateways'"
3. Selecting "the appropriate versions, whether it be print, electronic, multimedia, or a combination thereof"
4. Providing the metadata "essential to situating the information so that users can find, use, and then understand what it is that they have found"
5. "Organizing resource sharing and content delivery systems that are sensitive to the variety of cooperative and for-profit arrangements that will be available in the networked world"
6. "Dealing with issues of copyright in a way that protects the interests of the academic community while still meeting the legal obligations of an evolving copyright law"
7. Continuing "to mediate between authors and readers"[113]

Ultimately, Budd and Harloe view professional content managers—and particularly librarians as content managers—as the "indispensable go-betweens as we move further into the 21st century."[114] This sentiment is echoed in Boiko's *Content Management Bible*: "Librarians are the gurus of the future."[115]

NOTES

1. "Public Affairs: The Bloom Is off the Rose," *U.S. Investor-Eastern Banker,* February 25, 1974, 9–11.

2. Jim Bryant, "Frameworks of Inquiry: Or Practice across the Hard-Soft Divide," *Journal of the Operational Research Society* 39 (May 1988): 423–35.

3. D. McGregor, "Geographic Information System Trends" (paper presented at the AM/FM International European Division, Automated Mapping/Facilities Management European Conference IV: Focus on Corporate Benefits, Montreaux, Switzerland, 1988).

4. Michael Feldstein, "What's Important in a Learning Content Management System," *eLearn,* May 31, 2002, http://elearnmag.org/subpage.cfm?section = tutorials&article = 4–1 (accessed February 10, 2007).

5. Chris Kartchner, "Fulfilling the Promise of Content Management," *Bulletin of the American Society for Information Science and Technology* 28 (October/November 2001): 18.

6. Stephen E. Arnold, "Content Management's New Realities," *Online* 27 (January/February 2003): 37.

7. Bob Boiko, *Content Management Bible*, 2nd ed. (Indianapolis, IN: Wiley, 2005), 148–71.

8. Kartchner, "Fulfilling the Promise," 18.

9. Bob Boiko, "Understanding Content Management," *Bulletin of the American Society for Information Science and Technology* 28 (October/November 2001): 8.

10. "Glossary," *DM Review,* http://www.dmreview.com/rg/resources/glossary.cfm (accessed February 13, 2007).

11. AIIM International, "What Is ECM?" http://www.aiim.org/about-ecm.asp (accessed February 13, 2007).

12. ARMA International, "What Is 'Records Management'? Why Should I Care?" http://www.arma.org/pdf/WhatIsRIM.pdf (accessed February 13, 2007).

13. Len Asprey and Michael Middleton, *Integrative Document and Content Management: Strategies for Exploiting Enterprise Knowledge* (Hershey, PA: Idea Group, 2003), 12.

14. Paul R. Gamble and John Blackwell, *Knowledge Management: A State of the Art Guide* (London: Kogan Page, 2002), 177.

15. Arnold, "Content Management's New Realities," 40.

16. Ibid., 38.

17. Barclay T. Blair, "An Enterprise Content Management Primer," *Information Management Journal* 38 (September/October 2004): 65.

18. Fred Leise, "Metadata and Content Management Systems: An Introduction for Indexers," *Indexer* 24 (October 2004): 71–72.

19. Boiko, "Understanding Content Management," 8.

20. AIIM International, "What Is ECM?"

21. M. Binder and B. T. Clegg, "A Conceptual Framework for Enterprise Management," *International Journal of Production Research* 44 (September/October 2006): 3813.

22. Blair, "An Enterprise Content Management Primer," 64.

23. *Columbia Encyclopedia,* 6th ed., s.v. "Aristotle."

24. Lawrence E. Sullivan, "Circumscribing Knowledge: Encyclopedias in Historical Perspective," *Journal of Religion* 70 (July 1990): 315.

25. David S. Ferris, "Post-modern Interdisciplinarity: Kant, Diderot and the Encyclopedia Project," *MLN* 118 (December 2003): 1260.

26. Ibid.

27. G. Brown Goode, "The Ideal Index to Scientific Literature," *Science* 16 (April 19, 1895): 433–37.

28. A. Liversidge, "The International Catalogue of Scientific Literature," *Science* 22 (October 6, 1905): 441–43.

29. Gabriel Naudé, *Instructions Concerning Erecting of a Library, 1661,* translated by John Evelyn (London: Dawsons of Pall Mall, 1966), 19–20.

30. Thomas Kapke, "From the World Brain to the First Transatlantic Information Dialogue: Activities in Information and Documentation in Germany in the First Half of the 20th Century," *IFLA Journal* 2003, no. 4 (29): 367.

31. Tefko Seracevic, "Digital Library Evaluation: Toward an Evolution of Concepts," *Library Trends* 49 (Fall 2000): 350–51.

32. Christine L. Borgman, Marcia J. Bates, Michelle V. Cloonan, Efthimis N. Efthimiadis, Anne J. Gilliland-Swetland, Yasmin B. Kafai, Gregory H. Leazer, and Anthony B. Maddox, "Social Aspects of Digital Libraries," http://is.gseis.ucla.edu/research/dl/UCLA_DL_Report.html (accessed February 19, 2007).

33. Digital Library Federation, "A Working Definition of Digital Library," http://www.diglib.org/about/dldefinition.htm (accessed February 19, 2007).

34. "Internet World Stats Usage and Population Statistics," http://www.internetworldstats.com/stats.htm (accessed February 19, 2007).

35. Ian H. Witten, Michael Loots, Maria F. Trujillo, and David Bainbridge, "The Promise of Digital Libraries in Developing Countries," *Communications of the ACM* 44 (May 2001): 82–85.

36. Paul Otlet, "Something About Bibliography," in *International Organisation and Dissemination of Knowledge: Selected Essays of Paul Otlet,* translated and edited by W. Boyd Rayward (Amsterdam: Elsevier, 1990), 14.

37. Ibid., 16.

38. Ibid., 17.

39. Paul Otlet, "The Science of Bibliography and Documentation," in *International Organisation and Dissemination of Knowledge: Selected Essays of Paul Otlet,* translated and edited by W. Boyd Rayward (Amsterdam: Elsevier, 1990), 73.

40. Ibid., 72–73.

41. Otlet, "Something About Bibliography."

42. Ibid.

43. Ibid.

44. Ibid., 19.

45. Ibid.

46. Ibid.

47. Ibid., 18.

48. Paul Otlet, "Transformations in the Bibliographic Apparatus of the Sciences," in *International Organisation and Dissemination of Knowledge: Selected Essays of Paul Otlet,* translated and edited by W. Boyd Rayward (Amsterdam: Elsevier, 1990), 149.

49. Ibid.

50. W. Boyd Rayward, "Visions of Xanadu: Paul Otlet (1868–1944) and Hypertext," *Journal of the American Society for Information Science* 45, no. 4 (1994): 238.

51. H. G. Wells, *World Brain* (Garden City, NY: Doubleday, Doran, 1938), 13.

52. Ibid., 17.

53. Ibid.

54. Ibid.

55. Ibid., 18.

56. Ibid., 19.

57. Ibid., 20.

58. Ibid., 24.

59. Ibid., 24–25.

60. Ibid., 25.

61. Ibid., 21.

62. Ibid.

63. Ibid., 23.

64. Ibid., 27–28.

65. Ibid., 28.

66. Ibid.

67. Ibid., 29.

68. Ibid., 50.

69. Ibid., 66.

70. Ibid., 67.

71. Ibid., 59.

72. Ibid., 61.

73. Ibid., 68.

74. Ibid., 69–70.

75. Ibid., 70–71.

76. Ibid., 74.

77. Tim Berners-Lee, "The Original Proposal of the WWW, HTMLized," http://www.w3c.org/History/1989/proposal.html (accessed February 22, 2007).

78. Ibid.

79. Ibid.

80. Ibid.

81. Ibid.

82. Ibid.

83. Ibid.

84. Ibid.

85. Ibid.

86. Ibid.

87. Ibid.

88. Ibid.

89. John M. Budd and Bart Harloe, "Collection Development and Scholarly Communication in the 21st Century: From Collection Management to Content Management," in *Collection Management for the 21st Century: A Handbook for Librarians,* edited by G. E. Gorman and Ruth H. Miller (Westport, CT: Greenwood Press, 1997), 7.

90. Ibid., 8.

91. Ibid.

92. Ibid.

93. Ibid.

94. Ibid.

95. Ibid., 9.

96. Ibid.

97. Ibid., 11.

98. Ibid.

99. Ibid.

100. Ibid., 12.

101. Ibid.

102. Ibid., 13.

103. Ibid.

104. Calvin N. Mooers, "Mooers' Law: Or, Why Some Retrieval Systems Are Used and Others Are Not," *American Documentation* 11 (July 1960): ii.

105. Budd and Harloe, "Collection Development," 13.

106. Ibid., 14.

107. Ibid.

108. Ibid., 15.

109. Ibid.

110. Ibid.

111. Ibid., 20.

112. Ibid., 22.

113. Ibid.

114. Ibid., 23.

115. Boiko, *Content Management Bible,* 167.

8

Taxonomies and Ontologies

taxonomy A classification of anything.

1960 *Times Lit. Suppl.* 29 Apr. 277/4 Professor Goldschmidt . . . has constructed what he calls a "taxonomy" of human societies.

ontology, *n.* As a count noun: a theory or conception relating to the nature of being. Also in extended use.

1855 A. POTTER *Lect. on Evid. Christianity* 197 [Rationalism] might do but little harm in . . . disporting itself with its own fanciful creations . . . respecting necessity and spontaneity . . . , quiddities and ontologies.

IN THIS CHAPTER

KEY CONCEPTS

Definitions of Taxonomy
Digital Information and Taxonomies
Categorization: A Fundamental Human Process
Taxonomy and Classification
Natural and Constructed Languages
History of Classification
Taxonomy/Classification Fundamentals
Surrogation
Vocabulary Control
Specificity and Exhaustivity

Warrant
The Thesaurus
Approaches to Classification
Content and Containers
Metadata and Information Architecture
Metadata Schema
Ontology and Purpose
Ontologies and Knowledge Management

KEY PAPERS

Charles A. Cutter, *Rules for a Printed Dictionary Catalog*
Jesse Shera, "Social Epistemology, General Semantics, and Librarianship"
B. C. Vickery, "Ontologies"

DEFINITIONS OF TAXONOMY

Taxonomy has three prominent dictionary definitions: (1) "the classification of organisms in an ordered system that indicates natural relationships," (2) "the science, laws, or principles of classification; systematics," and (3) "division into ordered groups or categories."[1] The distinction among these definitions is fairly subtle; each has meaning in the knowledge management context.

DIGITAL INFORMATION AND TAXONOMIES

The most direct relationship between the dictionary definition of taxonomy and knowledge management comes through the third definition and has to do with the need to systematically organize recorded knowledge. This is not in any way a new or recent concern, but it is one that has been greatly heightened by the introduction of Internet-based digital information systems into all kinds of organizations and endeavors. Although in many cases an organization is actually dealing with no more information than before, the imposition of an intranet or content management system frequently has the effect of making more people more aware of the volume of information being handled by the organization, the dangers of losing access to information through inappropriate management, and the difficulty of creating an effective information management structure.

Organizations have had to deal with bodies of internal information of various kinds and of varying sizes and varying complexity for centuries. In paper-based environments and internal "legacy" automated systems, the structures and procedures for managing information resources have frequently been relatively informal, sometimes to the point of being truly ad hoc. Information was typically retained in the system at the level of the individual document or file, with little or no perceived need to manage information at a finer level or to create and use links across documents or files. Such systems were generally quite tolerant of idiosyncrasy and error. Problems introduced by inconsistency or error were amenable to seemingly automatic human resolution.

Internet-based content management systems that provide access to content within documents—and may even disaggregate the content within documents—and provide complex linkages among documents and elements of content are much less amenable to informal structures. In such systems, which typically emphasize searching for specific content rather than browsing text as the fundamental form of access to information, the nature of the content cannot be readily divorced from the structure of the system. Pushing from the informal to the truly ad hoc is a recipe for disaster in such systems; realized or impending disasters of this kind are typical motivations for employing structured content management systems.

Bruno and Richmond outlined three roles for taxonomies in business settings: (1) determining where and how information should be stored "by filtering, categorizing, and labeling information," (2) making it possible to infer "additional information on a topic . . . by seeing where the entry is placed in context within the taxonomy" and providing "serendipitous guidance," and (3) improving information retrieval.[2]

CATEGORIZATION: A FUNDAMENTAL HUMAN PROCESS

"There seems to be a basic drive for humans to organize."[3] This drive is reflected in the structure of human languages and in the human traits that are ascribed positive value. Physical items such as tools or surgical instruments are organized to maximize ease of location and use. Workspaces are organized to facilitate the intersection between the employee, tasks to be accomplished, and tools for approaching those tasks. Geographic locations are identified by addresses or coordinates that identify their relationships. One of the most flattering statements that can be made about an individual in nearly any context is praise for the impressive extent to which he or she is organized.

TAXONOMY AND CLASSIFICATION

The Montague Institute has published this definition: "A taxonomy is a system for naming and organizing things into groups that share similar characteristics."[4] This definition is essentially identical to the dictionary definition of classification: "the action or process of classifying something according to shared qualities or characteristics."[5] The dictionary also specifically identifies classification as a synonym for taxonomy. Svenonius employed a very simple definition: "Classification brings like things together."[6] To Kwasnik, "classification is the meaningful clustering of experience."[7] Taylor contrasted categorization and classification, noting that "during the twentieth century, classification has come to be associated with assigning some kind of notation to physical information packages."[8] Warner essentially dismissed the differences in terminology, identifying thesauri and synonym rings as additional synonyms. "All of the terms . . . controlled vocabularies. That means that they are organized lists of words or phrases, or notation systems, that are used to initially tag content, and then to find it through navigation or search."[9]

Foskett noted a fundamental problem with organizing knowledge: "Knowledge is multi-dimensional: that is to say, subjects are related one to another in many different ways."[10] Svenonius expanded on this:

> Organizing information would seem to be no different from organizing anything else. The
> assumption that this is the case has led to attempts to interpret it as a routine application

of the database modeling techniques developed to organize entities like the employees, departments, and projects of a company. But there are important differences. One that is particularly important, because it is at the root of many of the complexities unique to organizing information, is that two distinct entities need to be organized in tandem with respect to each other: works and the documents that embody them.[11]

In other words, organizing knowledge requires distinguishing between essential content and the container or package that holds and identifies the content. Further complexity is introduced by the possibility that the same content may appear in different packages, and that different versions or editions of the content may exist. "The essential and defining objective of a system for organizing information . . . is to bring essentially like information together and to differentiate what is not exactly alike."[12] This is a fundamentally and deceptively difficult task.

NATURAL AND CONSTRUCTED LANGUAGES

Organization of information addresses two primary purposes: (1) making it possible to effectively use the structure used to organize the things that are referenced by the information and (2) making it possible to gain access to the information so that its content can be used. An example of the first can be found in the organization of household items, such as dishes and utensils, in a kitchen cupboard. Most people tend to stack plates, put cutlery together in one drawer, store glasses separately from cups, and the like. The pegboard organization of an efficient home tool collection is a similar example. The actual organizational structure of these systems is defined by the objects themselves and is rarely expressed or even thought of in explicit terms. There is an inherent "rightness" to the structure that frequently seems inviolable to the individual who has organized the objects. The descriptive language used to describe the organizational structure can be extremely informal. "The drawer next to the refrigerator" and "the third screwdriver from the left" are sufficient descriptions for purposes of communicating with someone other than the individual responsible for the organizational scheme. The language of such systems is fundamentally natural and essentially organic. Ambiguity within such a language is generally limited, and the potential negative impact of any existing ambiguity is relatively trivial and easily corrected. Although the color blue is an ambiguous concept in that there can be many variations in tone, hue, saturation, and related features, an organizational structure that dictates storing all the blue coffee mugs together is almost completely unambiguous and requires no conscious symbolic expression.

Organization of information content, however, requires a more explicit structure and a more formal descriptive language, usually a symbolic one. Such languages are inherently artificial and are deliberately constructed to serve specific purposes. Although some language structures are so universally familiar that they seem to be natural and organic, they are not. Alphabetization, for instance, is used to organize information in a vast variety of contexts; the very notion of a prescribed order for the letters of the alphabet is completely artificial and the standard order in widespread use is completely arbitrary. Even a system so seemingly simple as alphabetization requires rules for combating ambiguity. Sources of such ambiguity include the distinction between "Mc" and "Mac" in surnames, the inclusion or exclusion of initial articles as components in determining alphabetical position, and letter-by-letter vs. word-by-word alphabetization.

These more complex organizational structures can be expressed in a wide variety of ways: words, phrases, sentences, and texts; word-like combinations of letters and numbers; visual symbols and images; and sounds. They cannot, however, be expressed without creating some symbolic link between the expression and the content the expression represents. Even something as simple as an ATM that beeps to indicate that either the user's input has been accepted or action on the part of the user is required necessitates a complex one-to-many relationship between the audible signal and its context-dependent meaning. There is nothing in the nature of the sound generated by the ATM that is inherently or permanently related to its meaning.

HISTORY OF CLASSIFICATION

Early attempts to devise classification schemes were based on the general classification of knowledge rather than classification of documents. Aristotle attempted to categorize all human knowledge on the basis of his understanding of the natural order of the universe. He divided knowledge into 10 broad categories based on the characteristics of different kinds of knowledge: substance, quantity, quality, reason, place, time, position, state, action, and affection. According to Aristotle, "the aim of science [is] to unambiguously classify all phenomena by their essential (true) qualities."[13] Francis Bacon's primary division of knowledge distinguished between "sacred theology revealed to man by God and human knowledge acquired by man's unaided powers." The latter was subdivided into "History, Poesy, and Philosophy," each of which had many subdivisions and sub-subdivisions.[14] Jean Le Rond d'Alembert adapted Bacon's scheme, without the provision for divine knowledge, for Diderot's *Encyclopédie*. According to Taylor, these classical theories of categorization dominated until the mid-twentieth century and were very influential in the development of classification schemes for libraries and related organizations.[15] Thomas Jefferson's library, for instance, was organized using a classification scheme based on D'Alembert's adaptation of Bacon's approach to categorizing knowledge.[16]

Other than for philosophical purposes, there is little need to classify until some collection of objects of interest becomes sufficiently large that differentiating among objects and finding objects in the collection become difficult. Classification of documents rather than abstract knowledge arose only after the printing explosion of the sixteenth century began to be accompanied by the rise of libraries that were tangibly different from the monastery libraries of the medieval period. The practices of the monastery libraries were not easily abandoned, and the development of explicit classification systems for use in libraries progressed slowly and sporadically during the sixteenth, seventeenth, and eighteenth centuries. Although many library classification schemes were developed during that period, none rose to prominence, and most were used only in a single library.

Modern library classification has its origins in the latter half of the nineteenth century, when many competing classification schemes were introduced and gained greater or lesser favor among librarians. Dewey's Decimal Classification, the first standardized classification scheme for libraries, was based on the classification in use at the

St. Louis Public School Library, which was based on the system developed for the St. Louis Mercantile Library, which in turn was based on D'Alembert's interpretation of Bacon.[17] Dewey's scheme, which was published anonymously in 1876, presented three notable features: (1) rather than assigning books to fixed shelf positions, books would be numbered and arranged in order by their numbers, (2) an unusually detailed division into subject classes, and (3) the provision of a "relative index" that provided an alphabetical list of the names of classes and their numbers. Foskett asserted that the value of these three features may have had more to with the success of the Dewey classification than the inherent benefits of the classification scheme itself.[18]

Many other library classification schemes were introduced during the great era of library classification schemes that characterized the late nineteenth and early twentieth centuries. Cutter's Expansive Classification, which was intended to tailor the level of detail to the size or type of library, was published in incomplete form between 1891 and 1893.[19] The Library of Congress Classification (LC) was published sequentially beginning in 1898.[20] Originally intended entirely for internal use, the Library of Congress Classification eventually became the dominant classification scheme for university and research libraries. The Universal Decimal Classification (UDC), an adaptation of the Dewey Decimal Classification (DDC), was introduced in 1905 as part of Paul Otlet and Henri La Fontaine's efforts to achieve universal bibliographic control. Although it was initially very similar to DDC, UDC rapidly evolved into a much more modern facet analysis-based classification. Bliss's Bibliographic Classification was published in outline form in 1910 and gained a following among libraries in Britain.[21] One of the most important classification schemes from a conceptual viewpoint was Ranganathan's Colon Classification, which was first published in 1933 and introduced facet analysis as a basis for classification.

TAXONOMY/CLASSIFICATION FUNDAMENTALS

Designing, building, and using a taxonomy or classification scheme is a complex process that requires systematic analysis and significant effort. Approaching taxonomy development in a casual or ad hoc way is a guarantee of inefficiency at best, and chaos at worst. An effective taxonomy consists of four essential components: (1) schedules, which are systematic listings of terms that reveal relationships among terms; (2) notation, which allows users to view the schedules from a symbolic viewpoint; (3) an index, usually in alphabetical form, to provide access to specific points in the schedules; and (4) a commitment and resources to make it possible to keep the taxonomy up to date.[22] The schedules are the heart of a taxonomy and provide the most direct representation of content. There are many ways in which schedules can be presented, and many pitfalls in constructing the artificial language that constitutes the schedules.

SURROGATION

Providing access to content generally requires some form of surrogation, in which a substitute is used to represent the content for some specific purpose. In a taxonomy or classification scheme, the language of the taxonomy acts as a substitute for the language of the content as encoded in some kind of information container or package. There are two prevalent forms of surrogation—textual and symbolic—each of which has a variety of subcategories.

1. Textual surrogates
   a. *Document as surrogate.* The availability of complete or mostly complete content in digital form raises the possibility of making the entirety of the content available for use, with no explicit surrogation process. The major attractions of such a system are (1) making the entirety of the document directly available for use, (2) making the entirety of the document searchable, and (3) eliminating the need for the process of translating the nature of the document into some other form of surrogate. The major disadvantages of making the whole content available rather than creating some kind of more compact surrogate are (1) the expense of storing full-content documents and (2) the difficulty and cumbersomeness of working with the complete text.
   b. *Language extraction.* Extraction is the process of creating a reduced version of the full document using the language of the document. There are two primary forms of surrogates created via extraction. A digest is a grammatically structured, readable version of a document that has been editorially trimmed to produce a version that conveys the essence of the full document in a more compact form. The *Reader's Digest* magazine is a prominent example of this approach to extraction. Although there have been many experiments with automatic digest creation, they have had limited success, and therefore most digests today are created by human editors. An extract is similar to a digest but lacks the characteristics of readability assured by the editorial process. In an extract, key sentences or phrases are simply taken from the full document and presented in some structured manner, with no expectation that the result will take the form of a sequentially readable text. Using the title of a document as a substitute for the document is a simple example of an extract. A bibliographic reference is a structured extract. Automatic extraction procedures have been used successfully with bodies of documents that share a core nature and structure, but have proved less effective for homogeneous document collections.
   c. *Language substitution.* Substitution is the process of creating a surrogate that in some way reflects the content of the document but consciously does not employ the language of the document. The most frequent example of language substitution is abstracting, in which typically some skilled abstractor summarizes the document in a structured manner in the context of a set of rules and processes defined by the organization responsible for the abstracting process. Automatic approaches to abstracting have generally been less than successful; thus most abstracting is carried out by human abstractors.
   d. *Word or phrase indexing.* This is the category of surrogation most closely associated with the current use of taxonomies in knowledge management. Words and phrases are selected to represent important concepts and presented in the form of a thesaurus that reveals not only the terms but also their relationships and may provide rules and guidelines for use.
   e. *Synthetic surrogation.* The process of creating documents on the fly, usually through some database-driven process that assembles content from more than one source to create what is essentially a custom impermanent document, is synthetic surrogation. Synthetic surrogation is the function of many computerized content management systems.

2. Symbolic surrogates

   a. *Mnemonic symbols.* One of the problems of any approach to surrogation that uses symbols rather than text is that of memorability. Mnemonic symbols are symbolic surrogates that in some way invite the user to associate the surrogate with what it represents. In the Library of Congress Classification, for instance, the symbol for the class Music is the letter *M*. Unfortunately, that principle does not apply broadly across LC classes. Foskett referred to this category of mnemonic as a literal mnemonic and distinguished it from systematic mnemonics. A systematic mnemonic is found in a taxonomy that always uses the same symbol to represent a concept: in the Dewey Decimal Classification, for instance, the number 2 in the final position of a main class number in Literature always means drama: 822 is English drama, 832 is German drama, 842 is French drama, and so forth.[23]

   b. *Structural symbols.* These are nontextual surrogates that provide access to the structure of the taxonomy. Library classification schemes, the Chemical Abstracts Service (CAS) Registry Numbers, and the Standard Industrial Classification are examples of structural symbolic surrogation. The Standard Industrial Classification (SIC), for instance, uses the symbol *B* to represent Mining, 10 to represent the major group Metal Mining, and 1 to represent the industry group Iron Ores; the Standard Industrial Classification notation B1011 represents Iron Ore Mining as an area of industrial activity. Structural symbols may or may not have mnemonic value.

   c. *Visual symbols.* Visual symbols rely on some sort of graphic or other visual characteristic to provide a surrogate representation for a document or other content. Simple examples of visual symbolic surrogates include the standardized shape of stop signs, the circle-and-bar combination that means "No," and the standard symbols for poisonous or radioactive substances. Color and pattern can also be used for symbolic surrogation: there is no obvious link between the color red and the need for traffic to stop, but a red light is universally understood to mean "Stop." Prior to the era of automated information systems, color coding was used to good effect to identify characteristics such as document type in information storage and retrieval systems, and it still plays a role in some systems. Medical examination rooms, for instance, are frequently equipped with colored flag systems that alert medical personnel to the status of the room or the patient. A major advantage of visual symbols is the immediate impact of the symbol on someone who knows what it means. Unfortunately, the major disadvantage is that a visual symbol typically has no meaning to an individual who is not familiar with the system of which the symbol is a part and with the specific symbol itself.

VOCABULARY CONTROL

Word or phrase indexing and symbolic surrogation systems require some sort of controlled vocabulary—an artificially constructed language in which the ambiguities of natural language are reduced or, ideally, eliminated. A controlled vocabulary is an organized list "of words and phrases, or notation systems, that are used to initially tag content, and then to find it through navigation or search."[24] Controlled vocabularies have two primary objectives: (1) to represent concepts systematically and (2) to facilitate comprehensive searching of a body of information.[25]

The concept of a controlled vocabulary is relatively easy to express and to understand. Building controlled vocabularies, however, tends to be more difficult. Some languages, such as those of the physical and biological sciences, are by their very nature relatively unambiguous and constitute controlled vocabularies in and of themselves. Many organizations enter into taxonomy development projects under the false impression that there must be a standardized, essentially organic structure and terminology that defines the organization's area of interest. The languages of most areas of interest, though, are flexible, changeable, and characterized by multiple ways of expressing concepts (synonyms) and words and phrases with multiple possible meanings (homographs). A major first step in vocabulary control, then, is separating those elements of language that will be included in the controlled vocabulary and consciously rejecting those that will not, which can be a complex and time-consuming process even for a fairly tightly defined domain of interest. Devising ways to distinguish homographs is an equally challenging task.

SPECIFICITY AND EXHAUSTIVITY

A controlled vocabulary must, within the confines of the domain of interest it supports, provide two essential elements of functionality. First, it must be capable of accurately representing the nature of content. This is the principle of specificity: "the extent to which the system permits us to be precise when specifying the subject."[26] If the subject of a document being described is "trade with France," the term "international trade" is inadequate in terms of specificity. On the other hand, "trade with the town of Ganagobie" may be unnecessarily specific. Creating a controlled vocabulary that is sufficiently specific to meet system needs without being excessively specific requires substantial knowledge of the organization the vocabulary is intended to serve, the functions of the organization the vocabulary supports, and the content of the documents to which the system will provide access. Ensuring adequate specificity also dictates that the vocabulary is capable of being modified to accommodate new or changed terminology.

Exhaustivity describes the extent to which the vocabulary and the system that is supported by the vocabulary make it possible to completely describe content. If multiple concepts are represented in a single document, then ideally all those concepts should be included in the vocabulary and used to describe that document. Where specificity is a function of the controlled vocabulary itself, exhaustivity is a function of management policy or processing decisions.

WARRANT

The process of selecting and expressing terminology in a controlled vocabulary is guided by the concept of *warrant*, which has to do with the fundamental principles that guide terminological choices. Warrant has two possible origins. Document warrant, also known as literary warrant or bibliographic warrant, relies primarily on the language of the content the controlled vocabulary is intended to represent. User warrant relies primarily on the language of the people who are expected to use the controlled vocabulary, which includes both the people who will be charged with associating the controlled vocabulary with content and the people who will use the controlled vocabulary to search for content. In some environments, the language of documents and the language of users are sufficiently identical that there is no particular need to think in terms of a defined approach to warrant. A system designed to provide medical information to medical practitioners, for instance, can probably be designed with the assumption that there is no meaningful potential for confusion or ambiguity. A system designed to provide medical information to consumers, however, must bridge the gap between the technical language of medicine and the everyday language of consumers. Designing a system to meet the needs of multiple user groups obviously adds complexity to the task.

THE THESAURUS

A thesaurus is a means of presenting a controlled vocabulary. "In essence, a taxonomy is a hierarchical classification of headings constructed using the principles of classification, and a thesaurus supplies the commentary and links to navigate the taxonomy."[27] The primary role of the thesaurus is to make the classification of information provided by the controlled vocabulary understandable and usable. A traditional thesaurus typically takes the form of a book in which terms and their relationships are presented in a manner designed to eliminate the ambiguity of synonyms and homographs and to show hierarchical or parallel relationships among terms. Current thesauri are more typically presented as structured Web sites or as searchable databases.

Hundreds of thesauri exist, some of them published and readily available. Standard thesauri such as those developed by the Education Research Information Clearinghouse (ERIC), BIOSIS, and the Standard Industrial Classification may be directly applicable in some organizational environments. Although preexisting thesauri are available from various commercial and noncommercial sources, the investment in licensing fees and the need to customize for local needs frequently dictate that organizations create and implement specialized controlled vocabularies internally.

APPROACHES TO CLASSIFICATION

Kwasnik identified four fundamental approaches to classifying knowledge: (1) hierarchies, (2) trees, (3) paradigms, and (4) faceted analysis.[28]

1. *Hierarchical classification.* Taylor suggested that the origins of the hierarchical approach to classification lie in Aristotle's "classical theory of categories" and that the Aristotelian understanding of the nature of classification was dominant until the mid-twentieth century.[29] Wason contended that "the most typical form of a taxonomy is a hierarchy."[30] A hierarchy connotes a genus-species relationship of the kind sometimes referred to as a paradigmatic relationship.[31] This is the structure, in which a lower position in the hierarchy indicates that a concept is part of the larger concept at the next higher position, that is encapsulated in the first dictionary definition of taxonomy. This is sometimes referred to as an "is a" relationship or a parent-child relationship. A springer spaniel is a spaniel, which is a dog, which is a mammal, which is a vertebrate, which is an animal. Unfortunately, many domains of interest are not readily broken into genus-species relationships. According to Kwasnik, "hierarchies are excellent representations for knowledge in mature domains in which the nature of the entities, and the nature

of meaningful relationships, is known. Hierarchies are useful for entities that are well defined and have clear class boundaries. In general, some theory or model is necessary to guide the identification of entities, the rules of association and distinction, and the order in which these rules are invoked."[32]

2. *Tree classification.* A tree is very similar to a hierarchy but does not require a true genus-species structure. This conforms to the kind of relationship known as a syntagmatic relationship, in which the nature of the relationship is impermanent but directional. Ranks in a personnel classification are examples of syntagmatic relationships. Kwasnik uses the example of military rank, in which generals are higher in the tree than colonels, colonels are higher than majors, majors are higher than captains, and so on.[33] There is no "is a" relationship implied: a captain is not a type of major, and a major is not a type of colonel. Many domains of interest can be expressed in terms of syntagmatic trees. "Trees are useful for displaying information about entities and their relationships along one dimension of interest. They require fairly complete knowledge about a domain or at least about one aspect of a domain. A tree representation is good for displaying the relative placement of entities with respect to each other and their frequency at any node."[34]

3. *Paradigms.* Kwasnik uses the term "paradigm" to describe a relationship that spans two concept areas. This relationship can be visualized as a matrix or graph with one concept area on the *x* axis and one on the *y* axis. For example, Ford, General Motors, and Daimler-Chrysler are all manufacturers of cars, vans, SUVs, and light trucks. The intersection of the "manufacturer" category and the "vehicle type" category defines a paradigm. "Paradigms are good tools for discovery. They reveal the presence or absence of names for entities defined by pairs of attributes. They can be used for comparison and for the display of patterns and anomalies with respect to the variety and distribution of terms. Paradigms are heuristic in that they present a clear view that can then be analyzed and interpreted."[35]

4. *Facet analysis.* The origin of facet analysis is generally credited to S. R. Ranganathan, who introduced the concept as a fundamental feature of the Colon Classification. Many concepts can be examined from the viewpoint of a variety of characteristics. Ranganathan identified five somewhat esoteric "fundamental categories": (1) personality, (2) matter, (3) energy, (4) space, and (5) time. This structure is referred to by the acronym PMEST. A more general and understandable categorization that can be used in many domains of interest is "Things—Kinds—Parts—Materials—Properties—Processes—Operations—Agents."[36] A classification scheme based on facet analysis consists of some way of naming and defining facets and a consistent process for listing facets in describing content. A faceted classification allows "at least some systematic way of viewing the world without the necessity for a mature and stable internal framework in which to view it."[37]

CONTENT AND CONTAINERS

A common misunderstanding regarding the historical origins of classification is the belief that librarians have historically been primarily interested in the management of collections of information containers, books being the primary example, and have been uninterested in managing the content of those containers. It is, however, accurate to state that for most of the history of librarianship it has been necessary to manage content primarily by means of managing containers. Although the conceptual framework for deeply and exhaustively managing content within containers has been understood for nearly two centuries, the physical nature of books and the economics of library practice have mitigated in favor of relatively simplistic and limited approaches to managing content. There has never been a library-based scheme for the organization of materials, other than the fixed location systems of medieval monastery libraries, which concentrated on the thing rather than its content. In a very real sense, every system for managing and providing access to information is limited and controlled by the nature of the physical environment, regardless of whether that environment emphasizes books on shelves or disaggregated information in a content management system. The need to manage content primarily by managing content containers is in all likelihood a permanent challenge.

METADATA AND INFORMATION ARCHITECTURE

"The task of the information architect is to create web sites where users can actually find the information they are looking for."[38] Controlled vocabularies produce the metadata that are used to organize Web sites in two ways: (1) by providing structure for the navigational scheme of the page or site, "which should use unambiguous labels and where the primary organization is usually hierarchical," and (2) by ensuring optimal performance of the searching system, "where search terms are selected and organized for tagging content and searching for them."[39] A controlled vocabulary in a Web information architecture context is primarily a mechanism for implementing the effective use of metadata.

The standard definition of metadata is "data about data," but in practice it usually means "'information about objects' . . . that is, information about a document, an image, a reusable content module, and so on. . . . In general, metadata is best understood as 'any statement about an information resource,' regardless of what it is being used for, which metadata vocabulary is being used, and how the metadata is represented."[40] Taylor examined competing definitions of metadata and found that "what they all have in common is the notion that metadata is structured information that describes the attributes of information packages for the purposes of identification, discovery, and sometimes management."[41] Metadata are used for two prominent purposes: (1) to describe documents as objects or containers and (2) to describe document content. Both are important. The metadata that describe the document provide context for the content and help distinguish among similar sources of information. The metadata that describe document content help facilitate subject retrieval and group similar sources of information.

Taylor distinguishes three major categories of metadata: (1) administrative metadata, (2) structural metadata, and (3) descriptive metadata. Administrative metadata are most closely associated with the document as property and may include such features as the source of the document, document ownership and rights, legal information related to the document, locational information, document use statistics, and information regarding retention and preservation.[42] Structural metadata have to do with the document as physical entity and may address such factors as technical documentation related to the document, specifics of the physical nature of the document, creation or revision date, version or edition control, information about the software or browser processes required to use the document, compression or resolution information, encryption or password access information, and search protocol identification.[43] Descriptive metadata are those that identify the intellectual and conceptual characteristics of a document and include information directly of value to the user of the content of the document, such as title, responsibility, date of creation, institutional affiliation, authority, links to other documents, and access to document content through a taxonomy, keywords, or other items intended to facilitate retrieval and use.

METADATA SCHEMA

Although standard markup languages such as HTML and XML provide for flexible use of metadata to describe Web content, the flexibility that is a positive characteristic of general purpose markup languages translates into a negative due to the absence of metadata standardization in markup languages. The solution to this is generally thought to be found in metadata schema. "A metadata schema consists of a set of elements designed for a specific purpose, such as describing a particular type of information resource."[44] Many competing metadata schemata have been developed, some designed to achieve general purpose use and some for highly specialized purposes. Metadata schema are intended to do for the organization and representation of information on the Web what bibliographic standards such as the Anglo-American Cataloging Rules did for libraries.

Any metadata schema is a form of artificial language, but metadata schema differ from controlled vocabulary in that a metadata schema makes no attempt at being a complete listing of usable terminology. Metadata schema possess three essential characteristics: (1) syntax, (2) semantics (content), and (3) structure.[45] Any of these characteristics may be implemented at a variety of levels ranging from fundamentally simple to extremely complex.

According to Gorman, metadata "arose from the desire of non-librarians to improve the retrievability of Web pages and other Internet documents."[46] Gorman places metadata schema and their use "between the free-text searching of search engines (which is quick, cheap, and ineffective) and full cataloguing (which is sometimes slow, labor-intensive, expensive, and highly effective)."[47] Interestingly, though, perhaps because of the similarity between metadata schema and the standards and systems used by librarians for many decades, metadata schema have been somewhat embraced by the library and information communities and largely ignored elsewhere.

ONTOLOGY AND PURPOSE

Ontology is "the branch of metaphysics that deals with the nature of being."[48] Alternatively, it is "the theory or study of being as such; i.e., of the basic characteristics of all reality."[49] The *Stanford Encyclopedia of Philosophy* provides a somewhat more colloquial definition: "the study of what there is."[50] Ontology is a complex discipline that explores the nature of what is, the ways in which existence can be determined and understood, the general nature of existence, and the characteristics of things that are.

The term "ontology" and the modern philosophical discipline of ontology came into being in the eighteenth century, although there certainly were distinct ontological themes at least as early as Aristotle's exploration of metaphysics. There are two prominent classical views of ontology. Wolff proposed an essentially Newtonian view of ontology, which reduces the evidence of existence to its simplest components. In this view, "most of what appears significant . . . is irrelevant."[51] Leibniz developed a contrasting view based on the principle that God despises waste and therefore would not have created things that have no significance. Kant rejected ontology more or less outright "as a discipline that tried to confer metaphysical significance on every aspect of human experience."[52]

ONTOLOGIES AND KNOWLEDGE MANAGEMENT

The concept of ontologies as it is used in knowledge management was largely adopted from artificial intelligence research. Gruber defined an ontology as a "specification of a representational vocabulary for a shared domain of discourse—definitions of classes, relations, functions, and other objects."[53] Chandrasekaran, Josephson, and Benjamins defined ontologies as "content theories about the sort of objects, properties of objects, and relations between objects that are possible in a specified domain of knowledge," a definition much closer to the dictionary definition of ontology.[54] According to Wilks, "all modern use refers to hierarchical knowledge structures whose authors never discuss what there is but assume they know it and just want to write down the relations between the parts/wholes and sets and individuals that undoubtedly exist."[55]

An ontology is essentially an approach to looking at things and the language that accompanies that approach. The word "ontology" has taken on a variety of new overlapping but not identical meanings in the knowledge management context. According to Chan, "the ontology of a system consists of its vocabulary and a set of constraints on the way terms can be combined to model a domain," a definition remarkable similar to that of taxonomy.[56] Roche described an ontology as "an agreed upon vocabulary of common terms and meanings shared by a group of people," a description also similar to definitions of taxonomy but adding the element of an ontology as a consciously social construct.[57] Brachman and Levesque used this definition: "the kinds of *objects* that will be important to the agent, the *properties* those objects will be thought to have, and the *relationships* among them."[58] Sowa's definition was "a catalog of the types of things that are assumed to exist in a domain of interest *D* from the perspective of a person who uses a language *L* for the purpose of talking about *D*."[59] Sowa provided an extensive glossary and a sample ontology that shares most of the characteristics of schedules, notation, index, and commitment described by Foskett. Edgington, Choi, Henson, Raghu, and Vinze defined ontology as "the basic structure or armature around which a knowledge base can be built" and emphasize that ontology "is not merely vocabulary, nor is it merely taxonomy."[60] Wilks, however, referred to "the conflation of ontologies (construed as hierarchical classifications of things or entities) and thesauri or taxonomies (hierarchical classifications of words or lexical senses)."[61] Wilks appeared to be of the opinion that there was no need to maintain a precise distinction between taxonomy and ontology.

Charles A. Cutter, *Rules for a Printed Dictionary Catalog* (Washington, DC: Government Printing Office, 1875).

Charles Ammi Cutter (1837–1903) entered Harvard College at age 14 and graduated four years later. In 1856 he enrolled at Harvard Divinity School. While a student employee in the library there, he completed a completely new catalog of the library's holdings. He was appointed assistant librarian in the Harvard College library in 1860. From 1868 to 1893 he was librarian at the Boston Athenaeum. During his tenure at the Athenaeum, he formulated *Rules for a Printed Dictionary Catalog* and the Expansive Classification. Although the Expansive Classification was never completed and failed to gain popularity in libraries, the Cutter tables used to identify authors in other classification systems are based on the principles of the Expansive Classification. He also originated many practices that later became standard in libraries, including recording book information and due dates on paper pockets glued inside books, interlibrary loan, and book services for the homebound. From 1893 until his death in 1903 he was librarian at the Forbes Library in Northampton, New Hampshire, where his innovations included a system of branch libraries, open stacks, and a "traveling library" that predated modern bookmobiles. *Rules for a Printed Dictionary Catalog* has had a profound impact on cataloging and bibliographic control and has generated more than two hundred citation entries in the *Social Sciences Citation Index*.

Cutter's *Rules for a Printed Dictionary Catalog*, although copyrighted 1875, actually appeared in print in 1876, the same year as the first publication of the Dewey Decimal Classification, the foundation of the American Library Association, in which both Cutter and Dewey played pivotal roles, and the publication of the first issue of *Library Journal*. Cutter's *Rules* was the first effort to establish a systematic approach to developing, presenting, and fostering the use of a vocabulary for representing and retrieving information. Although the bulk of the *Rules* has to do with description of items, proper names, and titles, the 14 pages devoted to "subjects" established a set of principles for vocabulary control that have enduring value and are quite worthy of attention in efforts to exploit taxonomies for modern purposes.

LIBRARIES AS SYSTEMS

Cutter was a systems thinker long before the era of systems analysis and general systems theory, and even before the word "systemics" entered the English language as a name for the study of systems. Miksa traced Cutter's dedication to systematic design and action to his exposure to the Boston-Cambridge intellectual community of the late nineteenth century, his deep interest in a scientific approach to the thought processes of everyday life, his familiarity with the works of Scottish realist philosophers such as Thomas Reid and Dugald Stewart, and in particular to the principle of enculturation that the realists espoused.[62]

"Cutter considered democracy to be the highest expression of man's political nature."[63] Enculturation of the populace via "the pursuit of true knowledge" was essential to the success of a democracy; "the chief method by which an individual could engage in the enculturating process was reading."[64] Although Cutter clearly distinguished between reading in pursuit of the noble cause of enculturation and reading for less lofty purposes, he was convinced that all reading was beneficial. This semi-egalitarian view of the role of reading was an essential component in Cutter's view of libraries as information systems in that "it placed the basic motivation for library work in the personal and essentially moral realm"; enculturation "provided a reason for being systematic."[65]

Cutter's view of the library was that "it was, or least had the potential to be, a rational interrelationship of parts and processes."[66] In a manner unprecedented for the time, he viewed the system as including not only the intellectual and content components of information, but also the processes through which access to information was provided and even the physical facility that housed information objects. He was possibly the first person to explicitly recognize the influence of heat and humidity on collections of information objects.

Cutter's dedication to systems thinking played a profound role in his design of classification systems and in his design and development of the *Rules.* The 261 rules of the first edition, which expanded to 369 by the 1904 fourth edition, do not individually stand on their own but rather collectively constitute a system that defines the life cycle of a library catalog. Cutter is known primarily for his direct contributions to the practice of library cataloging, but his real influence on the systematic nature of taxonomies and classification resides in his application of the systems approach.

CUTTER'S OBJECTS

Cutter was interested exclusively in the organization and creation of library catalogs, with the first two editions of the *Rules* focused explicitly on the creation of catalogs in the form of printed books, the dominant format at the time, although Cutter was also a pioneer in the implementation of catalogs in card form. Later editions of the *Rules* dropped the word "Printed" from the title.

Cutter identified three essential roles or "objects" for a catalog: (1) to assist in finding information, (2) to reveal the nature of information in a collection, and (3) to distinguish among sources of information in a collection. Cutter phrased this entirely within the context of books, but the general principle applies to any type of information.

Cutter's Objects

1. To enable a person to find a book of which either
   (A) the author
   (B) the title   } is known
   (C) the subject
2. To show what the library has
   (D) by a given author
   (E) on a given subject
   (F) in a given kind of literature
3. To assist in the choice of a book
   (G) as to its edition (bibliographically)
   (H) as to its character (literary or topical)

SYNDETIC STRUCTURE AND HIERARCHY

The hierarchical structure found in most modern taxonomies has its direct origin in Cutter's concern with syndetic structure. A dictionary definition of syndetic is: "of or using conjunctions."[67] Cutter provides a more detailed definition:

> *Syndetic.* connective, applied to that kind of dictionary catalogue which binds its entries together by means of cross-references so as to form a whole, the references being made from the most comprehensive subject to those of the next lower degree of comprehensiveness and from these to their subordinate subjects, and vice versa. These cross-references correspond to and are a good substitute for the arrangement in a systematic catalogue. References are also made in the syndetic catalogue to illustrative and coordinate subjects, and, if it is perfect, from specific to general subjects.[68]

Syndetic structure is one of those ideas that seem so obvious as to be organic; it is exceptional in that no one had previously formulated it and in how succinctly and carefully it is stated.

It is impossible to overstate the importance of syndetic structure in Cutter's *Rules*: it is the organizational system that drives relationships among concepts. Although Cutter thoroughly—perhaps even excessively—supported the use of natural language for headings, he explicitly recognized the limitations of a purely alphabetical arrangement, which he likened to a mob, asserting that "by a well-devised net-work of cross-references the mob becomes an army, of which part is capable of assisting many other parts."[69] A common misunderstanding is that Cutter "restricted the links in practice to downward references, *ie* from broader to narrower subjects, and suggested that we should ignore on economic grounds both upward links . . . and links from one term to another of equal rank."[70] It is clear, however, that Cutter viewed a "perfect" syndetic system as one that provided robust links of all kinds.

SPECIFIC ENTRY

A fundamental principle of the *Rules* is that of specific entry, which dictates that the primary identifying term for a concept should be the most specific term available in the vocabulary to describe the concept, "as distinct from entering it in a class which includes that subject."[71] The user of information system should have access to the hierarchy within which a term lies but should also have direct access to that term. Cutter did recognize that there may be emerging concepts for which terminology has not been standardized, and suggested that the only solution for such concepts is to identify them by a broader term. He also recommended, however, that some specific term should be used as soon as there is sufficient agreement on that term. Cutter, then, viewed vocabulary as being explicitly evolutionary, rather than bound by the constraints of changing use.

USER CONVENIENCE

An extremely important component in the design of Cutter's *Rules* is his focus on the convenience of the users of information systems. "The convenience of the public is always to be set before the ease of the cataloger," even when "the public's habitual way of looking at things" requires "a sacrifice of system and simplicity."[72] Although Cutter is unquestionably a proponent of standardization, it cannot be an absolute goal but must be applied within the general objective of making the system as usable as possible. Cutter is particularly insistent that usage provides the fundamental warrant for the choice of language in an information system: "Usage . . . is the supreme arbiter,—the usage, in the present case, not of the cataloger but of the public in speaking of subjects."[73] This is not quite the same as literary warrant, in that Cutter favored using the language of the people, not the language of content. Even this was not an absolute. Although Cutter favored resolving the choice of synonymous terms by granting preference to the term "that is most familiar to the class of people who consult the library," he suggested that a scientific term "may be preferable when the common name is ambiguous or of ill-defined extent."[74]

Jesse Shera, "Social Epistemology, General Semantics, and Librarianship," *Wilson Library Bulletin* 35 (June 1961): 767–70.

Jesse Hauk Shera (1903–82) earned a bachelor's degree in English from Miami University of Ohio and a master's degree in English from Yale University. He embarked on a career in librarianship immediately after completing his master's degree, first at the Scripps Foundation for Research in Population Problems and later, briefly, at the Library of Congress. He later earned a doctoral degree from the Graduate Library School at the University of Chicago. After a short post–World War II period of service with the Central Information Division of the Office of Strategic Services, he joined the faculty of the Graduate Library School. In 1951 he was named dean of the School of Library Service at Case Western University, where he remained until his retirement in 1970. Shera was a founding member of the American Documentation Institute, the forerunner of the American Society for Information Science & Technology, and was a major proponent of information science. Shera was a prolific author and profound thinker whose works have received more than five hundred entries in the *Social Sciences Citation Index*.

THE SEARCH FOR THE FOUNDATIONS OF LIBRARIANSHIP

Shera was undoubtedly one of the greatest library and information science philosophers of the twentieth century. He was particularly interested in generalizing a theory that would apply to all information and knowledge processes, both within and beyond the library context. His association with Margaret Egan at the University of Chicago Graduate Library School led him to explore epistemology, especially social epistemology, as the basis for that theory. Shera later explicitly credited Egan with the origin of the term, noting that although she apparently never used it in writing, "she used it frequently in class lectures and in conversation."[75]

THE NATURE OF KNOWLEDGE

Shera begins "Social Epistemology, General Semantics, and Librarianship" with a quote from John Rader Platt on the fundamental needs of humankind. Platt had added to the "traditional needs of man for air, water, food, and shelter" a fifth need for "'information,' for a continuous, novel, unpredictable, nonredundant, and surprising flow of stimuli."[76] Extending from Platt's idea, Shera contends that "the brain exists in order to organize and to weave patterns from information presented to it, and it becomes seriously deranged if this essential opportunity is denied. This activity of organizing information not only characterizes the sane mind, but also is necessary to the maintenance of sanity."[77] Shera echoes Popper and Polanyi by noting that such information must be supplied from outside the individual brain.

> External stimuli are necessary for the proper operation of the human nervous system. Without them the brain cannot reason, for it generates new information through clues and analogies, and it solves problems by fragmenting them into manageable parts with familiar connotations. Moreover, not only does the brain search for and process information telegraphed to it by the senses, but it also has closure. This is the ability to fill in informational gaps so that a conclusion can be achieved or a conceptualization formulated . . . despite the fact that a fragment of sensory evidence may be missing. Thus can be generated information that is anticipatory and, in a measure, independent of sensory perception.[78]

COLLECTIVE KNOWLEDGE

Shera is not, however, primarily interested in knowledge as it is characterized by the individual process of converting stimuli to absorbable information and from information to personal knowledge. His concern is with the nature of shared knowledge. "As the need for information drives the individual, so also it drives societies. It is the basis of collective, as well as individual, behavior."[79] Consideration of collective knowledge must include not only the roles of stimulus and perception, but also the roles of communication and language. "Knowledge and language are inseparable, for language is the symbolic structuring of knowledge into communicable form, and because it is the instrument by which knowledge is communicated, language itself can determine both individual and group conduct and behavior."[80] Increasing sophistication in the development of languages, first in oral form and later in graphic form, served not to increase the effectiveness of individuals, but to increase the effectiveness of and ensure the survival of groups and societies. Shera defines culture as "a duality of action and thought, bound together by the communication process."[81]

Cultures are highly dependent on the structures of language and communication. "The recorded history of the world of thought suggests that as man's knowledge increases in volume and complexity, it becomes increasingly interdependent, and tends toward fragmentation, centrifugation, and what we today glibly call specialization."[82] Shera calls for a new science of communication to concentrate on exploring and understanding this interdependence of language, communication, and culture. Although he is not directly dismissive of the fields of mass communication and communication studies, he does not feel that they have the focus of background to address this need. He similarly fails to find the necessary resources in psychology or philosophy. "Neither epistemologists nor psychologists have developed an ordered and comprehensive body of knowledge about intellectual differentiation and the integration of knowledge within a complex social organization."[83]

THE NATURE OF SOCIAL EPISTEMOLOGY

Shera finds in the failures of communication studies, philosophy, and psychology a need for a new discipline, "which, for want of a better name," he terms social epistemology. The purpose of social epistemology as a discipline is to "provide the social framework for the effective investigation of the entire complex problem of the intellectual processes of society—a study by which society as a whole seeks a perceptive relation to its total environment."

Social epistemology will "lift the study of intellectual life to that of a scrutiny of the individual to an inquiry into the means by which a society, nation, or culture achieves understanding of the totality of stimuli which act upon it. The focus of this new discipline will be upon the production, flow, integration, and consumption of all forms of communicated thought throughout the entire social pattern."[84] With this lofty set of goals, Shera extends librarianship as a discipline far beyond a concentration on the purposes, policies, practices, and processes of libraries and previews later definitions of information science and knowledge management.

Shera does not see social epistemology as an academic discipline divorced from the realities of practice, however. "Though social epistemology will have its own *corpus* of theoretical knowledge, it will be a very practical discipline, too."[85] Although "Social Epistemology, General Semantics, and Librarianship" doesn't extensively explicate the practical side of social epistemology, Shera does suggest that the discipline will play a role in determining the relationships between people and machines, particularly those "machines that extend man's mental power" for which "society is as yet psychologically and socially quite unprepared."[86] Shera was undoubtedly familiar with Wiener's *The Human Use of Human Beings* and provides a very Wieneresque assertion that "a society will permit itself to become subservient to machines only if it first allows itself to place a higher value on technology than it does on creative thought."[87]

Shera expanded on the role of social epistemology in 1965, stating that

> If the librarian's bibliographic and information systems are to be structured to conform as closely as possible to man's uses of recorded knowledge, the theoretical foundations of his profession must eventually provide answers to such questions as:
>
> > The problem of cognition—how man knows.
> >
> > The problem of social cognition—the ways in which society knows and the nature of the socio-psychological system by means of which personal knowledge becomes social knowledge.
> >
> > The problem of the history and philosophy of knowledge as they have evolved through time and in variant cultures.
> >
> > The problem of existing bibliographic mechanisms and systems and the extent to which they are in congruence with the realities of the communication process and the findings of epistemological inquiry.[88]

Although Shera was still vague about the practical applications of social epistemology, he provided a preview of many of the concerns of knowledge management, including the social nature of knowledge and the challenges of transforming tacit knowledge into explicit knowledge to achieve a collective benefit.

SOCIAL EPISTEMOLOGY, LIBRARIANSHIP, AND KNOWLEDGE MANAGEMENT

"The aim of librarianship, at whatever intellectual level it may operate, is to maximize the social utility of graphic records. . . . The librarian is the supreme 'time-binder,' and his is the most interdisciplinary of all the disciplines, for it is the ordering, relating, and structuring of knowledge and concepts."[89] This very knowledge management–oriented view of librarianship has its ultimate expression in Shera's conviction that "fundamentally, librarianship is the management of knowledge."[90]

LIBRARIANSHIP AND GENERAL SEMANTICS

Although Shera includes "General Semantics" in the title of his article, he actually has very little to say about general semantics. His assertion that "librarianship and general semantics should be natural allies, closely interrelated, and converging at many points" seems almost to be a throwaway, even when backed up with the explanation that "both are interdisciplinary to the highest degree, both are vitally concerned with the utilization of information by the human nervous system, both are important links in the communication chain, both are deeply involved in language, symbolism, abstraction, conceptualization, and evaluation," and, perhaps most importantly in Shera's mind, "both are fundamentally epistemological."[91] All this exploration of general semantics comes in the final paragraph of "Social Epistemology, General Semantics, and Librarianship," after the article really seems to have come to a natural end with a strong statement about the relationship between knowledge and machines. This seemingly tacked-on section on general semantics may be a direct result of the fact that Shera's ideas were based on a presentation at a colloquium sponsored by the Institute of General Semantics. Shera's article in the *Wilson Library Bulletin* was a condensation of an article with the same title that had earlier appeared in the *General Semantics Bulletin.*

In a 1962 talk at the University of Minnesota Library School, Shera revisited the links among semantics, epistemology, and librarianship, stating that "the bridge from semantics to epistemology is a natural one, for our knowledge about the nature of knowledge itself, how it is communicated through society and how it shapes a culture, is itself transmitted through a symbolic medium."[92]

THE IMPACT OF SHERA'S SOCIAL EPISTEMOLOGY

Shera's somewhat idiosyncratic use of the word "epistemology" may have mitigated against the impact he sought for his model of a philosophy for the information professions. Although Shera argued that social epistemology was something distinct from the sociology of knowledge, Budd's analysis indicated that Shera's thinking was much more closely allied with sociology than with epistemology.[93] The term "social epistemology" reappeared independently in the late 1980s to describe an emerging area of interest among epistemologists in the social nature of knowledge. Zandonade detailed the relationship, or lack thereof, between Shera's social epistemology and this later social epistemology as exemplified by the works of Steve Fuller.[94] Fuller presented the following fundamental question to be addressed by social epistemology: "How should the pursuit of knowledge be organized, given that under normal circumstances knowledge is pursued by many human beings, each working on a more or less well defined body of knowledge and each equipped with roughly the same imperfect cognitive capacities, albeit with varying degrees of access to one another's activities?"[95] Fuller later defined social epistemology as

> An intellectual movement of broad cross-disciplinary provenance that attempts to reconstruct the problems of *epistemology* once knowledge is regarded as intrinsically social. It is often seen as philosophical science policy or the normative wing of *science studies*. Originating in studies of academic knowledge production, social epistemology has begun to encompass knowledge in *multicultural* and public settings, as well as the conversion of knowledge to *information technology* and *intellectual property*.[96]

This is remarkably similar to Shera's definition of social epistemology, especially given that Fuller did not cite Shera and was apparently at the time unaware of Shera's earlier work. In 1996 Fuller acknowledged Shera's contribution and specifically recognized the similarity of orientation of his ideas and Shera's. Fuller's explanation that the difference in theoretical bases was an important distinction seems somewhat disingenuous.[97]

Ultimately, Shera's social epistemology looks very much like a general model for what is now being called an ontology, a way of looking at and thinking about the world that leads to explicit decisions about representing and organizing knowledge. Shera may have doomed his core philosophy to extinction by aligning it with the wrong branch of philosophy.

B. C. Vickery, "Ontologies," *Journal of Information Science* 23 (1997): 277–86.

B. C. Vickery (1918–) was born in Australia and earned a master's degree in chemistry from Oxford University. He was appointed librarian at the Akers Research Laboratories of Imperial Chemical Industries in 1946 and later held positions at the National Lending Library for Science and Technology and the University of Manchester Institute of Science and Technology. From 1966 to 1973 he was research director for Aslib. In 1973 he became director of the School of Library, Archive and Information Studies at University College London, where he remained until his retirement in 1983. Vickery's works have generated more than five hundred citation entries in the *Social Sciences Citation Index*.

SEEKING CLARITY OUT OF CONFUSION

Vickery recognizes the confusion inherent in the emerging use of the term "ontology" and attempts to ameliorate it by tracing the origins of current usage, comparing and contrasting definitions, and providing examples of ontologies and their use. He finds the direct origin of the concept in artificial intelligence and the shift that took place in the 1980s from attempts to model human thought to attempts to model instead those domains that are the objects of human thought. "By the end of the 1980s it was accepted that 'domain conceptualisation' was a necessary part of knowledge acquisition for a knowledge-based system."[98] Vickery also links ontologies to Hayes's concept of "task-independent conceptual analysis."[99]

DEFINING ONTOLOGIES

Vickery turns to Gruber's definition of ontology, which he asserts "seems generally to be accepted." An ontology is "an abstract, simplified view of the world that we wish to represent for some purpose . . . an explicit specification of a conceptualization."[100] This definition appears to have three fundamental characteristics: (1) an ontology is an artificial construct that may have a link to a naturally occurring phenomenon, (2) an ontology is a tool for knowledge representation, and (3) an ontology is an explicit but abstract and simplified conceptualization. "Ontologies, writes Gruber, are often equated with taxonomic hierarchies of classes, with class definitions and the subsumption relation, but they need not be limited to these forms."[101] Vickery does not provide any guidance as to other forms an ontology may take and ultimately, even though he cites a number of commentaries on the nature of ontologies, fails to provide a concise definition. He does indicate that one of the variables in definitions of ontology is that the definition is a function of the purpose for which an individual wishes to use the term. Vickery especially notes the distinction between "those who aim to build a general ontology, taking all knowledge for its province, and those who are concentrating on an ontology for a specific domain."[102]

EXAMPLES OF ONTOLOGIES

The bulk of Vickery's article consists of descriptions of four ontology-based systems: CYC, MIKROKOSMOS, GALEN, and ENTERPRISE. CYC is an attempt at a general ontology, "a formalised representation of a vast quantity of fundamental human knowledge: facts, rules of thumb, and heuristics for reasoning about the objects of everyday life."[103] It is a formal logical system in which assertions are linked to form statements. CYC employs an extremely complex and specific system of symbolic notation to build explicit hierarchies.

MIKROKOSMOS was designed to support transporting information among systems that use different internal structures. In MIKROKOSMOS, "interlingual meaning representation for [machine translation] is derived from representations of word meanings in computational lexicons and from representations of world knowledge in ontologies."[104] The fundamental purposes of the system are (1) "representing meanings of different languages," (2) "representing meanings of natural language texts," and (3) "sharing knowledge between different lexical knowledge bases."[105] The structure of MIKROKOSMOS resembles Ranganathan's PMEST system but somewhat simplified. Each concept is represented by three essential elements: (1) an object, which can be physical, mental, or social; (2) an event, which can also be physical, mental, or social; and (3) a property, which can be either an attribute or a relation. Overall, the system strongly resembles a well-designed thesaurus for an information storage and retrieval system. MIKROKOSMOS has been used experimentally to translate between Spanish and English language knowledge bases.

GALEN, the Generalized Architecture for Languages, Encyclopedias, and Nomenclatures in Medicine, is "a 'semantically sound' model of clinical terminology."[106] GALEN models fundamental clinical concepts (bone, fracture, humerus), orientations (left, right), and relationships in a complex medical coding system.

ENTERPRISE is an ontology system for business. ENTERPRISE uses a very compact language of about one hundred terms that can be combined to represent business activities and products. Terms are grouped into four roles: (1) activities and processes, (2) organizations, (3) strategies, and (4) marketing. This nonhierarchical dictionary resides within the context of a "metaontology" that defines relationships among the four categories. Relationships include roles, attributes, and actors.

BUILDING AND USING ONTOLOGIES

Vickery devotes about one-and-a-half pages to the processes and methods of constructing ontologies, relying mostly on the works of other authors. He summarizes the general process as follows:

> Clearly, the domain to be covered by the ontology must first be decided, and a specification document must be drawn up. Concept terms are collected by scanning the literature of the domain, and by consulting domain experts. A "brainstorming" session with experts is recommended, to produce significant terms and their relative importance.[107]

Vickery then describes the process of grouping terms, resolving synonyms, developing cross-references and definitions, and deciding on the structure of the meta-ontology. He cites Mahesh's guidelines for "ontological engineering," which include (1) the inherently artificial nature of ontologies, (2) the need to make ontologies task specific, (3) usability, (4) the ability to accommodate new concepts and new relationships, (5) granularity, and (6) redundancy.[108] Overall, the process and problems as described are remarkably similar to Lancaster's guidance on the creation of a thesaurus.[109]

Vickery recapitulates the nature of ontologies by writing, "An ontology may be regarded as a database with information about what categories and/or concepts exist in the world/domain, what properties they have, and how they relate to each other."[110] This is very straightforward and is the clearest definition yet, but it is inherently rather dissatisfying. Defining concepts, properties, and relationships is the central function of a well-constructed controlled vocabulary. Vickery's definition seems to imply that an ontology is essentially a database with a good thesaurus, which is probably not what is meant by most people writing about ontologies.

Fortunately, Vickery has not missed the analogy with vocabulary control and suggests that the primary difference is that "the uses intended for ontologies are not the same as for classifications and thesauri."[111] Vickery laments, however, that "ontological engineers" appear to have been largely ignorant of the work that has gone before them in the domains of bibliographic organization and information science. Vickery further notes that, with a few notable exceptions, "there is not much appreciation that constructing an ontology is not such a new activity" and traces ontology development to Wilkins's work in 1668 and Roget's 1852 thesaurus.[112] Vickery closes his article with an expression of hope "that all involved will continue to learn about each other's experience."[113]

NOTES

1. *American Heritage Dictionary of the English Language,* 4th ed., s.v. "Taxonomy."

2. Denise Bruno and Heather Richmond, "The Truth about Taxonomies," *Information Management Journal* 37 (March/April 2003): 45.

3. Arlene G. Taylor, *The Organization of Information,* 2nd ed. (Westport, CT: Libraries Unlimited, 2004), 1.

4. "Ten Taxonomy Myths," *Montague Institute Review,* November 2002, http://www.montague.com/review/myths.html (accessed March 1, 2007).

5. *American Heritage Dictionary of the English Language,* 4th ed., s.v. "Classification."

6. Elaine Svenonius, *The Intellectual Foundations of Information Organization* (Cambridge, MA: MIT Press, 2000), 10.

7. Barbara H. Kwasnik, "The Role of Classification in Knowledge Representation and Discovery," *Library Trends* 48 (Summer 1999): 24.

8. Taylor, *The Organization of Information,* 297.

9. Amy J. Warner, "A Taxonomy Primer," http://www.lexonomy.com/publications/aTaxonomyPrimer.html (accessed March 1, 2007).

10. A. C. Foskett, *The Subject Approach to Information,* 2nd ed. (Hamden, CT: Linnet & Clive Bingley, 1969), 26.

11. Svenonius, *The Intellectual Foundations,* 10.

12. Ibid., 11.

13. Kwasnik, "The Role of Classification," 24.

14. Leo E. La Montagne, "Historical Background of Classification," in *The Subject Analysis of Library Materials,* edited by Maurice Tauber (New York: Columbia University School of Library Service, 1953), 19.

15. Taylor, *The Organization of Information,* 298.

16. La Montagne, "Historical Background," 19.

17. John P. Comaromi, "The Foundations of the Dewey Decimal Classification: The First Two Editions," in *Melvil Dewey: The Man and the Classification,* edited by Gordon Stevenson and Judith Kramer-Greene (Albany, NY: Forest Press, 1983), 136.

18. Foskett, *The Subject Approach to Information,* 208.

19. Ibid., 297.

20. Ibid., 290.

21. Ibid., 257.

22. Ibid., 84.

23. Ibid., 135.

24. Warner, "A Taxonomy Primer."

25. F. W. Lancaster, *Vocabulary Control for Information Retrieval,* 2nd ed. (Arlington, VA: Information Resources Press, 1986), 7–8.

26. Foskett, *The Subject Approach to Information,* 21.

27. Bruno and Richmond, "The Truth about Taxonomies," 45.

28. Kwasnik, "The Role of Classification," 24–42.

29. Taylor, *The Organization of Information,* 298.

30. Thomas D. Wason, "Dr. Tom's Taxonomy Guide," http://www.twason.com/drtomtax onomiesguide.html (accessed March 1, 2007).

31. Foskett, *The Subject Approach to Information,* 43.

32. Kwasnik, "The Role of Classification," 30.

33. Ibid.

34. Ibid., 35.

35. Ibid., 38–39.

36. Foskett, *The Subject Approach to Information,* 93.

37. Kwasnik, "The Role of Classification," 42.

38. Lars Marius Garshol, "Metadata? Thesauri? Taxonomies? Topic Maps! Making Sense of It All," *Journal of Information Science* 30, no. 4 (2004): 378.

39. Warner, "A Taxonomy Primer."

40. Garshol, "Metadata? Thesauri? Taxonomies?" 379.

41. Taylor, *The Organization of Information,* 139.

42. Ibid., 148.

43. Ibid., 150–51.

44. Lois Mai Chan and Marcia Lei Zeng, "Metadata Interoperabiity and Standardization—a Study of Methodology. Part I: Achieving Interoperability at the Schema Level," *D-Lib* 12, no. 6 (June 2006), http://www.dlib.org/dlib/june06/chan/06chan.html (accessed March 6, 2007).

45. Sherry L. Vellucci, "Metadata and Authority Control," *Library Resources & Technical Services* 44 (January 2000): 44.

46. Michael Gorman, "Authority Control in the Context of Bibliographic Control in the Electronic Environment," *Cataloging & Classification Quarterly* 38, no. 3/4 (2004): 15.

47. Ibid.

48. *American Heritage Dictionary of the English Language,* 4th ed., s.v. "Ontology."

49. *Encyclopaedia Britannica Online Academic Edition,* s.v. "Ontology."

50. Thomas Hofweber, "Logic and Ontology," in *Stanford Encyclopedia of Philosophy,* edited by Edward N. Zalta (Stanford, CA: Metaphysics Research Lab, 2004), http://plato.stanford.edu (accessed March 7, 2007).

51. Steven Fuller, "If Everything Always Is, Why Hasn't There Always Been Ontology?" *IEEE Intelligent Systems* 19 (January/February 2004): 73.

52. Ibid., 74.

53. Thomas R. Gruber, "A Translation Approach to Portable Ontology Specifications," *Knowledge Acquisition* 5 (June 1993): 199.

54. B. Chandrasekaran, John R. Josephson, and V. Richard Benjamins, "What Are Ontologies, and Why Do We Need Them?" *IEEE Intelligent Systems* 14 (January/February 1999): 20–26.

55. Yorick Wilks, "Are Ontologies Distinctive Enough for Computations over Knowledge?" *IEEE Intelligent Systems* 19 (January/February 2004): 75.

56. Christine W. Chan, "From Knowledge Modeling to Ontology Construction," *International Journal of Software Engineering and Knowledge Engineering* 14, no. 6 (2004): 604.

57. Christophe Roche, "From Information Society to Knowledge Society: The Ontology Issue" (paper presented at the Fifth International Conference of Computing Anticipatory Systems, Liège, Belgium, 2001), 576.

58. Ronald J. Brachman and Hector J. Levesque, *Knowledge Representation and Reasoning* (Amsterdam: Elsevier, 2004), 32.

59. John F. Sowa, *Knowledge Representation: Logical, Philosophical, and Computational Foundations* (Pacific Grove, CA: Brooks/Cole, 2000), 492.

60. Theresa Edgington, Beomijn Choi, Katherine Henson, T. S. Raghu, and Ajay Vinze, "Adopting Ontology to Facilitate Knowledge Sharing," *Communications of the ACM* 47, no. 11 (2004): 86.

61. Wilks, "Are Ontologies Distinctive Enough," 75.

62. Francis L. Miksa, *Charles Ammi Cutter: Library Systematizer* (Littleton, CO: Libraries Unlimited, 1977), 29–34.

63. Ibid., 35.

64. Ibid.

65. Ibid., 44.

66. Ibid.

67. *American Heritage Dictionary of the English Language,* 4th ed., s.v. "Syndetic."

68. Charles A. Cutter, *Rules for a Printed Dictionary Catalog* (Washington, DC: Government Printing Office, 1875), 14.

69. Ibid., 57.

70. Foskett, *The Subject Approach to Information,* 55.

71. Cutter, *Rules for a Printed Dictionary Catalog,* 14.

72. Charles A. Cutter, *Rules for a Dictionary Catalog,* 4th ed. (Washington, DC: Government Printing Office, 1904), 6.

73. Ibid., 69.

74. Ibid., 70.

75. Jesse Shera, "An Epistemological Foundation for Library Science," in *The Foundations of Education for Librarianship* (New York: Becker and Hayes, 1972), 112.

76. Jesse Shera, "Social Epistemology, General Semantics, and Librarianship," *Wilson Library Bulletin* 35 (June 1961): 767.

77. Ibid.

78. Ibid., 767–68.

79. Ibid., 768.

80. Ibid.

81. Ibid.

82. Ibid., 769.

83. Ibid.

84. Ibid.

85. Ibid.

86. Ibid.

87. Ibid., 770.

88. Jesse Shera, "An Epistemological Foundation for Library Science" (paper presented at the Foundations of Access to Knowledge: A Symposium, Syracuse, NY, 1965), 9–10.

89. Shera, "Social Epistemology," 770.

90. Ibid.

91. Ibid.

92. Jesse Shera, "The Propaedeutic of the New Librarianship," in *Documentation and the Organization of Knowledge* (Hamden, CT: Archon, 1966), 66.

93. John M. Budd, "Jesse Shera, Sociologist of Knowledge?" *Library Quarterly* 72 (October 2002): 423–40.

94. Tarcisio Zandonade, "Social Epistemology from Jesse Shera to Steve Fuller," *Library Trends* 52 (Spring 2004): 810–32.

95. Steve Fuller, "On Regulating What Is Known: A Way to Social Epistemology," *Synthese* 73, no. 1 (1987): 145.

96. Steve Fuller, "Social Epistemology," in *The Norton Dictionary of Modern Thought,* edited by Alan Bullock and Stephen Trombley (New York: W. W. Norton, 1999), 801.

97. Steve Fuller, "Recent Work in Social Epistemology," *American Philosophical Quarterly* 33, no. 2 (1996): 149.

98. B. C. Vickery, "Ontologies," *Journal of Information Science* 23, no. 4 (1997): 277.

99. Ibid., 278.
100. Ibid.
101. Ibid.
102. Ibid., 279.
103. Ibid.
104. Ibid.
105. Ibid., 280.
106. Ibid., 281.
107. Ibid., 282.
108. Ibid., 283.
109. Lancaster, *Vocabulary Control.*
110. Vickery, "Ontologies," 284.
111. Ibid.
112. Ibid.
113. Ibid., 285.

9

Informatics and Information Technology

cybernetics The theory or study of communication and control in living organisms or machines.

1948 N. WIENER *Cybernetics* 19 We have decided to call the entire field of control and communication theory, whether in the machine or in the animal, by the name Cybernetics.

informatics

1967 *FID News Bull.* XVII. 73/2 Informatics is the discipline of science which investigates the structure and properties (not specific content) of scientific information, as well as the regularities of scientific information activity, its theory, history, methodology and organization.

IN THIS CHAPTER

KEY CONCEPTS

The Uneasy Link between Knowledge Management and Technology
Technology and People
Knowledge Management Applications of Technology
Challenges to the Role of Information Technology in Knowledge Management
The Impact of Technology
Social Informatics
Applications of Social Informatics

KEY PAPERS

Norbert Wiener, *The Human Use of Human Beings: Cybernetics and Society*
Rob Kling, "Towards a Person-Centered Computer Technology"
Rob Kling, "What Is Social Informatics and Why Does It Matter?"

THE UNEASY LINK BETWEEN KNOWLEDGE MANAGEMENT AND TECHNOLOGY

Knowledge management is, to some people, primarily about the effective application of technology to solve knowledge and information problems. In one of the earliest commentaries on knowledge management and technology, Worthley expressed concern that in the 1975 *Public Administration Symposium,* "the computer was not mentioned yet alone discussed and analyzed."[1] A 2004 news feature in *Nature* pictured knowledge management systems in terms of software that "builds up a picture of who knows what in an organization, and uses the information to connect queries with answers."[2] Chou and Lin stated that "Information technology . . . is a powerful enabling factor for capturing the organizational knowledge and sharing it internally and accessing others' knowledge externally."[3] According to Alavi and Leidner, "advanced computer storage technology and sophisticated retrieval techniques . . . can be effective tools in enhancing organizational memory."[4] Frappaolo and Capshaw included technology in their core definition of knowledge management: "Knowledge management refers to the practices and technologies that facilitate the efficient creation and exchange of knowledge on the organizationwide level."[5] Flanagin's view was that "recent developments suggest that technological tools are progressively more capable of providing meaningful support for KM applications."[6]

To others, knowledge management has little or no relationship with technology. McDermott, in an exploration of the past and future roles of information technology in knowledge management, referred to the false expectations that can accompany technological solutions. "Information technology has led many companies to imagine a new world of leveraged knowledge. . . . As a result, many companies are rethinking how work gets done, linking people through electronic media so they can leverage each other's knowledge."[7] Stromquist and Samoff shared this concern regarding potentially unattainable expectations and extended it to a broader societal level. "With the advent of widespread use of computer-mediated communications technologies, such as e-mail and the World Wide Web, has come the expectation that information and its more complex articulation—knowledge—will become more accessible, focused to meet needs of specific social sectors and their decision-makers, and able to improve the basis on which public policies are made."[8]

Gamble and Blackwell commented that "trying to implement a knowledge management system of any scale without technology is extremely difficult but the technology of itself does not make the knowledge management system work; it can facilitate and enable connections and communications but it will not make them happen."[9] Wiig's take was similar: "Information technology . . . and related technologies are significant, but secondary factors. They serve mostly as passive infrastructure and are not as central for competitive superiority as it was generally thought in the 1990s. This may change if IT becomes smarter and more sophisticated."[10]

This tension regarding the real and potential roles of technology in knowledge management arises at least in part from the motives that lead organizations to seek technological solutions. According to Tiwana, "technology drivers from knowledge management are either motivated by new opportunities that have arisen for companies to compete through knowledge process differentiation using technology or through their failure to compete sustainably using technology. . . . Technology, by itself, is simply an entry-precursor and core-capability *leveler,* not a competitive differentiator."[11]

A further concern has to do with expectations regarding the immediacy of the impact of technology. Tiwana suggested that "the companies that will truly thrive are those that can use their information technology assets to leverage their people's knowledge in ways that are immediately applicable."[12] Gamble and Blackwell, however, noted the inevitable lag time in achieving results through implementation of technology. "Another important point to recognize is that if technology is going to be used, not only is the enterprise going to spend money, perhaps lots of it, but it is also probably going to reduce performance in the short term before a medium- or longer-term improvement is realized."[13]

TECHNOLOGY AND PEOPLE

For many commentators, the focus on information technology in knowledge management inappropriately draws attention away from people. Wiig, who titled his book *People-Focused Knowledge Management: How Effective Decision Making Leads to Corporate Success,* expressed concern that "during the last decade, the perception was often that technology was central to success. However, the business world is increasingly realizing that the effectiveness of enterprises rests upon people."[14] Tiwana echoed that sentiment: "As we move further into the information age, the interesting counterintuitive shift that becomes evident is that of the firm's anthropocentricity—dependence on people."[15] Gamble and Blackwell wrote in a similar vein: "Since first and foremost knowledge management involves working with people and their ideas, what needs to be thought about is what kind of technology will fit with each small community, small grouping or small department as appropriate. . . . This is not a case where one size fits all."[16] This last concern about the potentially unitary application of technological solutions resonated with Tanriverdi: "It is not appropriate to standardize all aspects of the IT infrastructure since business units need autonomy for meeting their specific IT needs."[17]

It is not at all clear, however, how focusing on people rather than technology advances the purposes of knowledge management. Even authors whose major premise is the need to focus on people cannot avoid discussing the role of technology. Wiig wrote that "apart from increased work complexity, the workplace itself is equipped with sophisticated work-aids that often take considerable understanding to handle and exploit" and offered a list of technology-based "work-aids."[18] Many early expositions on the role of technology in business espoused the benefits of directly replacing people with machines. There is a difficult dynamic tension in the knowledge management literature regarding the core focuses of knowledge management, which clearly have to do with communication and transformation of the workplace to enhance shared learning, and the tools and techniques necessary to support organizational activities, which are primarily tied to computer information technology.

HUMAN AND SOCIAL CONCERNS IN KNOWLEDGE MANAGEMENT

Many commentators have expressed concern that knowledge management in practice, as opposed to knowledge management theory, lacks an appropriate focus on human factors and the role of knowledge management as a fundamentally social process. Thomas, Kellogg, and Erickson expressed concern that knowledge management "pays little attention to human and social factors."[19] They concluded that knowledge management requires the creation and support of a knowledge community, "a place within which people discover, use, and manipulate knowledge, and can encounter and interact with others who are doing likewise."[20] They promoted social computing and knowledge socialization as approaches to supporting knowledge communities. "Social computing has to do with digital systems that draw upon social information and context to enhance the activity and performance of people, organizations, and systems. . . . Knowledge socialization . . . describes a constellation of projects around the use of stories and storytelling in business settings."[21]

Moffett, McAdams, and Parkinson found that a plurality of firms were approaching knowledge management initiatives from a primarily technology-centered viewpoint, while only 14 percent of the firms they studied were focused primarily on human factors and transformation of organizational culture.[22] Stromquist and Samoff expressed concern that knowledge management systems carry the risk of "presenting access to knowledge in fragmented and decontextualized ways, introducing a layer of mediators whose view of knowledge and intentions about its use may not coincide with those of the primary users. . . . Notwithstanding its democratic potential and promise, KMS approaches are likely to reinforce existing power relations . . . [and] may foster the growth of an intellectual elite."[23]

KNOWLEDGE MANAGEMENT APPLICATIONS OF TECHNOLOGY

Flanagin identified two major focuses for the application of technology to knowledge management that align directly with the distinction between explicit and tacit knowledge. "The dominant strategy has been to identify and develop technologies for the capture, storage, retrieval, and dissemination of explicit knowledge. The chief concern has been how to extract an individual's knowledge, place it in a format and location that are accessible to relevant others, and ensure that this knowledge is utilized in the achievement of organizational goals."[24]

According to Gamble and Blackwell, "technology support can be divided into two broad classes": (1) "transfer and exchange systems" and (2) "data analysis and performance support."[25] Transfer and exchange systems include databases, knowledge repositories, expertise banks, and similar technologies for encoding and preserving knowledge. Data analysis and performance support technologies include "data to knowledge conversion systems, data mining decision support and real time intelligent data analysis."[26]

Frappaolo and Capshaw identified four essential functions of technological solutions to knowledge management needs:

1. "Intermediation, which refers to the connection of people to people"
2. "Externalization, the connection of information source to information source"
3. "Internalization, the connection of explicit knowledge to people or knowledge seekers"
4. "Cognition, which connects knowledge to process"[27]

Gallupe's analysis provided four major categories of goals or purposes for knowledge management technologies:

1. "Encouraging serendipity," which Gallupe equated with problem recognition. Tools that contribute to this goal include chat rooms, environmental scanning, and search functions.
2. "Knowledge creation" focuses on problem solving and includes such solutions as computer-mediated discussion groups, online knowledge forums, and digital brainstorming.
3. "Knowledge acquisition" technologies have to do with codification and storage of knowledge and include knowledge repositories and knowledge mapping tools.
4. "Mentoring and training" tools support learning and knowledge transfer. These tools include those that support formal online learning and informal interpersonal communication.[28]

Bowman's categorization concentrated not on purposes or functions, but on specific types of application software, including intranets, Web authoring tools, document and content management systems, search engines, office productivity suites, collaboration tools, and enterprise portals.[29] Given that all these technologies have multiple purposes, many of which have no permanent relationship to knowledge management, their identification as specifically being knowledge management technologies is questionable. Luan and Serban's grouping is similar in specificity, but slightly more knowledge management oriented, including business intelligence, knowledge bases, collaboration systems, content and document management, portals, customer relationship management, data mining, workflow analysis, searching, and e-learning.[30]

CHALLENGES TO THE ROLE OF INFORMATION TECHNOLOGY IN KNOWLEDGE MANAGEMENT

This diversity of approaches to identifying and defining those technologies or technology functions essential to knowledge management is a major obstacle to understanding and communicating the role of technology in knowledge management. Many technology-centered knowledge management initiatives have been colossal money-wasting failures. A 2005 study, for instance, indicated that 51 percent of large-scale technology projects were finished later than scheduled and over budget; only 10 percent of the corporate representatives polled felt that the return from information technology investment was high.[31] Damodaran and Olphert attributed these failures, at least in part, to the technology-centric focus on "technology push," which they identified as "not sufficient to achieve the necessary organization culture and context which will promote organizational learning."[32]

Flanagin identified three major issues related to the application of technology to knowledge management (KM):

1. There is a "tendency to artificially reduce knowledge complexity with the use of technologies for KM. In essence, the trend in KM has been to condense knowledge to less than it is in order to increase the capacity to process it efficiently."
2. "KM applications may be limited by focusing primarily on the individual as the source of knowledge. Recent changes in organizational structures, forms, and the nature of association, however, endorse a richer view of the location of knowledge."
3. "Because tacit knowledge is viewed as tremendously personal and contextual, it is often seen as an inappropriate candidate for technological support in KM applications."[33]

THE IMPACT OF TECHNOLOGY

Tanriverdi studied information technology relatedness, which is defined as "the use of common IT infrastructures and common IT management processes across business units."[34] IT relatedness has four components: (1) relatedness of IT infrastructures, which is evidenced by the use of "common standards for general-purpose hardware, software, and communications technologies," (2) relatedness of IT strategy-making processes, which is reflected in "a common IT strategy-making process that provides a general strategic direction for the IT decisions of the business units" and "allows the business units to develop their unique IT strategies, but . . . also increases their adherence to corporate objectives," (3) relatedness of IT human resource management processes, which is found in "sharing of common goals, principles, values, and language among the IT talent in the business units," and (4) relatedness of IT vendor management processes, such that vendor relationships are managed "as an interrelated portfolio of relationships while allowing the business units to source their IT needs from the vendors of their choice."[35] Tanriverdi found that these factors are indeed related to knowledge management performance: "IT relatedness has a significant effect on the KM capacity, and KM capacity, in turn, has significant effects on market-based and accounting-based firm performance. IT relatedness also has significant indirect effects on market-based and accounting-based performance of the firm through the mediation of KM capacity."[36]

Mitchell looked at the relationship between technology and knowledge management from an essentially opposite viewpoint from that of Tanriverdi, exploring the link between knowledge integration and technology project performance. She specifically examined the influences of access to external knowledge, evidenced in such factors as "frequency of communication with external colleagues" and other approaches to "importing new knowledge through external communication channels," and internal knowledge integration, evidenced by "social interaction among individuals using communication channels for knowledge transfer to arrive at a common perspective for problem solving," on on-time project completion.[37] Her results demonstrated that "higher levels of integrative capability minimize IT delays through better prediction and execution, thereby promoting timely project completion."[38]

Heintze and Bretschneider's study of almost six hundred county-level public organizations found that the introduction of information technology had no meaningful impact on organizational structure, communication, or decision-making processes. They observed that "little restructuring occurs in local government agencies as a result of IT implementation. When restructuring does occur, it has only a very small impact on the performance of the agency."[39] They did, however, find that the introduction of information technology had an impact on overall organizational performance.

SOCIAL INFORMATICS

The most cogent and compact definitions of social informatics are perhaps those from Kling's 1999 article, "What Is Social Informatics and Why Does It Matter?"

> A serviceable working conception of "social informatics" is that it identifies a body of research that examines the social aspects of computerization. A more formal definition is "the interdisciplinary study of the design, uses and consequences of information technologies that takes into account their interaction with institutional and cultural contexts."[40]

The origin of the term "social informatics" is unclear, although it was in use at least as early as 1989.[41] Halavais suggested a much broader definition: "Social informatics aims to understand the relationship of technological systems to social systems."[42]

Social informatics is closely related to and overlaps community informatics, which has been defined as "a multidisciplinary field for the investigation and development of the social and cultural factors shaping the development and diffusion of new ICTs and its effects upon community development, regeneration and sustainability."[43] Bishop and Bruce added to this definition of community informatics the characteristic of "enabling communities with information and communications technologies," which seems to emphasize a direct role in influencing action as much as a research orientation.[44]

Sawyer identified a number of other related terms, including "the social analysis of computing, human-centered computing, social studies of information technology and the sociology of computing." According to Sawyer, the name is less important than the perspective that social informatics provides, which is "complex, situated, multi-level, multi-effect and socio-technical."[45] Halavais provided the additional terms "social computing," "sociable media," and "social software," as well as "computer-mediated communication, computer supported collective work and human-computer interaction."[46]

Sawyer outlined five common findings about information and communication technology (ICT) that had emerged over the course of "more than 30 years of careful empirical research in the social informatics tradition":

1. Uses of ICT lead to multiple and sometimes paradoxical effects.
2. Uses of ICT shape thought and action in ways that benefit some groups more than others.
3. The differential effects of the design, implementation and uses of ICTs often have moral and ethical consequences.
4. The design, implementation and uses of ICTs have reciprocal relationships with the larger social context.
5. The phenomenon of interest will vary by the level of analysis.[47]

Sawyer's final point about variations in level of interest and analysis is an important one. Commentators on social informatics are quite mixed in their approaches. Halavais adopted a deliberately high-level approach in which social informatics could be applied to the study of doorknobs.[48] Sawyer took a more middle-of-the road stance in which social informatics examines problems in their "institutional and cultural contexts, including organizations and society."[49] Davenport assumed a much narrower focus, concentrating on "workplace or organizational computing."[50]

APPLICATIONS OF SOCIAL INFORMATICS

Social informatics has both an explanatory role in fostering understanding of the relationships between people and technology and a potential pragmatic role in driving systems design. Davenport described social informatics as "a research approach that is embedded in practice" but provided little evidence or explanation of ways in which social informatics directly affects practice.[51] Karamuftuoglu asserted that "information retrieval research has been somewhat slow in recognizing the power latent in social relations that tie the users of information systems together."[52] He concluded that current approaches to information retrieval have two fundamental limitations: (1) they assume that information seeking is exclusively an information transmission process and (2) they assume that information seeking is entirely individual.[53] Karamuftuoglu presented a theoretical model in which collaboration could effectively lead to the production of new knowledge and identified newsgroups, e-mail, and similar online collaboration tools as primitive examples of the potential role of collaboration in information retrieval.[54] Tang also presented a model for "participative design" in which "users' social context and relationships [would] be considered in the design and evaluation of [information retrieval] systems" and suggested that the traditional measures of retrieval system performance—precision and recall, which are both based on the concept of relevance—may be inadequate for "a more user- and use-centered concept of relevance."[55] It is unclear whether any of these ideas resulted in the transformation of information and communication technology systems design. Although social informatics has direct implications for the social networking environment proposed as the basis for Web 2.0, neither the social informatics literature nor the knowledge management literature has drawn any direct links to or from Web 2.0. The ultimate benefit of social informatics may lie in its explanatory qualities rather than its contributions to action.

Norbert Wiener, *The Human Use of Human Beings: Cybernetics and Society* (Boston: Houghton Mifflin, 1950).

Norbert Wiener (1894–1964) was born in Columbia, Missouri. A child prodigy in mathematics, he graduated from high school at age 11 and received a bachelor's degree in mathematics from Tufts College at age 14, and a PhD in philosophy from Harvard University at age 18. Following the completion of his doctorate, he studied with Bertrand Russell at Cambridge University for two years. Wiener joined the faculty of the mathematics department at the Massachusetts Institute of Technology in 1920 and remained there until his retirement in 1960. *The Human Use of Human Beings: Cybernetics and Society* is a popularization of his earlier *Cybernetics, or Control and Communication in the Animal and the Machine* (Cambridge, MA: Technology Press, 1948), in which he introduced the term "cybernetics." *The Human Use of Human Beings* has received more than 150 citation entries in the *Social Sciences Citation Index*. Wiener has received more than four thousand citation entries.

CYBERNETICS DEFINED

A dictionary definition of cybernetics is "the theoretical study of communication and control processes in biological, mechanical, and electronic systems, especially the comparison of these processes in biological and artificial systems."[56] Wiener grounded his definition of cybernetics in terms of the "study of messages, and in particular of the effective messages of control."[57] His specific definition is found in his *Cybernetics, or Control and Communication in the Animal and the Machine:* "We have decided to call the entire field of control and communication theory, whether in the machine or in the animal, by the name Cybernetics."[58] The word has its origin in the Greek word for "the art of pilot or steersman."[59] The *Oxford English Dictionary* notes that a similar word, *cybernétique,* entered the French language in 1834.[60]

Wiener came to cybernetics by a fairly circuitous route. When he joined the mathematics faculty at MIT, the department was in the midst of a transition from a primarily pragmatic and practice-oriented program designed to meet the needs of engineers to a more explicitly theoretical identity. This was a highly productive environment for Wiener, who early on "solved the problem of integration in function spaces," developed a mathematical model for Brownian motion, formulated a set of axioms for what later became known as Banach spaces, and dabbled with potential theory.[61]

WAR AND AUTOMATION

Wiener developed a close relationship with the engineering department, but his work remained primarily in the more theoretical areas of mathematics until the late 1920s, when he worked closely with Vannevar Bush on the development of the Differential Analyzer. As was true of many other developments related to automation and computers, Wiener's initial work on what he later termed cybernetics was an outgrowth of his work toward the war effort. His relationship with Bush had a transformative impact after the beginning of the war; in late 1940, Wiener wrote to Bush, "I . . . hope you can find some corner of activity in which I may be of use during the emergency."[62] Wiener's subsequent interest in computer development and prediction theory emerged from this inquiry.

Wiener's specific war-related initiative had to do with the design and use of the control mechanisms of antiaircraft guns. His mathematical background led him to seek mathematical solutions to the fundamental problem of predicting an airplane's future position based on data regarding its past positions. He was the first researcher to explicitly model the role of feedback in predictive decision-making. His formula proved to be very broadly useful, encompassing not only targeting systems for weapons but also noise reduction in radar systems. The first published product of this work was *Extrapolation, Interpolation and Smoothing of Stationary Time Series with Engineering Applications,* which, although not publicly published until 1949, was actually completed in 1942 and was widely used in the war effort.

THE IMPORTANCE OF HUMAN BEINGS

Although a dedicated mathematician and scientist, Wiener was also fundamentally a humanist whose doctorate in philosophy heavily influenced his thought and his work.

One of his earliest published works, "The Highest Good," which he wrote while a doctoral student at Harvard, was an exploration of ethics in which he rejected the very notion of a universal "highest good" as a model for understanding ethical behavior.[63] Another early work, "Relativism," provided a wide-reaching logical, epistemological, and ontological discussion of the nature of experience and perception, leading to the conclusion that the work of scientists is inherently relativistic in nature and that the relativistic nature of science exhibited in the form of "approximate knowledge" is a strength rather than a weakness.[64] He returned to this theme in "Is Mathematical Certainty Absolute?" In this article he concluded that although the degree of uncertainty that can be found in mathematics and logic is so small as to be truly insignificant, there is no support for the assertion that there is no such uncertainty.[65]

Wiener's 1936 article "The Role of the Observer" explored the relationships among logic, psychology, and epistemology through the lenses of the myth of universal truths and the principle of uncertainty.[66] This notion of the essential nature of the observer was extended to scientific models in 1945.[67] In 1943 he was coauthor of an article on "Behavior, Purpose, and Teleology" that presented the core for some of the ideas that later appeared in *The Human Use of Human Beings*, including the notion that machines are not necessarily intrinsically purposeful and that behavior may be either purposeful or nonpurposeful. This article provided one of the first explorations of the role of feedback—particularly negative feedback—in purposeful behavior and introduced "the behavioristic analysis of machines" and the notion that machines and animals can be understood in parallel terms. Although this article didn't coin the term "servomechanism," it was probably responsible for introducing it into general use.[68] By 1949 Wiener was part of a team exploring the potential for translating sound into tactile messages that could be "heard" by deaf people. Although similar projects were being performed at Bell Laboratories and elsewhere, a unique characteristic of the work being carried out by the team to which Wiener belonged was an emphasis on the affective benefits of sound.[69]

Wiener's focus on the human condition finds its apex in *The Human Use of Human Beings*, in which he brings together many ideas from his earlier works, including *Cybernetics, or Control and Communication in the Animal and the Machine,* to build a holistic view of the emerging cybernetic world.

MACHINE BEHAVIOR AND HUMAN BEHAVIOR

The starting point for *The Human Use of Human Beings* is Wiener's observation that some machines "have shown an uncanny ability to simulate human behavior, and thereby to throw light on the possible nature of human behavior."[70] To Wiener, the emergence of machines that can emulate human activity creates "an immediate need of discussing the powers of these machines as they impinge on the human being, and the consequences of this new and fundamental revolution in technique."[71] The stated purpose of *The Human Use of Human Beings* "is both to explain the potentialities of the machine in fields which up to now have been taken to be purely human, and to warn against the dangers of a purely selfish exploitation of these possibilities in a world in which human beings, human things are all-important."[72] Wiener strongly emphasizes, however, that although it is seemingly inevitable that machines will transform society, machines themselves must remain subservient to people.

In an attempt to "define" man, Wiener concludes that what distinguishes humans from other animals is that a human is an animal that talks. Although other animals exhibit social behavior, the central defining characteristics of the human animal is the "necessity for communication," which "is the guiding motive of their whole life."[73] The role of language and communication in human existence constitutes a pattern or set of patterns; Wiener suggests that these patterns are fundamental and are among "the most interesting aspects of the world."[74] Although Wiener somewhat belabors the concept of patterns, his ultimate point is that certain kinds of patterns constitute messages, and that the nature of messages is important to understanding both human and nonhuman communication. The patterns defined by messages constitute a communication system. In keeping with the general principles of systems thinking, understanding communication necessarily requires understanding communication systems. "It is the thesis of this book that society can only be understood through a study of the messages and the communication facilities which belong to it; and that in the future development of these messages and communication facilities, messages between man and machines, between machine and man, and between machine and machine, are destined to play an ever-increasing part."[75]

Wiener is directly offended by and explicitly protests the "inhuman use of human beings. . . . In my mind, any use of a human being in which less is demanded of him and less is attributed to him than his full status is a degradation and a waste."[76] Wiener is particularly opposed to any form of manual labor in which a person is essentially employed primarily as a source of energy. "It is simpler to organize a factory or galley which uses individual human beings for a fraction of their worth than it is to provide a world in which they can grow to their full stature. Those who suffer from a power complex find the mechanization of man a simple way to realize their ambitions."[77]

ENTROPY

Three essential interrelated themes recur throughout *The Human Use of Human Beings*: entropy, feedback, and information. Wiener explains entropy, which is defined by Clausius's second law of thermodynamics, in terms directly reminiscent of Shannon's mathematical theory of communication, with which he was undoubtedly familiar.[78] Entropy in the thermodynamic context is the principle that disorder in a closed system tends over time to reach some maximum value that undermines the functionality of the system. The probability of entropy (disorder) decreasing in a closed system is zero.

Wiener's "qualitative formulation" of the principle of entropy is stated as: "A message can lose order spontaneously in the act of transmission, but cannot gain it."[79] Examples of entropy include the loss of information on a noisy telephone connection and the impossibility of producing a precise translation from one language to another, which inevitably results in the loss of some of the original author's meaning. Wiener also echoes Shannon in describing the potential for measuring information quantitatively, where information "is essentially a measure of order."[80]

PROGRESS

Wiener links entropy to progress, which he defines as "essentially an assessment of the direction of change of the world according to certain values."[81] Progress can be assessed in the primarily physical terms of entropy or in terms that are "relevant to our normal human schemes of moral values."[82] Wiener suggests that either approach to assessment can take on the characteristics of either pessimism or optimism. In the simplest physical sense, entropy suggests that the universe will over time "run down." From an equally simplistic optimistic social point of view, all change is good and inherently constitutes evidence of progress. Wiener states that the "idea of progress has two aspects: a factual one and an ethical one."[83] The factual aspect has to do with the evolution of ideas, processes, and machines and "the discovery of new techniques for controlling the human environment."[84] From this point of view, which emphasizes the processes of invention, change is evidence of progress, and progress can be measured in terms of the frequency and extent of change. Wiener's conclusion is that although change is not evidence of progress from an ethical point of view, it is often interpreted as such.

In the context of measuring progress, Wiener laments the tendency of the "scientifically illiterate" to think only in terms of linear processes in which the measurable aspect of an effect has a direct one-to-one correspondence with the measurable aspect of its cause. Wiener points out that very few processes of nature even closely approximate a linear structure, and that for many phenomena, "very small causes will produce very great effects."[85] Furthermore, the "long-time results of two nearly identical causes may diverge" over time.[86]

Wiener discusses the difficulty of obtaining a historical perspective on change sufficient to really analyze progress, noting that some tools and processes of ancient origin have had very long useful lives and may still be in use, and that close examination reveals that seemingly major advances are actually quite subtle. Nonetheless, he notes an important set of changes associated with the industrial revolution that have no parallels in earlier times.

One of the most important distinctions between the physical point of view and the social point of view is that physics has typically concentrated on measuring disorder, while a purely social view tends to highly value order. An important consideration is that the physical definition of entropy is generally applied to closed systems, but systems thinking emphasizes that there are no naturally occurring closed systems. It is therefore possible, particularly in a societal system, for entropy to decrease, and Wiener is of the opinion that human society constitutes "an island of decreasing entropy."[87] Wiener calls particular attention to the relationship between quantitative and qualitative changes, which is almost never linear in nature.

FEEDBACK

Much of *The Human Use of Human Beings* has to do with the cybernetic concept of feedback, the "control of a machine on the basis of its *actual* performance rather than its *expected* performance."[88] A feedback system is essential to any machine operation that requires a variable response to external stimuli. A simple example is an automatic elevator, which must be capable not only of delivering the elevator to the correct floor but also of detecting that the elevator is completely in place at that floor before opening the door. Feedback systems generally work both most effectively and most efficiently when they are truly automatic. Feedback systems in animals, for instance, are primarily autonomic and require no conscious decision or designed action.

Wiener's thesis is "that the operation of the living individual and the operation of some of the newer communication machines are precisely parallel. . . . In both of them there exists a special apparatus for collecting information from the outer world at low energy levels, and for making it available in the operation of the individual or of the machine."[89] Sophisticated feedback mechanisms are required to make this possible.

LEARNING

Learning is an extremely important and fundamentally complicated form of feedback that "influences not merely the individual action, but the pattern of action."[90] Where "feedback is the control of a system by reinserting into the system the results of its performance," learning is a form of feedback in which "the information which proceeds backward from the performance is able to change the general method and pattern of performance."[91] Much of Wiener's work during World War II had to do with developing algorithms for machine learning. Although he confesses to a lack of success, he is confident that it is possible to design "a machine which contains a certain element of learning," and describes in general terms work under way at MIT to develop such machines.[92] Interestingly, although Wiener demonstrates considerable familiarity with the binary digital nature of most computers, he looks for success in machine learning to an analog model, "in which the quantities with which we deal are measured rather than counted."[93]

INFORMATION

An important point in Wiener's discussion of information is the notion that although "we ordinarily think of a message as sent from human being to human being," it is quite possible for a message to be sent from a human to a machine, from a machine to a human, or from a machine to a machine.[94] Simple examples of these include any act that a human undertakes that involves pressing a switch (human to machine), any audible alarm (machine to human), and the control of heating or cooling via a thermostat (machine to machine).

Wiener asserts that modern machines possess characteristics that are directly analogous to the sensory organs of animals in the form of "receptors for messages coming from the outside."[95] Although simple versions of the machine that is "conditioned by its relation to the external world, and by the things happening in the external world," have been in existence for a long time, such machines are increasingly becoming more complex as they are made more effective.[96] Wiener describes system complexity in terms parallel to those of computer design. "A complex action is one in which the combination of the introduced, which we call the *input*, to obtain and effect on the outer world, which we call the *output*, may involve a large number of combinations. These are combinations, both of the data put in at the moment and of the records taken from the past stored data which we call the *memory*."[97]

LANGUAGE

Humans require language for the communication of information, which leads Wiener to an exploration of the nature of language. His specific goal is to demonstrate "that language is not an exclusive attribute of man, but is one which he may share to a certain degree with the machines he has constructed."[98] Wiener addresses three components of language necessary for understanding the ways in which language can be used by machines: (1) the phonetic aspect, which is represented in humans by the association between sound and meaning and in machines by the association of electrical impulses with meaning; (2) the semantic aspect, which is concerned exclusively with meaning; and (3) the experiential aspect, which has to do with the relationship between meaning and action.[99] These components correspond closely with Shannon's three communication problems: (1) the technical problem, which has to do with the physical nature of communication; (2) the semantic problem, which has to do with communicating meaning; and (3) the effectiveness problem, which has to do with the relationship between intent and outcome.[100] Unlike Shannon, who was primarily concerned with solving the technical problem, Wiener essentially dismisses the phonetic aspect of language as irrelevant to the use of language by machines and concentrates on the semantic and behavior aspects, which he contends can be addressed statistically.

TWO INDUSTRIAL REVOLUTIONS

Wiener explores the role of machines in the future in the context of two industrial revolutions. The first is the familiar industrial revolution of the eighteenth century, in which scientific developments for the first time began to play a significant role in the fundamental processes of society. Developments of this era include increasingly sophisticated navigational systems that made long-distance exploration and commerce possible; the steam engine that replaced humans and animals as sources of energy and transformed both water and land transportation; the introduction of electricity; and the invention of the vacuum tube.

Wiener describes a second industrial revolution leading to "a more completely automatic age" in which routine processes such as those carried out on assembly lines are controlled and operated by computers.[101] He foresees very clearly the replacement of the vastly expensive, uniquely designed, and custom-built machines that constituted the first generation of computers with specialized, mass-produced computers inexpensive enough and capable enough to be infused into routine manufacturing and business processes. Although he doesn't use the term "robotics," he accurately describes the nature of robotics in manufacturing, mining, and other applications. He also envisions increasingly complex machine input, manipulation, and feedback systems that will make it possible for machines to perform an expanding range of tasks. And finally, he also sees a future role for machines in analysis and learning.

The future promised by the second industrial revolution is not inevitably an entirely positive one. Wiener emphasizes that "the automatic machine, whatever we think of any feelings it may have or not have, is the precise economic equivalent of slave labor. Any labor which competes with slave labor must accept the economic conditions of slave labor."[102] Wiener predicts that the second industrial revolution will be associated with extensive unemployment that will make "even the depression of the thirties . . . seem a pleasant joke" and suggests that even those industries that embrace the new order and benefit most may not survive.[103] The second industrial revolution "may be used for the benefit of humanity, assuming that humanity survives long enough to enter a period in which such a benefit is possible. If, however, we proceed along the clear and obvious lines of our traditional behavior, and follow our traditional worship of progress and the fifth freedom—the freedom to exploit—it is practically certain that we shall have to face a decade or more of ruin and despair."[104]

POLITICS AND POTENTIAL

The Human Use of Human Beings was written at a very politically charged time. The red scare was its height, fears of Fascism loomed in the aftermath of World War II, the cold war was at its peak, and the nuclear age had been ushered in with great fear and trepidation. Much of Wiener's book reflects those turbulent times. He addresses the relationship between law and communication, the uneasy relationship between humanists and scientists, and the rigidity of totalitarian regimes and religious bodies.

Ultimately, Wiener poses no specific solution to the world's problems, nor even to the problem of ensuring that, in a machine age, human beings are in fact used in a human manner. The book ends on a fairly unsatisfying note of concern that increasingly intelligent machines can be used for good or for ill, to fight rigidity and oppression or as instruments of propaganda and suppression. Although Wiener doesn't reference Orwell's *Nineteen Eighty-Four,* which was published in 1949, there is an element of Orwellian doom in *The Human Use of Human Beings.*

The book is not, however, fundamentally pessimistic or fatalistic. Wiener clearly believes that humans can survive and thrive and that the second industrial revolution—the machine age—has the potential for doing good rather than evil. His ultimate warning has to do with the nature of machines and decision making.

> Any machine constructed for the purpose of making decisions, if it does not possess the power of learning, will be completely literal-minded. Woe to us if we let it decide our conduct, unless we have previously examined the laws of its action, and know fully that its conduct will be carried out on principles acceptable to us! On the other hand, the machine . . . which can learn and can make decisions on the basis of its learning, will in no way be obliged to make such decisions as we should have made, or as will be acceptable to us. For the man who is not aware of this, to throw the problem of his responsibility on the machine, whether it can learn or not, is to cast his responsibility to the winds, and to find it coming back seated on the whirlwind.[105]

Rob Kling, "Towards a Person-Centered Computer Technology" (paper presented at the ACM
National Conference, Atlanta, GA, 1973).

Rob Kling, "What Is Social Informatics and Why Does It Matter?" *D-Lib* 5, no. 1 (1999), http://
www.dlib.org/dlib/january99/kling/01kling.html.

Rob Kling (1945–2003) earned a bachelor's degree at Columbia University and master's and doctoral degrees in artificial intelligence at Stanford University, where he also
worked in the Artificial Intelligence Center at the Stanford Research Institute. He served
on the faculties at the University of California, Irvine, and the University of Wisconsin
before joining the faculty of the School of Library and Information Science at Indiana
University in 1996, where he was director of the Center for Social Informatics (now
the Rob Kling Center for Social Informatics). Kling described the focus of his work as
"the social opportunities and dilemmas of computerization for managers, professionals,
workers, and the public." His works have generated more than 1,600 entries in the *Social
Sciences Citation Index.*

CONTEXT AND SOCIAL INFORMATICS

A great deal of Kling's work lies in the area of exploration that has come to be known
as social informatics. Kling's first documented use of the expression appears to have
come in a keynote speech at the 1996 conference of the International Federation for
Information Processing, but his work in the area began at least 20 years earlier. A central
theme in Kling's work is the importance of *context* in understanding, using, and perhaps
designing information systems.

"Towards a Person-Centered Computer Technology" is one of Kling's earliest works
in this vein. This paper begins with a very straightforward assertion: "Contemporary
computer designers are largely machine centered."[106] Kling's goal is to explore "the ways
and means that computer technology can help foster a mature and humane society."[107]
Although Kling implies that there are many facets to building a person-centered technology, "Towards a Person-Centered Computer Technology" focuses explicitly on the
direct experience of people with computer systems.

COMPUTER AS TOOL VS. COMPUTER AS ENVIRONMENT

Kling distinguishes between the typical view of the computer as a tool and the possibility that "a person who works with a large scale computing system may well experience
it as an overwhelming total environment."[108] This comment would seem commonplace
in the networked world of the early twenty-first century. However, it seems nearly
prescient in the context of 1973, when Kling presented his paper at the annual conference of the Association for Computing Machinery. In 1973, time-sharing systems
allow online access to mainframe systems had been in existence for just more than a
decade and were far from ubiquitous. The first microprocessor had been introduced
only three years earlier and was in use only in expensive handheld calculators. The
first microcomputer in kit form was still two years away. The Apple I was three years
away and the first-generation IBM PC was eight years in the future. Kling's recognition

of the potentially extreme impact of the use of computing systems on users is quite remarkable.

Kling describes four possible positive outcomes of this immersion in the computing environment; he suggest that people who are so immersed may (1) "develop a more global and abstract 'system view,'" (2) "develop keener perspectives on their role in organizations," (3) "emphasize rationality," and (4) "consider efficiency as a primary criterion in selecting alternative designs."[109] Kling is concerned, however, that these potential outcomes are not at the heart of computer systems design, which tends to emphasize minimizing response time over all other considerations. "We have few means to deal with a person who may seek productive, satisfying work that makes coherent sense, challenges his talents, and fosters a personal sense of competence."[110]

MACHINE-CENTERED AND PERSON-CENTERED DESIGN

Kling described the differences between machine-centered and person-centered computer system design as follows. In a machine-centered design,

1. Efficiency is emphasized.
2. Human error is not tolerated.
3. Systems are designed in purely functional terms.
4. Jobs and procedures are simplified to simplify machine processing.
5. Users are forced to match the precision required by the machine.
6. System designs are imposed on users.[111]

The characteristics of a person-centered design are quite different:

1. Systems are valued that increase personal competence and pride in work.
2. Acceptance of people as nonrational and error-prone.
3. Jobs are designed to be personally satisfying. Automated procedures are designed to fit job needs.
4. Places the burden of precision on the machine. Systems are forgiving.
5. Easy for users to obtain/create systems that meet their needs.
6. Users can initiate, veto, and collaborate in system designs.
7. Designs and assumptions are intelligible to users through appropriate technique (modular structures) and clear documentation.[112]

Kling sees both sets of characteristics as being idealized and emphasizes the need to understand specific rather than generalized contexts. These are "criteria that are within the purview of computer system designers," not universal concerns. "The determinants of satisfaction are complex, but we know that there are strong correlations between work effectiveness, personal sense of competence and job satisfaction."[113]

THE EFFECTS OF COMPUTER USE

Kling notes that using computer systems has both direct and indirect impacts on users. Systems designers and "utopian themes" concentrate primarily on the direct impacts of reducing what Wiener referred to as the inhuman use of human beings and supporting "a society of abundance which provides high quality service for all."[114] The side effects are considerably more difficult to assess or even identify but may have an overall greater impact than the direct effects of computer use. Among the side effects Kling notes are the tendency for formerly low-level decisions to be made at higher levels, reduced interpersonal communication in the workplace, and potential unintended changes in organizational structures.

REQUISITES FOR PERSON-CENTERED COMPUTING

Kling's assessment of the overall computing environment of the early 1970s is that it is dominated by "large bureaucratic organizations that typically do not foster humanly vital contexts."[115] His perspective, which seems little more than wishful thinking in the context of the mainframe computing era, is that developing person-centered computing may necessitate first the creation of person-centered organizations.

From his discussion of the distinction between machine-centered and person-centered design, Kling synthesizes system design guidelines that emphasize (1) collaborative design, (2) software flexibility, (3) system intelligibility, (4) rewards for meeting addressing user needs, and (5) ready access to support personnel. "These proposals require little new technology. Rather, they effect the interpersonal process in the most immediate context that technology is used."[116]

Kling likens most computer systems design to public places designed by architects who are more interested in form and visual impact than in usability or public preference. An important distinction is that while redesigning a public space such as a park or plaza requires major reconstruction, redesigning software is a relatively low-effort task. A close parallel lies in the fact that, just as architects don't consider the public to be their clients, system designers don't consider the end users of systems to be their clients. In contrast, Kling encourages a "philosophy of collaborative design [that] must include some good means of identifying the various recipients of a system and including their diverse needs in the initial design phase."[117] A primary reason that such collaborative design does not normally take place is that designers are not rewarded for collaborating with or designing for end users; their reward instead come from managers who may have little or no contact with the system. Similarly, software flexibility is a user-centered concept that is also not rewarded. Furthermore, since computer systems are inherently intelligible to their designers, the designers place little emphasis on making them intelligible to users or on providing the support systems necessary for helping users understand the system.

Error messages, for instance, are frequently terse mnemonics that effectively serve to remind the designer of the nature of the error, but do little to assist the user.

Kling concludes his paper with a brief manifesto for user-oriented design: "A person-centered computer technology continually attends to the human cost of each design that restricts personal expressiveness, autonomy, and dignity. It attends to process as well as to content. . . . If our use of computing is to be humanely benign, it is not too much to ask that we foster experientially rich environments that enhance the sense of competence and self-acceptance of users."[118] Although Kling recognizes that user-oriented design may seem to some designers and managers to constitute "focusing on a small elite group of computer users," he also recognizes the future role of computers in serving "a larger public" and the necessity of person-centered design for making such a goal achievable.[119]

PERSON-CENTERED COMPUTING REVISITED: SOCIAL INFORMATICS

Kling's "What Is Social Informatics and Why Does It Matter?" was published 26 years after "Towards a Person-Centered Computer Technology." Not surprisingly, although the later work continues many of the themes of "Towards a Person-Centered Computer Technology," it is a substantially more mature presentation. Kling characterizes social informatics as simultaneously being a well-developed field that is "pertinent to understanding the design, development, and operation of usable information systems, including intranets, electronic forums, digital libraries and electronic journals" and being fragmented across multiple literatures, "including computer science, information systems, information science and some social sciences."[120] The diversity of terminology and scatter across literatures creates problems in collocating and understanding core contributions to the field. Kling hopes that adoption of the term "social informatics" will reduce the dispersal of ideas and improve general understanding of the field.

INFORMATION TECHNOLOGY AND SOCIAL CHANGE

Social informatics is in large part an organized, structured approach to studying the impact of information technology on society, as evidenced by its effects on both groups and individuals. The element of change is an essential component in social informatics. Kling notes that the relationship between technology and change is a favorite topic of "pundits" who approach that relationship not from the systematic point of view of social informatics but from a viewpoint that is largely based on anecdote and is frequently alarmist in nature. "Pundits play interesting social roles. The best pundits are entertaining, provocative and timely."[121] The works of pundits are also generally very visible, appearing in popular outlets such as magazines and deliberately popularized nonfiction books; pundits are increasingly taking their voices to online platforms. Although pundits are among the most visible sources of information, they are not necessarily the most reliable and may actually discourage research and analysis.

Reliance on anecdote and ad hoc assessment in the design, implementation, monitoring, and modification of information systems tends to lead to three very simple but deceptive criteria:

1. "use more advanced technology (whether it is faster or easier to use);
2. use 'better technologies,' (though there are different criteria for 'better' such as less expensive or compatible with other equipment); or
3. organize systems so that they are more efficient."[122]

Kling refers to these and similar criteria or guidelines as "context-free" and notes that such criteria "have not been good enough to help information technology professionals design or implement effective systems."[123]

INFORMATION TECHNOLOGY AND
THE PRODUCTIVITY PARADOX

Kling notes that historically economists, systems manufacturers and vendors, administrators and managers, and even workers closely associated with advances in computer technology and the increasing implementation of technological solutions with improved productivity. As the costs of computing declined, first with the introduction of minicomputers and then with the widespread use of personal computers, the expectation was that the balance of costs and productivity would shift favorably. The popular business literature has carried many stories touting the benefits of computerization but has also frequently published stories of technology failures and lost productivity. Kling refers to the "productivity paradox" of technology identified by economists, most notably Robert Solow, whom Kling quotes: "You can see the computer age everywhere but in the productivity statistics."[124] Economists differ on the origins and impact of the productivity paradox, but its existence is generally accepted. Kling notes that the productivity paradox also has social and personal ramifications but says that it is "glossed over by most of the pundits."[125] In particular, he calls attention to the vast differences between huge global increases in computing power, network connectivity, and speed, and similar measures of the adoption of technology and decidedly modest increased in productivity during the same period of time. He cites *Wired* author George Gilder's assertion that computing value increased by a factor of one hundred million between the 1950s and the 1990s and notes that there has clearly been no such increase in U.S. labor productivity. Even those studies that associate technology with increased productivity show substantial variability across organizations and settings. Kling concludes that the productivity paradox may be explained by the ways in which organizations incorporate information technology, and offers three "social explanations" for the paradox:

1. "Many organizations develop systems in ways that lead to a large fraction of implementation failure."
2. "Few organizations design systems that effectively facilitate people's work."
3. "We significantly underestimate how much skilled work is required to extract value from computerized systems."[126]

Kling does not propose to resolve the productivity paradox but rather suggests that the ultimate explanation and solution may lie in the domain of the field of social informatics.

DEVELOPMENTAL EMPHASES OF SOCIAL INFORMATICS

Kling's summary of the history of social informatics points out that much of the field has focused on the influence of information technology in organizational settings, primarily because the origins of the field lie in the pre–home computer era. As the role of the personally owned computer emerges and evolves, and especially as the social nature of the Internet is better understood, the focus of social informatics will necessarily expand and evolve.

Many of the questions asked about the impact of technology, both those asked by social informaticists and by others, have been "deterministic impact questions."[127] The ultimate deterministic impact question is "What is or will be the impact of technology?" This question can be applied to individuals, to groups, to organizations, to political entities, to continents, or to society as a whole. Kling asserts that many of the early explorations of the impact of technology were naively simple and led to uncertain and variable answers that essentially revealed that there "was no simple, direct effect."[128] Even when more complex questions were addressed, the answers were frequently no more satisfactory. "The analytical failure of technological determinism is one of the interesting and durable findings from social informatics research."[129] To Kling, the probable solution lies not in asking questions that explore the circumstances under which technology does or does not have an impact. "This kind of *contextual inquiry* illustrates the ways that social informatics researchers frame questions to develop an analytical understanding of information technologies in social life."[130]

THE IMPORTANCE OF CONTEXT

Kling illustrates the importance of context in social informatics research through a specific example from organizational practice. The example he uses is that of a corporation attempting to encourage knowledge sharing and interaction via an intranet. The company made a substantial financial investment in the software necessary to foster interaction and sharing but found the system was widely used only by the firm's information technology staff, who were not the intended primary beneficiaries. Other employees used the system modestly or practically not at all. The system was a commercial software product that had been used quite successfully in other settings, which made it hard to understand the mixed and mostly low levels of use in the firm.

Kling traces the failure of the collaborative software system to the specific context of the incentive systems of the company. Professionals in the firm were rewarded primarily in terms of their generation of billable hours. Use of the collaborative software, although potentially beneficial for its intended purpose, generated no billable hours. In fact, the time required to learn to use the system and then to use it as it was intended reduced the number of billable hours for which professionals could account. From the point of view of corporate incentives, then, use of the software system by the professionals it was intended to support inevitably led to a documentable decline in productivity. Employees who were not responsible for documenting billable hours, including the information technology staff, were not in any way penalized for using the system.

Kling's point is that "the 'social context' of information technology development and use plays a significant role in influencing the ways that people use information and technologies, and thus influences their consequences for work, organizations, and other social relationships."[131] Understanding the stratified social context of the firm in the example not only provides an explanation of why the collaborative software initiative didn't work, but also provides clues for ensuring that future efforts have an optimal chance for success. Context is not an obscure and abstract concept; it is concrete and knowable if one is aware of the techniques for examining it.

A second example concerns the unfulfilled promise of the paperless office. In an interesting parallel, he notes that the rise of the notion of paperless information systems was concurrent with increasing sales of laser printers. Although Kling recognizes that there is a certain tactile satisfaction element associated with the use of some paper-based information products, such as books and magazines, he finds it unlikely that "people like paper in the same way that people have an affection for dogs or cats" and particularly thinks it unlikely that there is any inherent tactile, visual, or other appeal to be found in 20-pound bond office paper.[132]

Again turning to the context in which people use office documents, Kling concludes that activities such as annotating, comparing, integrating and editing documents are sufficiently complex to be best achieved by most people via paper documents. Although the cost of computer systems capable of helping people carry out such tasks in a paperless manner may be a factor, Kling suggests that it is probably only a minor consideration, and that a large-scale migration from paper to fully digital document processing is unlikely. Even in environments in which computerized systems are dominant, such as airline reservations management and travel booking systems, people tend to use paper notes and "cheat sheets" liberally.

SOCIO-TECHNICAL SYSTEMS

These and other examples lead to a discussion of the roles of a socio-technical approach to understanding information and communication technologies based on the "concept of 'computerized information systems as social technical systems.'"[133] Echoing the discussion of computer as tool vs. computer as environment presented in "Towards a Person-Centered Computer Technology," Kling emphasizes the inappropriateness of discussing technologies "as tools or simple appliances, even when [referring] to complex arrangements of varied equipment, rules/roles/resources, and actual organizational practices."[134]

It is more interesting to view specific information technologies as socio-technical systems—a complex, interdependent system comprised of:

- People in various roles and relationships with each other and with other system elements
- Hardware (computers mainframes, workstations, peripherals, telecommunications equipment)
- Software (operating systems, utilities and application programs)
- Techniques (management science models, voting schemes)
- Support resources (training/support/help)
- Information structures (content and content providers; rules/norms/regulations, such as those that authorize people to use systems and information in specific ways; access controls).[135]

Kling emphasizes that these are not static, independent factors but are "interrelated within a matrix of social and technical dependencies."[136]

An important characteristic of a social informatics approach to designing and implementing a socio-technical system is that the designer must be immersed in the context in which the system will be deployed. This allows the designer to employ a number of "discovery processes," including but certainly not restricted to workplace ethnography, focus groups, and collaborative design that emphasizes user input and participation.

SOCIAL ACCESS TO TECHNOLOGY

Although physical access to information and communication technologies is demonstrably increasing rapidly, at least in the developed world, physical access is not sufficient to lead to ubiquitous use of such technologies. Kling introduces the additional factor of social access, which "refers to know-how, a mix of professional knowledge, economic resources, and technical skills, to use technologies in ways that enhance professional practices and social life."[137] Kling warns against the tendency to view social access as an "add-on" to physical access and technological infrastructures, noting that "social access is integral to the design and development of systems and services that are to be widely used. . . . Social access . . . is likely to prove vexing for many people, based on what careful studies of computer use and Internet use have shown us."[138] Kling notes that there have been few studies of computer use by "ordinary people," a concern that is still valid.

Although system designers and managers typically devote substantial attention to the technological infrastructure of a system and the organization that supports it, they rarely give any meaningful consideration to social infrastructure. "System infrastructure is a socio-technical system since technical capabilities depend upon skilled people, administrative procedures, etc.; and social capabilities are enabled by simpler supporting technologies. . . . Malfunctioning computer systems are not simply an opportunity loss, such as a book that is bought but not read. When people organize their days about the expectations that key technologies will work well—and they don't—they often spend considerable time tinkering to get systems to work, waiting for help to come, and so on."[139] Much of what is known about the social infrastructure of information and communication technologies comes from studies of failures. Although this knowledge base is limited, it is clear that "a weak socio-technical infrastructure can undermine the effective workability of computer systems, including those in people's homes."[140]

WHY SOCIAL INFORMATICS MATTERS

The section of "What Is Social Informatics and Why Does It Matter?" that actually addresses the issue of why social informatics matters is far from satisfying if removed from the context of what precedes it. Having provided a solid introduction to the nature of social informatics and many concrete examples of scenarios in which a social informatics approach would be useful in understanding and solving problems at the nexus of technology and the social nature of work, Kling summarizes in a rather cursory manner.

He does emphasize, however, the broad nature and implications of social informatics, pointing out that it "pertains to information technology use and social change in any sort of social setting, not just organizations."[141] This implication that social informatics applies at both narrower and broader levels than the organizational examples given earlier is important, particularly in light of developments since Kling's article appeared. "Social informatics researchers are specifically interested in developing reliable knowledge about information technology and social change, based on systematic empirical research, to inform both public policy debates and professional practice."[142] Here Kling returns to an earlier theme: the need to base understanding of the social forces exerted by technological change in scientific rather than anecdotal or alarmist terms. Unfortunately, although social informatics continues to grow as a field of study, it is unclear to what extent it truly has influenced either public policy or professional practice. The most accessible, most public literatures of many fields continue to be dominated by pundits and alarmists.

NOTES

1. John Worthley, "Letter to the Editor: No Mention of Computers," *Public Administration Review* 36 (July/August 1976): 470.

2. Philip Ball, "In the Know," *Nature,* April 1, 2004, 462.

3. David C. Chou and Binshan Lin, "Development of Web-Based Knowledge Management Systems," *Human Systems Management* 21 (2002): 155.

4. Maryann Alavi and Dorothy E. Leidner, "Knowledge Management and Knowledge Management Systems: Conceptual Foundations and Research Issues," *MIS Quarterly* 25 (March 2001): 114.

5. Carl Frappaolo and Stacie Capshaw, "Knowledge Management Software: Capturing the Essence of Know-How and Innovation," *Information Management Journal* 33 (July 1999): 44.

6. Andrew J. Flanagin, "The Elusive Benefits of the Technological Support of Knowledge Management," *Management Communication Quarterly* 16 (November 2002): 245.

7. Richard McDermott, "Why Information Technology Inspired but Cannot Deliver Knowledge Management," *California Management Review* 41 (Summer 1999): 103.

8. Nelly Stromquist and Joel Samoff, "Knowledge Management Systems: On the Promise and Actual Forms of Information Technologies," *Compare* 30, no. 3 (2000): 323.

9. Paul R. Gamble and John Blackwell, *Knowledge Management: A State of the Art Guide* (London: Kogan Page, 2002), 163.

10. Karl Wiig, *People-Focused Knowledge Management: How Effective Decision Making Leads to Corporate Success* (Amsterdam: Elsevier, 2004), 37.

11. Amrit Tiwana, *The Knowledge Management Toolkit: Practical Techniques for Building a Knowledge Management System* (Upper Saddle River, NJ: Prentice-Hall PTR, 2000), 38–39.

12. Tiwana, *The Knowledge Management Toolkit,* 39.

13. Gamble and Blackwell, *Knowledge Management,* 166.

14. Wiig, *People-Focused Knowledge Management,* 36–37.

15. Tiwana, *The Knowledge Management Toolkit,* 39.

16. Gamble and Blackwell, *Knowledge Management,* 166.

17. Tanriverdi, "Information Technology Relatedness," 316.

18. Wiig, *People-Focused Knowledge Management,* 9.

19. J. C. Thomas, W. A. Kellogg, and T. Erickson, "The Knowledge Management Puzzle: Human and Social Factors in Knowledge Management," *IBM Systems Journal* 40, no. 4 (2001): 864.

20. Ibid., 881.

21. Ibid., 872.

22. Sandra Moffett, Rodney McAdam, and Stephen Parkinson, "Technology and People Factors in Knowledge Management: An Empirical Analysis," *Total Quality Management* 14, no. 2 (2003): 215–24.

23. Nelly Stromquist and Joel Samoff, "Knowledge Management Systems: On the Promise and Actual Forms of Information Technologies," *Compare* 30, no. 3 (2000): 331.

24. Flanagin, "The Elusive Benefits," 243.

25. Gamble and Blackwell, *Knowledge Management.*

26. Ibid.

27. Frappaolo and Capshaw, "Knowledge Management Software," 45–46.

28. Brent Gallupe, "Knowledge Management Systems: Surveying the Landscape," *International Journal of Management Reviews* 3 (March 2001): 68–71.

29. Brent J. Bowman, "Building Knowledge Management Systems," *Information Systems Management* 19 (Summer 2002): 37.

30. Jing Luan and Andreea M. Serban, "Technologies, Products, and Models Supporting Knowledge Management," *New Directions for Institutional Research* 2002, no. 113 (2002): 85–86.

31. Andrew McAfee, "Mastering the Three Worlds of Information Technology," *Harvard Business Review* 84 (November 2006): 142.

32. Leela Damodaran and Wendy Olphert, "Barriers and Facilitators to the Use of Knowledge Management Systems," *Behaviour & Information Technology* 19, no. 6 (2000): 405.

33. Flanagin, "The Elusive Benefits," 244.

34. Huseyin Tanriverdi, "Information Technology Relatedness, Knowledge Management Capability, and Performance of Multibusiness Firms," *MIS Quarterly* 29 (June 2005): 316.

35. Ibid., 316–17.

36. Ibid., 327.

37. Victoria L. Mitchell, "Knowledge Integration and Information Technology Project Performance," *MIS Quarterly* 30 (December 2006): 923–24.

38. Ibid., 934.

39. Theresa Heintze and Stuart Bretschneider, "Information Technology and Restructuring in Public Organizations: Does Adoption of Information Technology Affect Organizational Structures, Communications, and Decision Making?" *Journal of Public Administration Research and Theory* 10, no. 4 (2000): 827.

40. Rob Kling, "What Is Social Informatics and Why Does It Matter?" *D-Lib* 5, no. 1 (January 1999), http://www.dlib.org/dlib/january99/kling/01kling.html (accessed March 22, 2007).

41. A. D. Ursul, "On the Shaping of Social Informatics," *International Forum on Information and Documentation* 14, no. 4 (1989): 10–18.

42. Alex Halavais, "Social Informatics: Beyond Emergence," *Bulletin of the American Society for Information Science and Technology* 31 (June/July 2005): 13.

43. Leigh Keeble and Brian D. Loader, "Community Informatics: Themes and Issues," in *Community Informatics: Shaping Computer-Mediated Social Relations,* edited by Leigh Keeble and Brian D. Loader (London: Routledge, 2001), 3.

44. Ann Peterson Bishop and Bertram (Chip) Bruce, "Community Informatics: Integrating Action, Research and Learning," *Bulletin of the American Society for Information Science and Technology* 31 (August/September 2005): 6–10.

45. Steve Sawyer, "Social Informatics: Overview, Principles, and Opportunities," *Bulletin of the American Society for Information Science and Technology* 31 (June/July 2005): 9.

46. Halavais, "Social Informatics," 13.

47. Sawyer, "Social Informatics," 11.

48. Halavais, "Social Informatics," 13.

49. Sawyer, "Social Informatics," 11.

50. Elisabeth Davenport, "Social Informatics in Practice: A Guide for the Perplexed," *Bulletin of the American Society for Information Science and Technology* 31 (June/July 2005): 17.

51. Davenport, "Social Informatics in Practice," 19.

52. Murat Karamuftuoglu, "Collaborative Information Retrieval: Toward a Social Informatics View of IR Interaction," *Journal of the American Society for Information Science* 49 (October 1998): 1070.

53. Ibid., 1073.

54. Ibid., 1075–76.

55. Xiaoya Tang, "Social Informatics and Information Retrieval Systems," *Bulletin of the American Society for Information Science and Technology* 26 (February/March 2000): 20.

56. *American Heritage Dictionary of the English Language,* 4th ed., s.v. "Cybernetics."

57. Norbert Wiener, *The Human Use of Human Beings: Cybernetics and Society* (Boston: Houghton Mifflin, 1950), 8.

58. Norbert Wiener, *Cybernetics, or Control and Communication in the Animal and the Machine* (Cambridge, MA: Technology Press, 1948), 19.

59. Ibid., 9.

60. *Oxford English Dictionary Online,* s.v. "Cybernetics."

61. *American National Biography Online,* s.v. "Wiener, Norbert."

62. Quoted in Peter Galison, "The Ontology of the Enemy: Norbert Wiener and the Cybernetic Vision," *Critical Inquiry* 21 (Autumn 1994): 228.

63. Norbert Wiener, "The Highest Good," *Journal of Philosophy, Psychology and Scientific Methods* 11 (September 1914): 512–20.

64. Norbert Wiener, "Relativism," *Journal of Philosophy, Psychology and Scientific Methods* 11 (October 1914): 561–77.

65. Norbert Wiener, "Is Mathematical Certainty Absolute?" *Journal of Philosophy, Psychology and Scientific Methods* 12 (October 1915): 568–74.

66. Norbert Wiener, "The Role of the Observer," *Philosophy of Science* 3 (July 1936): 307–19.

67. Arturo Rosenblueth and Norbert Wiener, "The Role of Models in Science," *Philosophy of Science* 12 (October 1945): 316–21.

68. Arturo Rosenblueth, Norbert Wiener, and Julian Bigelow, "Behavior, Purpose and Teleology," *Philosophy of Science* 10 (January 1943): 18–24.

69. Norbert Wiener, "Sound Communication with the Deaf," *Philosophy of Science* 16 (July 1949): 260–62.

70. Wiener, *The Human Use of Human Beings,* 1.

71. Ibid.

72. Ibid., 2.

73. Ibid., 3.

74. Ibid.

75. Ibid., 9.

76. Ibid., 16.

77. Ibid.

78. Claude Shannon, *The Mathematical Theory of Communication* (Urbana: University of Illinois Press, 1949).

79. Wiener, *The Human Use of Human Beings,* 7.

80. Ibid., 21.

81. Ibid., 20.

82. Ibid.

83. Ibid., 27.

84. Ibid.

85. Ibid., 33.

86. Ibid., 34.

87. Ibid., 25.

88. Ibid., 12.

89. Ibid., 15.

90. Ibid., 69.

91. Ibid., 71.

92. Ibid., 72.

93. Ibid., 75.

94. Ibid., 8.

95. Ibid., 10.

96. Ibid., 10–11.

97. Ibid., 11.

98. Ibid., 85.

99. Ibid., 88–91.

100. Warren Weaver, "Recent Contributions to the Mathematical Theory of Communication," in *The Mathematical Theory of Communication,* ed. Claude E. Shannon and Warren Weaver (Urbana: University of Illinois Press, 1949), 96.

101. Wiener, *The Human Use of Human Beings,* 180.

102. Ibid., 189.

103. Ibid.

104. Ibid.

105. Ibid., 212.

106. Rob Kling, "Towards a Person-Centered Computer Technology" (paper presented at the ACM National Conference, Atlanta, GA, 1973), 387.

107. Ibid.

108. Ibid.

109. Ibid.

110. Ibid.

111. Ibid., 388.

112. Ibid.

113. Ibid.

114. Ibid., 389.

115. Ibid.

116. Ibid., 388.

117. Ibid., 390.

118. Ibid., 391.

119. Ibid.

120. Kling, "What Is Social Informatics," 1.

121. Ibid., 2.

122. Ibid., 2–3.

123. Ibid., 3.

124. Ibid.

125. Ibid., 4.

126. Ibid., 5.

127. Ibid.

128. Ibid., 5–6.

129. Ibid., 6.

130. Ibid.

131. Ibid., 9.

132. Ibid., 10.

133. Ibid., 14.

134. Ibid.

135. Ibid.

136. Ibid.
137. Ibid., 17–18.
138. Ibid., 18.
139. Ibid., 19.
140. Ibid., 20.
141. Ibid.
142. Ibid.

10

The Future of Knowledge Management

future, *n*. That period of time in which our affairs prosper, our friends are true and our happiness is assured.—Ambrose Bierce, *The Devil's Dictionary*

IN THIS CHAPTER

THE EVOLUTIONARY STATUS OF KNOWLEDGE MANAGEMENT

Although, as has been demonstrated in preceding chapters, the historical and cross-disciplinary origins of knowledge management extend back through many decades and, in some cases, centuries, knowledge management as a definable area of interest is quite young. As an emerging field, it is naturally lacking in form and structure. There is no one path to knowledge management either for an organization or for an individual, nor is there a standard job description for the role of the knowledge management professional. Any meaningful approach to studying knowledge management must begin with a consideration of the specific aspect or understanding of knowledge management to be studied. The literature, professional orientation, and educational opportunities related to knowledge management are diffuse.

COMMENTARY ON THE FUTURE OF KNOWLEDGE MANAGEMENT

Somewhat surprisingly, little reflection on the future of knowledge management has appeared in the literature. In 2005 Pollard contended that "most people left in KM are disillusioned."[1] He attributed such disillusionment to the culture of business and the inability of executives to cope effectively with creativity and innovation. Knowledge management professionals are "far more imaginative, more intelligent, more right-brained, more stimulated by ideas, and more idealistic than their organizational peers," but many are "misfits, nonconformists, constant questioners, thorns in the sides of managers who wished they would just shut up and do what they were told."[2] Although Pollard did not predict the absolute demise of knowledge management as a field, he felt strongly that knowledge managers must be brought to the forefront of business practice and that the way to do so is to make their abilities essential throughout the organization.

Miller explored the transition from corporate knowledge management to personal knowledge management in an era in which "knowledge workers facing ever-increasing sources of knowledge . . . need to find solutions to manage knowledge at the personal level."[3] Miller envisioned personal knowledge management as being both structurally and functionally separate from corporate knowledge management and, as such, in need of completely distinct solutions. In many ways his view of personal knowledge management is reminiscent of Bush's memex.

THE LITERATURE OF KNOWLEDGE MANAGEMENT

A search of *Ulrich's International Periodical Directory* using the title keyword expression "knowledge management" produced 37 entries, 17 of which are for refereed scholarly journals. Nine of the 17 titles actually contain the exact phrase "knowledge management." Of those 9, one is narrowly focused on nuclear energy and nuclear science management. Of the remaining 8, the oldest, the *Journal of Knowledge Management,* began publication in 1997. Six began publication since 2003. A search for the expression "information management" produced 215 entries, of which 44 were to refereed journals.

A search for the title keyword expression "knowledge management" in *Books in Print* yielded about 1,700 entries. By contrast, the expression "information management" produced more than 8,000 listings. The catalog of the Library of Congress lists 560 items to which the subject heading "knowledge management" has been applied. *Dissertation Abstracts International* lists 121 dissertations to which the subject term "knowledge management" has been applied. Although the oldest of these was completed in 1985, 113 were completed since 2001.

Concentrating on the term "knowledge management" as content in titles, however, is at best an imperfect representation of the literature of the field. None of the works identified as key papers for this book, for instance, contains the phrase in its title. None of the journals with titles containing the phrase "knowledge management" is among the 10 journals cited most frequently in articles on knowledge management topics. This is typical of an emerging literature. New ideas arise in the literatures of a diverse group of fields and are explored from a variety of viewpoints. Only as the idea matures and views become consolidated does the literature begin to concentrate on a unitary model of the idea. If such a model is successful, over time the dominant literature on the subject increasingly appears in publications dedicated to the subject, and the role of non-specialized publications diminishes.

KNOWLEDGE MANAGEMENT RESEARCH

Another way in which knowledge management as a field is lacking in self-examination is in its research orientation. In 1942, Beals characterized the literature of the emerging field of librarianship as consisting of "glad tidings, testimonial, and research," with research contributing very little to the overall corpus.[4] The literature of knowledge management in the early twenty-first century is subject to the same criticism. Much of what has been published is exhortatory in nature, encouraging the adoption of knowledge management as an overall organizational philosophy or the incorporation into organizational operations of certain aspects of knowledge management, such as the transfer of tacit knowledge or the development of content management systems. A secondary theme in the knowledge management literature is the exposition of success (only occasionally failure) in the specific application of knowledge management approaches and techniques in particular organizational settings. Trade publications such as *KMWorld* are dominated by news items primarily focused on software and hardware developments and market performance.

Research plays a distinctly tertiary role in the literature of knowledge management. Even those articles published in refereed scholarly journals tend toward very "soft" approaches to research, and many cannot really be considered research at all. Although quantification is only one aspect of rigor in research, it is informative to note that only 11 (17%) of the 66 articles published in the *Journal of Knowledge Management* during 2006 employed any sort of statistics. Only 3 of the 11 articles used inferential statistics or significance estimation. The remaining articles were primarily case studies, analytical literature reviews, visual models, and informed commentary. The lack of quantification in the articles published in the field's most mature scholarly journal does not suggest that the articles are of inferior quality, but it does provide a clue into the nature and focus of the field.

As early as 1998, Teece identified a set of targets for knowledge management research that included

- Assemble evidence to test the proposition that firm-level competitive advantage in open economies flows fundamentally from difficult to replicate knowledge assets.

- Make greater effort to quantify the value of intangible assets.
- Understand generic inputs, idiosyncratic inputs, and profitability.
- Explore the importance of entrepreneurial versus administrative capabilities.[5]

These all seem to be of enduring value as focuses for research in knowledge management, but little real progress has been made toward building a research knowledge base that addresses them.

THE PROFESSIONAL STRUCTURE OF KNOWLEDGE MANAGEMENT

Knowledge management as a field or discipline does not appear to have found a secure, consolidated home in a professional association. The *Encyclopedia of Associations* lists 21 entries that include the expression "knowledge management." The phrase does not actually appear in the names of any of these associations: knowledge management is mentioned in the textual descriptions of 13 associations; as the focus of a committee, special interest group, or other division of 7; and as the topic of a workshop for one. The names of the associations, which include the Workflow and Reengineering International Association, the Society of American Military Engineers, the National Study of School Evaluation, and the American Health Care Association, demonstrate a wide breadth of penetration but suggest that knowledge management is at best a side issue.

Several knowledge management organizations are not listed in the *Encyclopedia of Associations*. iKMS, founded in 2001 as an offshoot of an interest group that first came together informally in 1999, has fewer than two hundred members and is primarily centered around its headquarters in Singapore, where international conferences were hosted in 2004 and 2006. iKMS sponsors the *Journal of Information and Knowledge Management,* a refereed scholarly journal focusing on a broad range of topics and issues related to the management of information and knowledge. The Association of Knowledgework (AOK) is an explicitly virtual association self-described as a "Mom 'n' Pop organization."[6] The association is centered primarily around the efforts of its cofounders and acts primarily as a Web-based clearinghouse for information and events related to knowledge management. The International Knowledge Management Institute (KM Institute), founded in 2004 with a primarily trade association mission, has a membership base of approximately one thousand and describes itself as the "fastest growing knowledge management organization in the world."[7]

A much larger organization, the Knowledge Management Professional Society (KMPro), claims more than 120,000 members in 88 nations. KMPro is a largely virtual association with a strong emphasis on training centered in its certified knowledge manager program, a function that it absorbed from the formerly independent KM Certification Board. The *KMPro Journal* is a practitioner-oriented publication oriented largely toward opinion and news.

The Academy of Management, regarded by many observers as the premier membership association for business professionals, has no organizational unit devoted to knowledge management, nor does the American Management Association. The American Society for Information Science & Technology established a knowledge management special interest group in 2003. Also in 2003, the Information Resources Management Network, a special interest group of Aslib, the Association for Information Management, was transformed into the Aslib Knowledge and Information Management Network (KIMNET). The International Federation of Library Associations established a knowledge management section in 2004.

EDUCATION FOR KNOWLEDGE MANAGEMENT

Most knowledge managers came to their professional positions with no formal training in knowledge management, drawing on diverse backgrounds in an extremely wide variety of fields, disciplines, and professions. Although experience in business administration is possibly the most common credential, knowledge managers also have backgrounds in library and information science, public administration, health care, education, and many other areas.

Several knowledge management organizations concentrate on training programs leading to certification. This is the approach of KMCI.org, which offers five-day workshops leading to the CKIM certificate; KMPro offers a certified knowledge manager program, also based on a five-day workshop format. The Global Knowledge Economics Council maintains a list of certified knowledge manager programs but is not itself a recognized accreditation or certification body. The Knowledge Management Education Wiki lists 27 training programs worldwide.[8]

There are few formal degree programs in knowledge management. As is typical of an emerging field, many higher education opportunities in knowledge management exist as specializations within more broadly defined degree programs in areas such as business administration, management information systems, public administration, library and information science, and education. Master's degrees specifically devoted to knowledge management are found in only a handful of universities worldwide. The International Center for Applied Studies in Information Technology at George Mason University at one time maintained a list of degree programs, but the list has not been updated since February 2003, at which time it listed 18 master's programs and 4 doctoral programs worldwide; several of the master's programs and all the doctoral programs were actually specializations within more broadly defined disciplines. The Knowledge Management Education Wiki lists 63 university-based programs offering knowledge management education, with the largest numbers in the United States (17), the United Kingdom (14), and Australia (9). Many of these are non-degree experiences or concentrations within broader degree programs.[9]

Education for knowledge management has not been extensively studied, and many of the publications to date that have addressed education for knowledge management are opinion pieces. In 2005 Lai found that most ads for knowledge management positions listed an advanced degree as either required or preferred; 38.5 percent of the ads examined specified a degree in library and information science.[10] Sarrafzadeh, Hazeri, and Martin identified a central role for library and information science in knowledge management education but emphasized the need for a meaningful interdisciplinary approach. Their study revealed that 12.4 percent of knowledge management curricula were centered in library and information science programs, 3.5 percent were located in management programs, 3 percent were in information technology programs, and 62.8 percent were interdisciplinary programs spanning all three areas.[11]

SEEKING PROFESSIONAL IDENTITY

Pavalko identified seven key features of a true profession:

1. *A "theory of intellectual technique."* This is evidenced in "the extent to which there is a systematic body of theory and esoteric, abstract knowledge on which the work is based."[12] The professional's claim to expertise rests on presumed mastery of this body of knowledge. This body of knowledge is one of two factors that define the profession as a professional discipline as well as a field of practice.
2. *Relevance to basic social values.* The knowledge base, orientation, services, activities, techniques, and tools of a profession are applicable "to crucial, recurring human problems."[13]
3. *A training period.* This training period is characterized by four components: the amount of training involved, the extent to which training is specialized, the degree to which training is symbolic and ideational, and the content of what is learned. Control over education and training, and in particular the requirement of a higher education experience that usually involves earning a graduate degree as a professional credential, is a second factor in defining a professional discipline.
4. *Motivation.* This is reflected in the "degree to which work groups emphasize the idea of service to clients and the public as their *primary* objective and as one of the values of the occupational subculture."[14] An important ancillary factor is the extent to which the public service motivation is publicly acknowledged.
5. *Autonomy.* This is defined by the freedom of work groups to regulate their own work behavior. This freedom is expressed in two ways:
   a. Control of matters relating to the activities of members of the profession
   b. Individual autonomy that is resistant to undue influence or supervision from outside the profession
6. *Commitment.* Professionals have a personal commitment to the profession that takes on the form of a calling rather than an occupation. This commitment is generally assumed to be of a very long-lasting, perhaps permanent, nature.
7. *A sense of community.* Professionalism is a social phenomenon in which members of the professional community assume some manifestation of a "*common identity* and *common destiny.*"[15] The fate of the individual and the fate of the profession are inextricably intertwined.

Many fields, including architecture, business administration, education, engineering, and library and information science, have experienced long periods of uncertainty and questioning as to their identification as professions. Discussion of professionalism within such contexts has most frequently focused on the research base of the field in question but may extend to other factors as well. Knowledge management as a field appears to have not yet engaged in such self-questioning. The extent to which knowledge management currently constitutes a profession is uncertain but can be tentatively explored in terms of Pavalko's six criteria:

1. *Theory.* Examination of the professional literature, and particularly of the research base reflected in that literature, calls into question the existence of a defined body of knowl-

edge with a theoretical origin, although much of what has been published is couched in terms of the search for a theoretical base.

2. *Social relevance.* The largely corporation-oriented nature of much of the knowledge management literature and the largely trade orientation of many of the professional associations serving the field call into question the direct relevance of knowledge management to social or societal needs as opposed to matters related to the bottom line.

3. *Education and training.* No consolidated, widely recognized model for education and training has emerged, resulting in an environment in which formal preparation for a career in knowledge management may range from nothing to an advanced graduate degree.

4. *Motivation.* Knowledge managers, particularly those who write, speak, and participate in professional associations, appear to be highly motivated, frequently to the point of acting as proselytes for the field.

5. *Autonomy.* Autonomy is clearly quite varied and tied to the particular organizational setting in which a knowledge manager works rather than to membership in the profession.

6. *Commitment.* Commitment, like motivation, appears to be high among knowledge managers, who frequently pursue knowledge management initiatives in organizational settings that are directly hostile to the principles of knowledge management.

KNOWLEDGE MANAGEMENT AS A PROFESSIONAL DISCIPLINE

A professional discipline is an academic or intellectual discipline that has its origin in a field of professional practice. Squires defined professional disciplines as being "characterized by instrumentality, contingency and processuality."[16] Instrumentality refers to a professional discipline's impact on society, contingency is the factor that results in professional decisions and actions being based on the uncertainty of circumstance rather than the physical certainty of the empirical sciences, and processuality has to do with the role of techniques and rules in determining the actions of professions. Squires concluded that management could tentatively be viewed as a professional discipline. Grossman and Hooton emphasized the role of members of a professional discipline serving as "educational custodians of the discipline" by controlling both the professional literature and professional education.[17] It seems clear that, to whatever extent knowledge management can be defined as a profession, it has not taken on the characteristics of a professional discipline. Instilling professional values and motivating professional commitment will be essential components of professional education.

POSSIBLE FUTURES 1: EMERGENCE OF A PROFESSIONAL DISCIPLINE

There are two possible futures for knowledge management as a field, profession, and discipline that seem likely. In the first, which closely approximates the development of library and information science as a profession in the early part of the twentieth century, knowledge management will take on the characteristics of a professional discipline. The literature will shift toward a research base that encompasses appropriate quantitative and qualitative methodologies from other disciplines and will eventually begin to develop, test, refine, and export unique methodologies. The benefits of knowledge management to society at large will assume transcendent importance over the benefits to individual organizations. Graduate education in a university setting will first become a broadly accepted path to a knowledge management career, then will be viewed as the normal approach, and ultimately will take precedence as the only accepted credential for professional practice.

In this scenario, knowledge management professionals will coalesce into a truly professional cohort and create broad-based professional associations—or possibly a single association with multiple divisions, chapters, committees, and other organizational and governance components—that encompass knowledge managers, knowledge management educators, and other knowledge management professionals in support of the profession and its benefits to society. Members of those associations (or that association) will have meaningful control not only over the philosophies, ethics, practices, and membership of the profession, but over the status and image of the profession and its recognition as a discipline. To most observers of knowledge management, this is the best possible outcome for the field.

POSSIBLE FUTURES 2: FAILURE TO LAUNCH

The second likely scenario for the future offers what may be viewed as a more negative outlook than the first. Although those commentators who insist that knowledge management is completely unlike information management may be dismayed at the comparison, this scenario is typified by the history of the field of information management. Information management, like knowledge management, emerged as an area of interest with great potential for gaining a distinct identity as both a profession and a discipline. Like knowledge management, information management arose simultaneously with a broad array of other fields, including (but far from limited to) business administration, computer science, engineering, library and information science, mathematics, and records management.

Ultimately, information management as a field failed to break away from its roots in other fields and has never gained an identity or recognition as a field in and of itself. Those aspects of information management that were mostly closely related to and had their origins in other fields mostly returned to those fields, although there was substantial and beneficial interdisciplinary cross-pollination. One of the possible fates of knowledge management is that the core knowledge, ideas, and techniques of the field, all of which came from other fields of endeavor, will be reabsorbed into those fields.

SEEKING A HAPPY FUTURE

Although this second scenario seems dramatically less promising than the first, either can be a beneficial future for knowledge management as a field, assuming that the core concepts and values of knowledge management are not lost. As intangible as some of those essential values are, the goal of diffusing knowledge throughout organizations and, by extension, across society is wholesome, laudable, and natural. It seems inevitable that the essence of knowledge management will survive and thrive.

NOTES

1. Dave Pollard, "The Future of Knowledge," *Across the Board* 42 (January/February 2005): 54.

2. Ibid.

3. Ron Miller, "The Evolution of Knowledge Management: This Time It's Personal," *EContent* 28 (November 2005): 40.

4. Ralph A. Beals, "Implications of Communications Research for the Public Library," in *Print, Radio, and Film in a Democracy,* edited by Douglas Waples (Chicago: University of Chicago Press, 1942), 159.

5. David J. Teece, "Research Directions for Knowledge Management," California Management Review 40 (Spring 1998): 289–92.

6. Association of Knowledgework, "Four 'W's and 'H,'" http://www.kwork.org/who.html (accessed May 18, 2007).

7. International Knowledge Management Institute, "Frequently Asked Questions about the KM Institute," http://www.kminstitute.org/index.php?page = blank&subpage = faq (accessed May 18, 2007).

8. Knowledge Management Education Wiki, "KM Education Links," http://knowledge-management-education.wikispaces.com/KM+education+links (accessed May 21, 2007).

9. Ibid.

10. Ling-Ling Lai, "Educating Knowledge Professionals in Library and Information Science Schools," *Journal of Educating Media & Library Sciences* 42 (March 2005): 358.

11. Maryam Sarrafzadeh, Afseneh Hazeri, and Bill Martin, "Knowledge Management Education for LIS Professionals: Some Recent Perspectives," *Journal of Education for Library and Information Science* 47 (Summer 2006): 227.

12. Ronald M. Pavalko, *Sociology of Occupations and Professions* (Ithaca, IL: F. E. Peacock, 1988), 20.

13. Ibid., 21.

14. Ibid., 23.

15. Ibid., 27.

16. Geoffrey Squires, "Management as a Professional Discipline," *Journal of Management Studies* 38 (June 2001): 473.

17. Mary Grossman and Margaret Hooton, "The Significance of the Relationship between a Discipline and Its Practice," *Journal of Advanced Nursing* 18 (1993): 871.

Index

About the Author

DR. DANNY P. WALLACE is a professor in the School of Library and Information Studies at the University of Oklahoma. He has also held administrative and academic appointments at Kent State University, Louisiana State University, Indiana University, and the University of Iowa. Dr. Wallace holds a PhD in library and information science from the University of Illinois and an MA in library science from the University of Missouri. Dr. Wallace is a past coeditor of *Reference & User Services Quarterly*, the official journal of the Reference and User Services Association. He is responsible for more than one hundred publications, including *Library Evaluation: A Casebook and Can-Do Guide* (Libraries Unlimited, 2000), which he coedited with Dr. Connie Van Fleet. His professional service includes the American Library Association Committee on Accreditation and the boards of directors of the Association for Library and Information Science Education and Beta Phi Mu, the international library and information science honor society. Dr. Wallace was the recipient of the 2000 Association for Library and Information Science Education Award for Teaching Excellence in the Field of Library and Information Science Education.

The author extends thanks to the University of Oklahoma, which supported this book through a sabbatical, and particularly to the College of Arts and Sciences, which provided several faculty enrichment grants to fund travel related to the preparation of the book. Thanks are also due to a supportive family who lived through the writing process and to the editorial staff of Libraries Unlimited.

Recent Titles in the
Libraries Unlimited Knowledge Management Series

Danny Wallace, Series Editor

Cross-Cultural Perspectives on Knowledge Management
Edited by David J. Pauleen

.